Essays, Stories, and Poems

Second Edition

Joseph D. Schulman

For Dixie, with whom I laugh
when we can and cry when we must

Table of Contents

Introduction to the Second Edition

The essays, stories, and poems in this volume were written for the pleasures of creation and sharing with others. The topics vary widely. Some are humorous, others serious, but none are intended to lack substance.

The present edition incorporates all the articles previously published in the first edition of this book (2013) plus an almost equal number of additions. The essays and stories were mostly written between 1998 and 2017, and the short poems since 2010.

I am grateful for the positive comments of friends and family who have encouraged publication of assortments of my writings.

The reader may, of course, go through the entire book in the order in which the material appears. However, there is no master plan in the sequence in which the articles appear, each is a self-contained entity, and the range of topics is so broad that an alternative may be to start by choosing a few items of interest, then returning to the book over and over again for more.

It is almost impossible to say anything without annoying someone, and particularly hard to avoid every sensibility in an era where political correctness is a commonly observed orthodoxy. We are sensitive to the issue, though truthfulness is not always politically correct

In this spirit, the reader is reminded that all gender-specific terms in this document appear solely for purposes of convenience. Thus the word "female" is intended to refer equally to "male", "male" to "female", "wife" to "husband", "girl-friend" to "boy-friend", "she" to "he", "He" to "She", and so on. We acknowledge that literal interpretations of words like "woman" or "man" may be construed as improper, sexist, and anachronistic, and their mere employment may be attributed to unconscious expressions of chauvinism and homo- or hetero-phobia. These conventional terms are occasionally used in this volume with regret.

November, 2017

California Expands the Americans for Disability Act

As you know, California recently decided that wearing of eyeglasses constitutes a disability, and that myopics or presbyopics should be covered under the ADA. This is good news for me, since I'm at an age where I have a little of both, and I recently bought a home in Palm Springs. Now I should be able to get one or maybe two of those handicapped parking permits that you see on cars left near mall entrances by healthy, young adults who have kids with reading disabilities when they run in to shop for focaccia or truffle oil. I plan to use my handicapped permit to park near where I like to go jogging. I once completed a marathon, and the easier parking will facilitate my training for another 26 miles run.

The California law is a step in the right direction but it hardly goes far enough. It's sad that there are still so many people excluded from the benefits of being disabled. The law should be broadened. The best way to do this may be to formally recognize the pain and suffering associated with two almost universal problems: dental caries and halitosis.

Don't laugh. Dental caries really do hurt. And it's hardly reasonable to expect someone to work when their teeth are aching. Moreover, caries require treatment needing time away from the job, and the treatment itself is painful. Do you know how much it hurts to have somebody making holes in your teeth with a 50 megahertz drill?! Then if caries damage a tooth so badly that a cap is needed, several dental visits may be required and the amount of suffering is increased. The worst is a root canal.

Talk about pain!!! Dentists must be sadists. But in any case, if you really think about it caries are a much bigger and more disabling disease than most people recognize. I bet that caries cost billions of dollars per year in dental bills, millions of hours lost from work, hundreds of thousands of person-days wasted trying to find parking near dentists' offices. If that's not a disability, I don't know the meaning of the word.

And halitosis. How psychologically traumatic! How isolating! How humiliating to be called "garlic breath", and have people talk behind your back. Think how many women have been abandoned by their boyfriends and husbands because halitosis has driven them away. Consider all the children this creates without fathers. And we all know that children from fatherless families commit more crimes. And criminals are injured more frequently than average, even disabled or sometimes killed, by flying police bullets. Injured feelings, loneliness, sleepless nights, fatherless children, injured criminals - all of this, and more, is caused by bad breath. Obviously it's disabling.

I have just started lobbying in California to get caries and halitosis covered under the ADA. The dental lobby is solidly behind me. I also plan to seek support from the Genetic Alliance (www.geneticalliance.org) which recently featured photographs of individuals with genetic disabilities on its web site to "break down the public's fear of difference and turn discrimination into distinction". Like every other disability, caries and halitosis must have genetic components. Maybe the Alliance would like a picture of me exhaling with my fillings showing.

Aunt Anna and Uncle Rube

When I was growing up, my family considered that New York City was the only true model for civilization. People in the wilderness outside the five boroughs (ie., the rest of the world) were underprivileged, uncultured country bumpkins. We knew, of course, that there were rare exceptions, and if pushed could probably have named a few famous artists, musicians, or writers who inexplicably lived in "the country" while their work products were sold in New York's galleries, concert halls, or bookstores. The family's view of the universe was close to the one in Saul Steinberg's "Ninth Avenue" (1976), his famous bird's eye cartoon for the cover of New Yorker magazine: Manhattan and its buildings loom large in the foreground, beyond is a broad Hudson River, farther away is a flat wasteland about the size of Manhattan with indications of Chicago and the Rockies and Los Angeles, then the Pacific Ocean appearing about as wide as the Hudson, and on the horizon the minuscule nations of the Pacific Rim.

Nearly everyone in our family lived in the City (when capitalized, the word could only mean New York City). My father, his parents, his sister Celia and brother David and their spouses, and my three paternal cousins resided in Brooklyn. My mother's parents and her brother Jack (Julius) and Jack's wife, Maidie, also were Brooklynites. Mom also had various aunts and cousins who lived in Manhattan. There was only one closely-related exception to the family's uniform settlement pattern, an aunt and uncle who lived in a truly remote location, an upstate town called Newburgh. These were the "country Schulman's," my aunt Anna, her husband Rube (nobody ever called him by his given name of Reuben), and their only child, Marvin.

3

The country Schulmans were different. The rest of the family considered them isolated, unfortunate, and misguided. Perhaps because of Anna's husband's nickname, we thought of them as "rubes" - this label stuck to them all.

The country Schulmans were one of two marriages linking the Schulman and Grossman families. Anna Grossman was my mother's older sister, and she had been a high school friend of my father's sister, Celia Schulman. Through Celia, Anna met a second cousin from a remote branch of the Schulman clan which had misguidedly settled in Newburgh during the late 19th century. And this distant cousin of my father, Rube, became Anna's husband. Hence my mother and her sister - who both were Grossmans - both married Schulmans, and both carried the Schulman surname thereafter.

Anna was brilliant and outspoken, lovely in her youth with long dark hair, light complexion, regular features, and a full bosom. She became one of the first female Certified Public Accountants in the country. She had a well-paying job in Manhattan and seemed to have every advantage for making a good marriage. But then she fell in love with and quickly married this yokel Rube. The family couldn't believe it. And when Anna said she and Rube would live in Newburgh, they feared for her sanity and almost went into mourning.

Rube only had a high school education, while Anna was a graduate of New York's prestigious Hunter College and was also a respected professional CPA. Rube wasn't a professional at all - he was nothing but a shopkeeper. He had inherited the shop from his father. "R. Schulman's Department Store" sold toys, pots and pans, dry goods of

various types, and sat on Main Street in downtown
Newburgh. Anna not only married Rube, but she gave up
being a CPA to become the bookkeeper for his store. Oy
vey!

To the New York Schulmans, Newburgh was
"Nowheresville." Newburgh had no universities, no opera
house or concert hall, no museums, and almost no Jews.
People in Newburgh were mostly "goyim" (Yiddish for
non-Jews), and the lowest sort of goyim at that -
Protestants. In Brooklyn, over half our neighbors were
Jews, nearly half Italian, and only about 1-2% were
Protestant (the word Christian was almost never used in
Brooklyn). Protestants were poor and uneducated, holding
menial jobs. (The superintendent, or "super," of our
apartment house, the landlord's slave ever at the call of
tenants 24 hours a day, seven days a week was what we
believed to be a typical Brooklyn Protestant). If we had
had the advantages of modern diversity training, families
like ours and the Italians would have made the
impoverished Protestant minority the objects of charity.
We might even have raised money for them through 10K
races like "Run for Protestantism," or special "Marathons
for Methodism." Perhaps we would have helped organize a
Million Protestant March on City Hall (although we all
knew that there were too few Protestants to ever turn that
dream into reality).

There were other strange things about Newburgh.
For example, people there lived mostly in single family
homes, with front lawns, porches, backyards, driveways,
and garages. In New York City, everyone lived the normal
way - in tiny rent controlled apartments, so cheap that you
could save money even on a small salary (while the
landlord went bankrupt and the property deteriorated)
instead of squandering your money on a mortgage. We all

knew that it was normal to get our daily mail by descending several flights of stairs to the lobby and prying it out of a 2-inch-wide pigeonhole with a screwdriver, we were proud to be sophisticated enough to know how to use the noisy communal washing machine and dryer in the dank apartment house basement, we delighted in playing on concrete surfaces in steel-fenced backyards, bouncing pink rubber balls off stoops (front entrance stairs) of multifamily walkups, playing stick ball on side streets with manhole covers ("sewers") as the "plate" and second base while overhanging branches knocked down potential home runs, and automobiles threaded in and out between running boys. We kept our bikes locked up, chained to fences between rides, like everyone should. The "rubes" in Newburgh never even owned bike locks and chains. They had to walk a few blocks to play baseball in an open field. Their neighbors wouldn't let them bounce balls off their stoops. Nobody in Newburgh even knew how to play stick ball. Ugh!

In New York, everyone knew that the only sports that counted were baseball, basketball, and football - in that order. Baseball was the most important sport in the world. New York had three famous baseball teams - the Dodgers, the Yankees, and the Giants. Newburgh had none - zero. It was the pits. My parents and other New York relatives listened to local Dodgers games on radio or watched them on tiny black-and-white television screens, and sometimes bought tickets from scalpers to take their sons to Ebbetts Field. Meanwhile, Aunt Anna and Uncle Rube were doing things like playing golf --- GOLF! We were told they had even wasted their money by joining some kind of local club for golfers. What kind of "sport" was that? It was rumored that Rube had been a high school golf champion. So what! There wasn't even a golf team in my high school. Who cared about that dumb game anyway? Nobody thought Rube could ever have learned how to hit a home run.

There was another reason not to live in Newburgh. The politics were unbelievable. Many people who lived there actually voted Republican. In fact, my own mother's sister had abandoned the party of her ancestors, and turned into a Republican after moving to Newburgh. In New York City, EVERYONE was a Democrat. FDR was the Man-God local Jews believed in. He had won the War. He had ended the Depression. He had Saved the Jews from Hitler's ovens. He had helped the Unions. He was so Brave. He never complained about getting Polio. He and His wife Eleanor were so Good, so Kind, so Concerned about the Poor, so Compassionate, though they were born to wealth.

Aunt Anna had moved to Newburgh and gone over to the other side. She belonged to some kind of Republican association up there. She was trying to raise money to support Republican candidates. How out of it can you get!

The whole political thing reached its limit when Barry Goldwater became the Republican candidate for President. Anna and Rube had driven down from Newburgh to visit my mother and father. Marvin was away in his medical residency at Yale. I was a student at Harvard Medical School, but happened to be home in Brooklyn during their visit. Anna tried to tell us that Goldwater would be a good President. We all laughed. Worse, we tried - and to my eternal shame, with the advantages of my new Harvard education I tried even harder than my parents - to prove to Anna that Goldwater was a Fascist. This angered my aunt. Didn't we know, she said, that Goldwater was part Jewish, that he had fought in the War, that he hated Hitler? Sure, we said, but didn't he vote against civil rights? That proved for sure that he was

Fascist. Rube sat quietly and took it all in. I understand he later, of course, just as quietly voted for Goldwater.

The years passed. After I had learned to play golf, I stopped in Newburgh and visited with Anna and Rube. They had continued to live in the large, red brick home a few blocks from their former store. Some new business called Walmart had just come to town, but about two years ago they had sold their general store and real estate along Main Street and were comfortably retired. Rube was in the backyard, hitting whiffle balls off the lawn with a five iron. Over and over, with his natural, easy swing he hit the ball perfectly. The man was a terrific athlete, but only then had I suddenly figured that out.

Anna and Rube lived together with much evidence of love and harmony for over 50 years. Then Rube died, and shortly thereafter, tragically, Anna's only son died in an automobile accident. Years before, when young Marvin had finally progressed from Newburgh to the more sophisticated environment at Yale, he reportedly developed an affinity for alcohol which may have contributed to his premature demise.

Anna lived on in the house in Newburgh with an elderly caretaker, and died at age 94. One afternoon her heart action suddenly became irregular, she asked her caretaker not to call a doctor, said she was ready to go, and just fell over. A quick and painless death.

How strange it is to realize, so many years later, that Anna and Rube were probably the two most normal people in my original family. May they rest in peace, and their souls be united in heaven.

Beans

Note: alternative title: Ode to a Mexican Meal; to the
rhythm of Poe's "The Bells"

See the tacos with the beans -
Golden beans!
What a gastric contentment their goldenness forseems!
Yet they swell, swell, swell,
In the icy air of night!
While the stars that oversprinkle,
All the heavens seem to twinkle,
As you sleepless pass the night;
Keeping time, time, time,
In a sort of endless rhyme,
To the tintinnabulation that so musically keens,
From the beans, beans, beans, beans,
      Beans, beans, beans,
From the hooting and the tooting from the beans.

Bend Over, Here Comes the Change

Some of you may be inclined to think of me as a conservative. While accurate to some extent, as a scientist one must ask, "Compared to what?" Certainly not compared to my wife.

Allow me to illustrate. A couple of years ago a news headline blared that, shortly before quitting his elected office, "Ohio Governor Clears Death Row." At the time of the clearance, over 100 inmates were awaiting execution. On hearing of this, my wife said something like "It's about time". She was subsequently disappointed to discover that instead of executing all 100+ prisoners, for some inexplicable reason the Governor had *commuted the execution of all of them* – scores of murderers, rapists, drug lords, and other similar felons whose lawyers had repeatedly stalled the legal system until many of their clients were close to natural death from old age.

In a more recent example, my wife purchased online about 50 bumper stickers which had symbols and colors similar to those used in the 2008 Obama campaign and which bore the legend, "Bend Over, Here Comes the Change." The first of these she affixed to the bumper of the rental car we picked up in Minneapolis to start our latest Western travels. Hertz was doubtless pleased. The others were passed out free to the many folks we ran into who admired the sentiment being expressed. These included people as diverse as deer hunters, retired professors of sociology, and National Park Service employees in places like eastern Montana and Oregon's Harney Desert where ACORN doesn't carry much influence with the voters.

Sometime soon I hope to inform you about some of the people we chatted with on this journey, but first I'd like to philosophize on the hypermodern, ugly, and service-deficient hotel at Minneapolis in which we spent our one and only night in the People's Republic of Minnesota, where by the way nobody expressed appreciation for Dixie's bumper sticker. The spirit of the place can best be captured from some of the magazines placed in our room by the seemingly youthful management. My favorite was, "Dwell", which subtitles itself as a guide to being "At Home in the Modern World."

"Dwell" relentlessly depicts its version of the world of the future, in which every imaginable "family" group will happily inhabit tiny, environmentally friendly cells mostly in multi-story urban complexes. Featured articles in the latest issue of "Dwell" had such titles as "Harvesting Sunlight", "Organic LEDs Explained" (they really weren't), and "Light Pollution". One long photo-feature showed how two gays tore down an old hut in a lovely historic village, Landskrona, in Norway and replaced it with an outrageously ugly white box with three oddly-placed windows, and interior rooms divided into steel cages resembling storage bins. The magazine approvingly refers to this atrocity in the midst of an 18th century cobbled alley as "a minimalist mirage" – though unfortunately for the Norwegians it is quite real.

But my favorite in this month's "Dwell" was the one page story involving two ladies whose joint second-home-building experience is worth sharing in detail. With apologies to "Dwell" for possibly trampling its copyright, here are selected portions of the article, all quotations being from the original:

"Suzanne S.'s life work is making sustainable lifestyles attractive and accessible" as CEO of "a marketing company...that works exclusively with environmentally focused clients." She dreamed of a "little cottage to get away to" and a couple of years ago found what she and her partner, Corinne, wanted, "a funky piece of property" in the woods near a "man-made [sic] reservoir." The parcel had a "peculiar rhomboid shape", barely touched the water, and was so small that only a two-bedroom cottage would fit on it. "But the site's location next to a protected wetland sealed the deal for the duo."

A modernistic shack was created with the help of an architect such that "cedar panels backed with insect screens could be snapped to the steel framework" in only three days. "The more difficult task however was incorporating rainwater-harvesting and solar-power systems." Suzanne discovered that "being green is often not easy." An oversized 400 gallon cistern, the smallest "approved for potable water" was acquired and "badly needed a custom cover to keep it from being an eyesore". As for solar power, "installing the system was far more laborious and expensive than expected, since Tennessee does not offer solar power incentives. Selecting a DC system cost the pair significant sums, and it came with a catch. They needed to buy DC-compatible appliances to avoid constantly using the energy-hogging converter. The biggest problem however was having to fell more than 40 trees to use the solar system. [Suzanne said] 'We're only getting about 30 percent of the full power, but we're not willing to cut any more down.'"

The article concludes, "Despite the obstacles and approximately $10,000 in extra costs, Suzanne believes the efforts were worthwhile and necessary. 'How else could we have done it?', she asks. 'We would have had to pump water from the lake and purify it. That would have required energy, meaning we'd have had to run wires down from the [nearby] road.'"

The end-product created by the two women is basically a lean-to with a glassed-in front. An insert explains "Equipped with rain-water harvesting and solar systems, [Suzanne and Corinne's] 176 square-foot, off-the-grid lakeside pavilion sits softly in its wooded surroundings."

Anyone want to buy a house by a reservoir? Here is the green vision all laid out for you. Claustrophically tiny, expensive, awkward, inefficient, dependent upon government subsidies – but ideologically politically correct. If we must depend on people who think like this to "save the earth", our planet is doomed. Fortunately, however, not everyone does think like this. A true experience parodies the point. A few years ago, a teenage female stood on 5th Avenue near East 58th Street in Manhattan accosting people with the request to sign a petition to "save the environment". In front of Dixie and me a well-dressed man responded, as he briskly strode onward, "I'm a Republican. I hate the environment." The shocked look on the young lady's face was priceless. We laughed so hard that the man disappeared into the crowd before we could ask him to join us for a drink.

Beneath the Beltway

A little while ago I decided that I'd had enough of doctoring after 40 years and wanted to do something new and useful. Only trouble was, I couldn't think what. I kept my ownership in my organization and turned the rest over to Warren Buffett, and he alone was making so much money for me that I didn't need a job anymore. I could do whatever I wanted for the first time in my life. Now all I had to do was figure out what the meaning of "whatever" was. I considered consulting with Bill Clinton who first challenged us to think about the meaning of the word "is," but couldn't find his number in the Harlem phone directory, and the operator told me "it be unlisted." I'm going to have to figure this one out myself.

When I'm looking for answers, I try to read and some kind of thinking seems to go on in the background. Good ideas pop up all the time. At least they look good, until I think about them harder. But some stand up even after a while. We'll see what happens to the one that hit me today.

The idea came when I was reading a book my wife had convulsed over last night. We had picked up the paperback on one of our trips to the Far West, where we like to wander in places so remote that seeing a Pizza Hut means you've entered the local metropolis. The author is a really funny writer named Roger Pond, and his books are collections of humorous stories about rural life that he composes for a syndicated column called "The Back Forty." The particular book I was reading is called, "My Dog was a Redneck but We Got Him Fixed," and other titles by the same author include "It's Hard to Look Good When Your Car's Full of Sheep," "Things That Go 'Baa!' In the Night," and so forth. Examples of topics include the joys and tears of camping out in tents that provide no protection from wind and rain, trying to borrow back your hunting rifle from your teenager, burying your child's pet hamster, training cats, shoveling manure, feeding fish entrails to hogs ("Feed them all you have. If they get fat, sell them. If they skinny up, try barley and corn"), fishing with your wife, and so forth. Country life is funny all right if you tell your tales with the right mix of humor and irony. But really, I think life's even funnier in the cities.

First of all there are so many more people in cities these days. That means there are going to be lots more examples of silly behavior, since folks are pretty much the same all over. It's not like most of the idiots live in the country, while the geniuses all congregate in big towns. In fact, the opposite may be true. Just living in New York City probably means your IQ has got to be lower than the national standard, unless you live there because you have to. And how many people really *have to* live in New York?

American cities should be ripe topics for wry humor, and a few creative souls have written about this subject for their life's work. Art Buchwald comes to mind, and a few others. But most of these writers are firmly interconnected to the people they write about, and need local social approval to earn their bread. They gently chide, seeking warm chuckles from the reader, but open up with both barrels only after a target has been labeled politically incorrect by powerful insiders. Thus, they produce a kind of selected pseudo-parody. It's OK to make fun of rednecks and white males and businessmen, but wrong to laugh at welfare mothers or blacks or Indians (sorry, I mean African-Americans and Native Americans) or gays. Making fun of Richard Nixon was fine, but joking about Hillary or Teddy is only for right-wing extremists. If you want to get into print, you don't chide about Katherine Graham turning the Washington Post into the political opposite of everything her father stood for when he bought the paper in the 1930s. And so it goes.

Then there is the hilarious pomposity of many who write seriously about urban activities. One well-known newspaper runs a column whose title refers to observing what is going on along the shores of a mid-Atlantic river where politicians flock to feed. Why are the details of their deals of serious interest to normal mortals? Only other politicians and lobbyists care. The topic is so sordid that the column should be re-titled, "Beneath the Beltway." The columnist was recently seen at a local hotel with a lovely young woman whose beltway he was obviously getting inside of - that's what made me think of the new name. An alternative could be "Venality Watch."

So maybe I can fill a need if I write in a humorous way about the things other writers must ignore to stay employed. A little while ago I composed something about the political geniuses in Sacramento who expanded the Americans for Disabilities Act to cover people wearing eyeglasses. (When I'm back in Palm Springs, I'm going to get that handicap sticker for my car if I have to drive all the way to the State House and run in to pick it up personally.) I could do more writing like that. A lot more. There is an embarrassment of topics out there. My pen would never grow still. I could start, for example, with the California energy crisis, move onto Medicare, then to public school teachers, millionaire socialists, taxes, saving the wilderness, $100,000 fines for disturbing sea turtle nests -- the list is endless.

There's only one problem with this idea now that I've thought more about it. Human folly really isn't funny.

We laugh about it so that we don't burst out crying. If you do a lot of writing about it, you are going to do a lot of weeping. You might even become cynical, angry, depressed.

No, this is not for me. Not really. I'll figure out something else to do with my life one of these days.

Meanwhile I'm going to play golf, go sailing, and have a drink. Tempus fugit.

Rare High Altitude Winter Sighting of the Northeastern Biternu

Publisher's note: The Editor-in-Chief of "Birds Watching", Stellar Jay, has written the following informative discussion for the benefit of our readers. We hope you will enjoy it. Keep twittering!

On January 15, 2002 I was resting on the branches of a denuded shrub at the dead-end of a lane off Highway 168 near Mount Whitney in the Sierras. The altitude was over 8,000 feet, air temperature was typical for winter at this altitude, the mountain was blanketed in snow, and all was quiet. It was slightly after noon. I had just curled my head around to go to sleep when, to my great surprise, a four-wheeled vehicle containing two biternus stopped about 100 feet from me. As you know, biternus have rather poor vision, and this pair used ocular tubes to examine me. With my much better eyes, I, of course, could observe all their features clearly. They chirped to each other for a little while, then reentered their conveyance, and the male biternu steered as the machine rolled away down the mountain.

There can be no doubt that these two biternus were of the Northeastern variety, which as some readers will know is rarely seen at altitudes above sea level in winter. The remarkable nature of this sighting can be best appreciated by a review of the principal features of the Northeastern subspecies.

Biternus are featherless (*nu*de), *ter*restrial *bi*peds, somewhat smaller than ostriches but with larger heads. They started to arrive in large flocks on the American continent from Europe about 250 generations ago, with the largest migration about 50 generations ago into northeastern cities. Some readers may recall that the biternu was originally named the nuterbi, but at the Birds Watching World Conference some years ago that name was officially changed to the modern form which is easier to warble and chirp.

The Northeastern Biternu, the subject of this brief essay, has a characteristic dark crest and dark eyes, usually intensely brown, and - in many but not all cases - displays a prominent, slightly angulated, beak. The normal winter range is on the eastern and western marshes of Florida and the coastal regions of central and southern California, although wintering has been observed as far away as Israel. The winter range may also become the year-round habitat. This biternu has a particular aversion to cold, damp, snow, and heights, which will help readers appreciate the surprise this writer felt to observe a pair of them in the upper Sierras only days after the winter solstice. Two principal sub-types have been identified so far, the Jewish and the Italian variants, which differ slightly in feeding habits and other minor features, such as the markings (respectively star or cross) on the buildings to which the sub-type flocks on weekends; some Birds Watcher scientists believe other variants will be identified upon further research.

The Northeastern Biternu has additional features which assist Birds Watchers in their identification. Females generally have large breasts, which sometimes rapidly increase in size between ages 20 to 30 years; this sudden expansion is especially common among Northeastern Biternus who have settled in Los Angeles or Miami Beach. While it is common to observe older male Northeastern Biternus with grey crests, this is never seen in the female whose crest remains dark until death, or may sometimes convert to a bright yellow hue during adult life.

Thus the basic Birds Watchers rule: If it is a female biternu with a grey crest, it cannot be the Northeastern variant.

The female Northeastern Biternu has additional features which may aid in positive identification. This biternu is frequently adorned with a shiny yellow metal around its neck and on the lower tips of the ears. It is common also to see large pieces of clear or colored glass affixed to the claws. The female also gathers in large flocks in shopping malls.

The mating pattern of the Northeastern Biternu is generally abundantly polygamous after the initial period of sexual maturation, but once offspring appear is most commonly serially or quasi-monogamous. The young of the Northeastern Biternu rarely are allowed to leave the nest until an extremely advanced age, often 25 years or more. While the female typically feeds and raises the young, the Northeastern Biternu is remarkable in that the female often devotes more care to the rearing of her grand-offspring than of her own first-generation offspring. The young of the Northeastern Biternu are thus often observed in the presence of their grandmothers, usually distinguishable from the mothers by their coarser integument (but not, as noted above, by crest color). Newborn Northeastern Biternus are frequently protected by one or more adult Black or Hispanic Biternus. The latter variants (not discussed in this article) rarely interbreed with the Northeastern Biternu, despite the obvious - and so far unexplained - affinity for their young. There is also a genetic mystery regarding the Northeastern subtype, since the female biternu almost always breeds true: thus, for example, a cross between a Jewish biternu female and any type of biternu male almost always is Jewish.

The Northeastern Biternu can also be recognized by the remarkable difference in vocal power between the female and the male. The female chirps and calls almost continuously, and often forcefully, while the male is usually silent for long periods, and in some cases may actually be mute. The atretic vocal apparatus of the male Northeastern Biternu has been the subject of much research, and grants for further investigation of this subject, or of the maternal inheritance issue noted in the paragraph immediately above, may be applied for from the Birds Watching Foundation.

Both sexes of the Northeastern Biternu demonstrate an affinity for nesting inside cliff-like dwellings, although a preference for suburban woodlands is increasingly evident among the young. Wilderness areas are strictly avoided, with only the rarest exceptions. Favored nests are large, warm (often heated nearly to avian body temperature), soft, and concentrated in coastal regions. However, the Northeastern Biternu can survive, and even produce offspring, far from large bodies of water as long as other nesting conditions are appropriate, altitude is sufficiently low, and environmental temperature not excessively cold.

The alimentary habits of the Northeastern Biternu also help identify it. Feeders provided with smoked salmon attract these biternus in large numbers. Chinese food and pasta are also avidly consumed. Water, unless carbonated, is virtually ignored by the Northeastern Biternu. Raw sugar is never ingested, and all fluids must be non-calorically sweetened. Bird-baths with jets are favored for frequent cleansing of the featherless integument.

Additional high altitude winter sightings of any Northeastern Biternus would be of considerable interest to the writer. Please provide as much information as possible about the specifics of the sighting to:

Stellar Jay
c/o Birds Watching
400 S. Via Las Palmas
Palm Springs, CA 92262
E-mail: stellarjay410760@earthlink.net

Summary of features of the Northeastern Biternu:

Normal winter range is Florida or the coastal regions of Southern California; sometimes seen in Israel
Dark crest, dark eyes, and - in some cases - prominent beak
Females have large breasts, which often additionally enlarge in the 20s or 30s
Protective of young, who are not allowed to leave nest until age 25 or more
Females never develop grey crest, but sometimes the crest changes color from dark to light yellow
Drawn to feeders with smoked salmon
Fondness for Chinese food, pasta
Aversion to sugar, water must be artificially sweetened
Frequent hybridization with other Biternus
Mating is polygamous early in mature life, then sometimes quasi-monogamous as age sets in
Female determines type of building the offspring enter for the weekly flock congregation on Saturdays or Sundays
Females are frequently adorned with shiny yellow metal, and glass on the claws
City cliff dwelling is a common preference in the native area, although suburban woodlands are favored for younger birds in particular
Biternu definition - featherless (nude), bipedal, terrestrial, almost as large as an ostrich

Distinct aversion to cold or damp environments, high altitudes, wilderness areas in general

Female normally raises two generations of offspring, often devoting more time to care and feeding of the grand-offspring than the first-generation

Preference for large nests, large vehicles, skin of furry animals (for warmth)

Females chirp almost continuously and far more than males, who are sometimes totally silent and whose presence is easy to overlook

Females concentrate in large flocks in shopping malls

Vehicles almost always driven by the male

Major subspecies: Jewish, Italian

Major feeding locations: restaurants; rarely feeds in the nest except when nursing young

Children are commonly accompanied by Black or Hispanic variant Biternus (although these subtypes rarely interbreed with the Jewish or Italian strains)

What I Learned Playing Chess in Brooklyn

In the 1950s, Brooklyn was packed with human energy, talent, and competitiveness. There were of course excessively tough, waterfront areas like Red Hook, poorer outer regions like Canarsie, and actual slums, that we never went near, seemingly dominated by poverty and the rude laws of the jungle. But Flatbush, where I grew up, and indeed most of Brooklyn was inhabited by middle class, upwardly mobile Jews and Italians.

The parents of my friends were mostly first generation Americans. Their parents had been immigrants, part of the late 19th century migrant waves that flooded New York and overflowed into other major cities. My mother and father were typical, their own parents being Jewish immigrants from Russia and Austria. Many of the newcomers had settled on the Lower East Side of Manhattan, and when they had saved some money then moved to quieter and more spacious Brooklyn. Their children, my parent's generation, struggled upward toward the American dream through extreme hard work, family ties, and education. But they were limited by being first-generation Americans, only partially integrated into the mainstream, often challenged by ethnic discrimination of the same type they sometimes used against others. Full cultural melding and limitless opportunity would, they believed, belong to their children - but only if the kids were smart enough and tough enough to succeed. Both the Jewish and Italian cultures of Brooklyn pushed children hard. To be successful in school was to be successful in life. To win in competitive activities was practice for winning in life.

A form of competition common among Jews in New York involved the game of chess, a game of the mind. It is an oversimplification, but with much truth, that in junior and senior high school the Italian boys played football and baseball, and the Jews played chess. To those who take it seriously, chess is intensely competitive, a conflict of wills, a battle of brains.

The Jewish affinity for chess is poorly understood, but undeniable. While many early American chess greats like Paul Morphy were not Jewish, an exceptional fraction of America's and the world's leading chess players have been of Jewish ancestry. Bobby Fischer, the former U.S. and world chess champion, and the current world champion Gary Kasparov are only two well-known examples. In the 1950s, most of America's leading chess players were Jews living in New York, mostly in Brooklyn and Manhattan. I was to get to know nearly all of them.

I was much more passionate about science than chess, but in preadolescence I had played chess as a casual pastime, and developed a moderate skill. Working from books filled with the games of old masters, I would replay moves, read the analyses of the positions, and enter into the mental world of legendary chess geniuses like Capablanca, Lasker, Alekhine, and Reshevsky. I understood early that my interest in chess would never be at the highest level. I was too focused on other things. I saw little point in devoting my youthful years to a game rather than to science and medicine, which I felt were "real", and for which I believed I had some greater talent. But I loved the beauty of an elegant chess game, and appreciated genius expressed in the works of others. Chess to me was a kind of art form, an imaginative endeavor enjoyable by both creator and observer. I experienced chess more like music, painting, sculpture, or photography, than as the intensely competitive game it actually is for its true devotees.

I was destined to become far more involved in the world of chess than I had imagined. At age 16, I entered Brooklyn College as the first of many participants in a new early college admission program for gifted students. And a classmate in my very first course in chemistry, my major subject and one where I was a strong student, was Ray Weinstein. Ray was having trouble comprehending the electrochemical properties of a storage battery. I assisted him with this and some other homework assignments, and we became close friends. Ray was grateful for the help, and tried to think of something nice he could do for me. So one day he invited me to go with him to a chess club where he was a member. To my surprise, I learned that Ray belonged to the Marshall Chess Club in Greenwich Village. The Marshall and the Manhattan were the two leading chess clubs in America. How could Ray, who was quite poor, be a member of this posh place? I had read something of the history of the Marshall, knew that Frank Marshall had been a wealthy man and one of America's leading players of the prior generation. The Club was in a townhouse which had been Marshall's home, and it was now supervised by his elderly widow.

So one Saturday, Ray and I took the subway to the Village, and I entered - for the first time in my life - into the luxurious setting of a men's club. The interior was high-ceilinged, rather dark, deep worn leather armchairs, tall windows. Chess tables were set up in the main room and several side rooms, each table with its pair of chairs, dark and white pieces, double-dialed, brass buttoned chess clock, and table or floor lamp. Some of the men greeted Ray. He sat down with one of them and began to play rapid chess.

If you are old enough, can you recall the first time you listened and watched as Heifetz or Milstein played the violin, or Horowitz rendered Chopin on the piano? Try to remember how you felt when first you saw a Monet landscape. Bring back if you can the memory of your first taste of food in a great Parisian restaurant. Feel again how you felt when you first stood on the rim's edge of the Grand Canyon. Watching Ray play chess was like experiencing these things. He was a chess genius! He peered at the board through his thick glasses, moved the pieces quickly with his tapering fingers, touched his clock, and returned to a position of intense concentration, hunched with arms crossed, elbows on the table. Ray did not speak even after his first opponent, shaking his head at the inevitable, began to set up pieces for the next game, a signal of resigning. Ray continued to play for over an hour, against whoever sat down across the table. He won about 20 games, and lost none. Only later did I learn that some of the men playing against him were among the highest ranked at the Marshall. And it was not until we were walking back toward the subway for our return to Brooklyn that Ray told me his secret. At age 14, he had been the U.S. Junior Chess Champion. He was currently ranked as a Senior Master, played annually in the U.S. Open Championship, and was one of the 10 or 12 strongest chess players in America. My friend Ray, this shy, round-faced guy with weak eyes who couldn't understand simple chemistry, was a world class fellow at chess, the game of the intellectuals! Wow!! Now that was something to think about.

Through Ray, I got to meet at competitions, at informal chess parties, and in other social settings virtually all the leading U.S. players except Reshevsky. Reshevsky, the legendary child prodigy of Jewish American players, was a good deal older than Fischer and the other chess leaders of the 50s. I was told that, never able to support himself adequately through chess playing, he had become an accountant and now lived quietly in the suburbs with his family. I got to know especially well Herbert Seidman, another Senior Master who played regularly in the U.S. Open. Herb had a lovely wife who, by coincidence, played viola in the same amateur community orchestra where I played tympani. Herb was a statistician with the American Cancer Society, and found work for me there one summer as a coder in the landmark study that initially linked cigarette smoking to lung cancer. Herb was famous for a legendary game he had once played against Reshevsky, winning after sacrificing several pieces against the grandmaster. Ray and I spent many rainy afternoons at the home of a Brooklyn dentist, Harold Sussman, who played almost as well as Seidman. There we met Bernard Zuckerman, another Brooklyn college student and future Senior Master, and many other top players. It was at Sussman's house, at a chess party, that I first met Fischer. It must have been in 1959 or 1960.

Bobby Fischer, a boy raised in Brooklyn, was at this time easily the best chess player in America, and one of the best in the world, but at this time he had not yet won the world championship. Fischer had triumphed in the U.S. Open every year for the past 5 years or so. It was said that he had started to play chess when he was 8 or 9, initially learning from his sister, and at first had shown no indication of his future greatness. But when he began to enter pre-adolescence something changed. He began to win all his casual games against friends, then at the local chess club, and at the strong Manhattan clubs. He won the U.S. Junior Championship, and shortly thereafter, in his mid-teens, the U.S. Championship itself.

Fischer was the only player that Ray was afraid to play, and he was not alone in this fear. To play Fischer was to lose. Before his games against Fischer in the Open I would encourage Ray, but he would tell me that it was a waste of time to try to cheer him up, there was no way he was going to win, the best he could hope for was a draw. And he would be defeated, and take it hard. Polite and seemingly unaggressive in personal interactions, at chess Ray truly hated to lose. In this regard, he was like all good players - intensely, profoundly competitive at chess. In some hundreds of casual games against Ray, he never let me win, nor could I ever play well enough to win. He would always beat his father at the game. It was the same with Seidman, the gentlest of men. Herb once made a blunder in a casual game with me at his home, and it appeared that I would win; his genuine friendliness and paternal kindness were suddenly replaced by a frightening intensity of concentration. Playing his best, he was eventually able to force me to a draw. Then he relaxed back in his chair, smiled, and we continued our conversation on mathematics while his wife brought us cookies and hot tea.

Sussman's afternoon party was crowded by the time Ray and I arrived. Harold had set up about 7-8 chess tables in his living room and kitchen, and about 30 men were packed into the barely adequate space, moving from one game to another, watching, talking, joking, drinking sodas and coffee, playing. It was noisy and hot. The usual game was 3 minute lightening chess. Each chess clock is set to only 3 minutes of play for each opponent (in competition chess, the time for each side is usually about 2 hours or more) . Under the rules, you must move a piece and then, using the same hand, hit the button on top of your chess clock. This stops your own clock, and the clock of your opponent starts ticking. When he moves, and then hits his clock, it stops and yours starts. There is a small flag in each clock, and it drops when your 3 minute time is up. If your flag drops before your opponent's, you lose. If you are checkmated, you lose. You must checkmate your opponent before your flag drops to win. The loser makes way for another opponent of the winner, who keeps playing until he is himself defeated. Lightening chess against strong opposition is an amazing test of skill. I would never have tried to play it in this crowd. Moves were nearly instantaneous, based on unconscious knowledge, a strong positional sense, and instincts finely honed through thousands of past games. There were occasional blunders, and hilarious laughter from the observers as the victim of the oversight was speedily punished for his "stupidity" or for being a "potzer" (a sarcastic Yiddish term for a weak player). Then Fischer arrived.

He was younger and taller than most of the men, perhaps 17 or 18, clean shaven and tan haired, no glasses, rather handsome. One of the seated players immediately made way for him at his favorite table just inside the kitchen. Sussman's wife knew of Fischer's fondness for donuts, and a box of the plain variety covered with white confectioner's sugar was laid on the near left corner of his chess table. I forced my way to a position almost directly behind Fischer. He picked up the chess clock. He set his opponent's clock to 3 minutes. He set his clock to 30 seconds!! He took the black pieces, placing him at a slight disadvantage against white, who always makes the first move. He grabbed a donut with his left hand, took a huge bite, and the game began. What I then actually saw, I would not have thought possible. After each move of his opponent, Fischer's response was absolutely instantaneous. In a fraction of a second, in a single blindingly fast and confident action, he would move his piece and slam the clock. In the 30 seconds he had allowed himself, he could make 60 moves or more! But rarely were this many moves required for him to checkmate or force a resignation. He won game after game, with the same six-fold handicap in time, against anyone who sat down to play him. Meanwhile, he was eating donuts nonstop, talking, joking about potzers, about "weakies". His manner was both arrogant and joyful. His mind played undefeatable chess while simultaneously carrying out other simpler functions. It was a performance of unbelievable virtuosity. Never in my life had I seen anything to compare with it.

That afternoon, Bobby Fischer never lost. He never, as far as I could tell, came even close to losing a single game. After a long time, he got up, spoke to some of his friends, and departed. He then became the major topic of conversation. His genius was universally acknowledged. It was agreed that he would be the next world champion. Even the Russians could not beat this guy. Petrossian, Smyslov, they were all potzers compared to Fischer! I was ready to believe it. Nobody could play chess better than that - nobody. And indeed Fischer did of course later win the world chess championship, but not without some delays and very strong Russian opposition.

During my college years, my interest in chess continued mostly as an observer and friend to Ray. But my interest in chess led to a first "entrepreneurial" effort as well. I learned that Brooklyn College did not have a chess team. Apparently one had existed years ago, but it had been disbanded. So I organized and captained the Brooklyn College chess team, and a year later we became the U.S. collegiate champions. Chess team competitions involve 4 boards simultaneously. Each board gets 1 point for a win, 2 point for a draw, and 0 for a loss. Ray always played first board, and Bernie Zuckerman played second. Both were almost undefeatable in college play, so with this advantage we were hard to stop - especially as I generally did not play at all to make way for better 3rd and 4th board players. I learned much from this experience, but more about this later.

One other chess experience stands out in my mind, and it occurred a few years later, when my interest in chess was already waning, and I was deeply engaged in learning medicine. I heard that Bent Larsen, a Danish grandmaster who was then considered the strongest player in the "Free World" except Fischer, would be playing a simultaneous exhibition at the Manhattan Chess Club. I went to watch, but when the day came a few boards of the twenty were open and I decided to actually play Larsen. Of course, he would be walking around making a rather a quick move on each board in sequence while I and his other opponents had on average 20 times as much time to think about our moves. This initial handicap diminished as players lost and dropped out. But still, Larsen was a grandmaster, and even in a strong chess club he would be expected to win all or nearly all the games. When I decided to play, Larsen had not yet appeared. I had never met the grandmaster, and when he arrived I experienced an instant dislike for him. He was short, and I felt he seemed cocky, strutted in a Napoleonic manner, and disdained his weaker opponents. These were, of course, purely subjective interpretations on my part, unsupported by any data, and I had enough insight to know it - but I still had a strong antipathy to the man. Such an emotion is very rare with me, but I could not shake it.

Play started. I of course expected to lose my game. Larsen was one of the best in world, and I was playing just for fun. I had not, in fact, played a serious chess game for several years. After about 20 moves, my position was substantially worse than the grandmaster's, and he was threatening a combination that would win one of my bishops. If this occurred, I would have to resign.

And then to my amazement, a powerful emotion, a mixture of rage and hatred, suddenly seized hold of me. My heart pounded, my face felt hot. Winning that chess game became overwhelmingly the most important thing in my life. I could not bear to lose that game to that cocky little man. I could not - I would not - lose that bishop! But he was going to take it. I was filled with an urgent, primeval loathing for Larsen. I understood then how men can kill. I looked at the chess board in desperation.

And then I was transformed. Suddenly, I could see many moves ahead on the board. My mind raced, my ability to plan, calculate, visualize, was powerfully expanded. I could see 9, 10, 12 moves ahead! Never before had I been able to do this. I suddenly saw a plan, worked it out at hyperspeed, trembled with the intensity and complexity and boldness of what I was going to do. Only seconds remained before Larsen would complete his circuit of the boards and be in front of me again. He arrived and stared, waiting for me to move. There seemed to be a slight smile on his lips. Hesitating, I then moved my piece. He stepped slightly back, puzzled. He was unprepared for what I had done. I had initiated a combination that sacrificed my own queen, the most valuable piece on the chess board! Against a grandmaster! Larsen studied the position for a long time. He made the move I knew he would have to make. He saw what was coming. After another 9 moves by each of us which were forced by the combination I had set into place, I was a piece ahead of the grandmaster. He had defeated his other opponents by now. I had the advantage in the endgame, but I was now playing the grandmaster one-on-one. Could I actually keep this advantage, against such a great player? Would he not figure out a way to win after all? My fury was unabated. I could feel the flushing of my face, the tightness in my chest, hear my shallow, rapid breathing. I concentrated as hard as I could. After about 10 minutes of play, Larsen extended his hand to me, and resigned. He congratulated me. I had won!!

I rose and took Larsen's hand. I could barely stand. There was a darkness before my eyes, and I felt unsteady. I left the club immediately, more deeply ashamed of my behavior than at any time in my life. No game, no winning, could possibly be worth this anger, this fury, this fear and hate, this super-charged, adrenalin wave, this irrational desire to destroy an opponent. To myself I said, "Never will I do this again. Never again will I play in a chess competition." And simultaneously I understood why I had never before been able to play serious high level chess. I really had never cared enough about winning the game. The good players all thought winning was the most important thing. You had to really WANT to win. You had to want it so bad that nothing else mattered. And, with chess, I never did.

And, in this one game when I had cared enough, I had been aware of deep, dark powers. I had become almost supernaturally clever, devious, even deadly. I realized that I was not alone in being subject to such effects. I felt, as never before, just how dangerous and destructive human rage can be. I resolved to avoid confronting and threatening others if it could possibly be avoided, never to knowingly make others feel hunted and cornered. Man in that state is very, very dangerous. I remembered a short story read in my childhood. On a private island, the demented owner hunts human beings for sport; he does it because, as the story title says, man is "The Most Dangerous Game". **Man can indeed be deadly dangerous**, as I learned from playing chess.

There were other lessons of general importance that I learned from playing chess in Brooklyn. Some have served me well in life, although chess remains to me just a game. Here are a few.

1. **You can't expect to beat an expert at his own game**. How many times have apparently intelligent people forgotten this lesson, to their enduring harm! The expert starts with talent and then refines it by many years of extremely hard work. The effect is a depth of knowledge and performance nearly always unattainable by the amateur. You simply will not beat Fischer at chess. Yet, we all know patients who do not accept the recommendations of an outstanding physician, men and women who think they will manage their investments better than Warren Buffett, ignorant reporters who snidely critique the life work of geniuses. Human pride truly comes before the fall. To know thyself is to know how little one knows, and to live in accordance with this understanding.

2. **Success comes from making sound moves time after time**. This rule applies to life as much as chess. The cumulative impact of many thoughtful, well considered minor as well as occasional major decisions will lead eventually to great progress. This is true with career development, with running a company, with building a loving relationship. It is hard to recover fully from repetitive blunders due to lack of thinking or effort.

3. **Never ignore threats**. Circumstances may suddenly change. In chess, an opponent makes an unanticipated move which you do not at first understand. Consider carefully. What you don't initially comprehend may deserve consideration, and should not blithely be ignored. The nature of the game may have changed. Life is filled

with examples of this rule. The Holocaust provides one tragic illustration, where for a much too long time some European Jews failed to recognize the implications of Hitler's potential and then actual ascent to power, and paid for this oversight with their lives. After the Civil War, America's largest cash crop was hay for horses, and later there were many hay farmers who tried to ignore the significance of the automobile. Threats to the status quo are an important fact of life.

4. **A bad game is hard to win.** Sometimes, a game develops that is virtually unwinnable. It is best to recognize that fact and, if circumstances permit, quit and start a new game before becoming exhausted. In life there are often opportunities to start again in changed circumstances, with a chance of a better outcome. I am eternally grateful to my grandparents, who recognized that being a Jew in Czarist Russia or the Austro-Hungarian Empire was not a game there was much chance of winning, and who therefore emigrated to America.

5. **The captain does not have to play first board.** This means that in those innumerable life activities requiring group effort - a company, the family, community service - building a successful team may actually be impaired by a prideful focus on being the center of attention, the most prominent symbol, the nexus of power. What is best for the total effort must take precedence, and stimulating and inspiring that effort is the real test of mature leadership.

6. **Try to see as many moves ahead as possible**. This one is obvious.

7. **To win, you have to really WANT to win.** The Larsen game highlights this truism. This need not apply in many life situations, but in some it has to. If you are very sick, to

36

survive you have to really want to recover. If you are running a company, you have to really want it to grow and thrive. You can't just generally "hope" it will happen. As a successful financier asked the young man who asked the elder gentleman to teach him how to make money, "The first thing is, do you sincerely want to get rich?" Whether you say "no" or "yes" to this type of deep question, try to be sure you know your own answer, and live that aspect of your life accordingly.

8. Grandmasters don't play much weaker players; they have much more to lose than to gain. There are many life situations which illustrate the biblical injunction not to throw your pearls before swine, lest they be trampled underfoot. Consider carefully with whom you are choosing to speak or act, and back away if they do not appear to match your own level. This is true morally as well as in other ways.

9. A cornered, desperate opponent can be very dangerous. Try to avoid placing persons in situations where they feel cornered. Allow them to save face and dignity, to withdraw from a situation without excessive rancor or anger. This is prudence as well as kindness.

10. Decisions are really made by individuals, not by committees. This is true of course in chess games, and is applicable to many life situations. You must make up your own mind. And while a team or committee may sometimes appear to decide certain issues, the matter is really determined by what goes on in the individual hearts and minds of the persons composing the group.

11. Genius matters enormously, is extremely rare, and always has a limited life. An individual of genius cannot be replicated. This is an inescapable tragedy of the human condition. The rare genius, who can play chess like Fischer, achieves many, many times more than just a very good player. It is folly to pretend that Fischer, Bill Gates, Warren Buffett, Margaret Thatcher, Josef Haydn, or Claude Monet are "replaceable". It has been correctly said that, "There are only so many people able to address issues at a certain level of complexity". At the highest levels of genius, the number of such people is extremely limited, and may approach one.

12. **In a second, an outstanding player will see more and do more (make a better move) than an ordinary player who takes all day**. This is not just limited to chess. It is true of leading physicians, investors, scientists, generals, artists, lawyers, and so forth. Don't conclude that the doctor who spends the most time talking with you or examining you has the deepest understanding of your health.

13. **Watch your clock**. How important this rule is! We are all influenced by the passage of time. Do not waste time, nor lose awareness of how much time has already been used. In a chess game, you can calculate how much time you have left; life allows no such precision, except with regard to time consumed.

14. **An important move may deserve over 1,000 times more thought than an ordinary one**. There are certain branch points in life, key decisions of great importance. Try to recognize these situations, and if at all possible give them the large amount of extra thought they truly deserve. While our human foresight is limited, we must try our best to recognize when the right move is especially important, and when a position is unusually complex or dangerous. In life you do not have to make all your moves in two hours.

15. **The chess game may seem important, but it is not everything that is important.** Life has many aspects. Whatever game you are thinking about, it is not all of life. There is a difference, ignored at one's peril, between any game or issue, and the totality of existence. Chess can be only win/lose; life can sometimes be win/win, and these are often the best solutions. And, however great you may think you are, you will someday lose an important game. In fact, someday you will lose everything. Prepare for that time and recall that in our lives it is not given to man to decide all things.

Coon Tales

It all started when my wife determined that the lawn at our winter home in Palm Springs wasn't perfect enough. An area under the big olive tree on the south side of the property manifested distinct imperfections: a few square inches of tiny rounded leaves had appeared among the grass blades. I knew nothing about any of this at the time my wife contacted our lawn service. Indeed, I had even failed to spontaneously perceive the infinitesimal lesion in our grass. Anyway, my wife had determined that something had to be done about this flaw, and that's when the trouble began.

A few days later, a pungent and repellent odor was noted in our home. My wife said she thought it was coming from our neighbor's property. But the smell just didn't go away. Finally, I called our lawn service guy, who's known as Finn and whose employees are all Hispanic. (By the way, I don't know how Finn and his employees communicate, since he does not speak Spanish and none of his workers speak English, let alone English with a Finnish accent.) I asked Finn to check out the smell next door. He came around the next day. Our conversation went something like this:

Finn: "Vat do you think of the steer manure? It's the best stuff."

Wife: "What steer manure?"

Finn: "That's vat I put on the lawn to fix it. Grass just loves it. It's the best stuff."

Me: "It may be the best stuff, but it has a horrible odor. And it's been smelling like that for about a week. When will the smell go away?"

Finn: "Vell, it vill get better soon.

Wife: "I sure hope so, I'm giving a dinner party here in a couple of days."

Me: "Finn, before you do something like this again, please check with me first."

Finn: "Of course I vill."

But, of course what he meant was that he would check first with my wife next time. And that's what he did. The little round leaves just loved the steer manure even more than the grass did, and the defects under the olive tree became large enough that even I - though only upon close inspection - could actually see them.

So a couple of weeks later, I came home to find that all the grass south of the pool had been cut out - nothing was where the grass had once been except dark brown soil. I asked my wife about this, and she told me that she and Finn had decided to re-sod. It was felt that weed killers plus simple re-seeding wouldn't really get the lawn in good enough shape. It was, admittedly, far more expensive to re-sod rather than re-seed, but it would do the job SO much better.....

Next day, a truck arrived burdened with heavy rolls of sod. These were unrolled to form grassy squares. Scores of these squares were laid side by side on the bare earth like gigantic tiles. By the end of the afternoon, the job was done. The weeds were gone. The grass mosaic looked fine, except for the dark edges of each square which were destined to grow together and form a new, seamless perfection of lawn.

Next morning, I was awakened by a scream from the garden. My wife was standing near the re-sodded area. Many squares of the newly-sodded grass had been rolled up at the edges, and some were turned over completely. Some animal had come in the night and destroyed the lawn. My wife called Finn, and he speculated that it was a raccoon. He said they like to dig for grubs under the new sod. He didn't explain why he didn't tell us in advance that this problem might arise. He wasn't sure the best way to get rid of the raccoon if it came back, but he speculated it might never return.

So my wife and I rolled the edges of the grassy squares back into place, made the lawn look sort of whole again, and hoped for the best. But in the morning, our worst fears had been realized. The coon had come back after dark and helped itself to another meal of grubs. The lawn looked even worse than after the coon's initial feast.

Coon: 1. People: 0.

Finn then said to put lime on the sod. This was done liberally. The lawn was dug up again the next night.

Coon: 2 People: 0

We replaced the pieces of sod again, and went out and bought some nets. These we placed carefully over the sodded area. The next morning, the nets had been torn away, and the sod dug up once again.

Coon: 3. People: 0.

My wife then went to that modern source of all self-help, online information. She learned that a product called "mountain lion urine", which claims to really be made from the pee of mountain lions, has a powerful repellent effect on raccoons. She also called some friends who are long time residents of Palm Springs, who confirmed they had heard that mountain lion urine was effective against coons although none of them had actually used it and didn't know where to buy it. The Palm Springs City office also advised trying this substance. I thought the whole thing extremely funny, figuring that obtaining the stuff would be just about impossible.

But I was wrong. My wife found a local source, and went out and bought many gallons of actual mountain lion urine. These she proceeded to decant liberally all over the sod. She also poured the urine on the wall which surrounds the garden, on the gates leading into our property, and even on the mailbox near the gate. The following morning, the sod nevertheless was dug up as usual. Moreover, it shortly became apparent that the mountain lion urine had permanently discolored the pink paint covering the block wall around the garden, and corroded like strong acid the metal of the mailbox. Subsequently, repainting of the wall and replacement of the mailbox were performed.

Coon: 4. People: 0.

I had heard that devices were sold that emitted a very high pitched sound, audible to animals but not to humans, and which were used to keep dogs off people's properties. My wife checked this out online, and purchased several emitters which arrived by next-day air. They were activated by a motion sensor which detects an approaching animal. These were carefully implanted around the periphery of the lawn. During the night, we were awakened by the high-pitched shriek of the alarms going off. Apparently, my wife had obtained devices emitting in the frequency range of both human and animal audibility. My wife threw on her robe, and raced out into the garden. I am told that I cursed, rolled over, and somehow fell back asleep despite the noise. Next morning, I learned that as my wife emerged into the garden, she actually saw the raccoon digging away quite unconcerned within 3 feet of one of the emitters. The noise was so loud that my wife had to retreat into the house. After the alarm stopped and she went back out, much of the sod had been dug up again and the coon was gone, presumably after having enjoyed its night-time snack.

Coon: 5. People: 0

It was obviously time to end "do it yourself" and get some experienced professional assistance. We were referred to the local "raccoon man", an exterminator who claimed to have rid many properties of these pests. Apparently, in California it is not legal to kill coons, but they can be trapped using devices that cause them no physical pain; the trapped animals are then transported into the Jacinto mountains and released. The raccoon man came and set a wire cage with a trap door between our pool and the sodded region. Within the cage he placed an opened can of sardines. We savored the thought that tonight that raccoon was going to be history.

We awoke at dawn, and looking from our bedroom window in the feebly gray light perceived that at last we had done it. The animal was in the trap! I hastily dressed and went out to view the prisoner. But inside that trap was not a raccoon, but a snarling cat. And the lawn, by the way, had been dug up as usual. Getting the cat out of the trap was tricky, and required figuring out how the door could be sprung free while protecting oneself in heavy gloves. When at last the door popped open, the cat accelerated out of the box faster than a Ferrari and leapt out of the garden. I had never before seen an animal go from 0 - 60 in less than two seconds.

Over the next few nights, the trap was rebaited and reset. Some nights, we caught nothing. But we did imprison two other cats, and one small dog. The coon was too smart, kept digging the lawn, and never was trapped. Finally the raccoon man came and took his cage away. He had been paid up front, results not guaranteed.

Coon: 6. People: 0.

After telling the above story to a local friend, we heard about the time someone had called the same raccoon man to deal with a nest of coons living in their chimney. His fee, to be paid before commencing services, was $400 and for this problem he guaranteed success. After getting paid, the raccoon man borrowed from the homeowner a ladder, a roll of toilet paper, and some matches. He climbed onto the roof, tore off pieces of toilet tissue, rolled them into balls, set the balls on fire, and dropped them down the chimney. The raccoons immediately scampered out and disappeared. Upon finishing his work, the raccoon man presented several copies of his business card to the homeowner. He explained that the raccoons would doubtless find another chimney to live in, and he thought it might be helpful for the neighbors to be given one of his cards.

Yup, raccoons are smart, almost as smart as the raccoon man. A local resident claimed to have actually seen one coon pop open the door of a trap and free its mate. Springing the coon trap the first time (with the hissing cat inside) took me about 20 minutes, suggesting that in terms of IQs the correct descending sequence is raccoon man > coon > me.

Well, as the late economist Herbert Stein liked to say, "If something can't go on forever, it will stop." We went back to covering the new sod with nets, and laid upon those nets many long and weighty wooden poles. The coon came back for a few more nights, but the damage after each visit gradually diminished. I suspect he was getting tired of eating the same meal every night, and probably finding fewer grubs on each return trip. One night he stopped coming and never came back, retiring with dignity and undefeated.

The lawn looks fine now. The grass is the way it should be again. In fact, it looks just about as good as when we started trying to make it better.

A few of those little round leaves have reappeared under the olive tree, but we plan to ignore them. If they get real bad, I guess we'll just have to sell the house.

The Cracker Barrel

Hay, y'all. Well, hear we are in North Carlina on our way home from the mountins of Georga where Dick C.'s maw decided to orginize a gatherin of the hole family sept fur the four out of eight who couldn't git there.

Still we met some real nice peeple. Like Nancy, who ran the in we staid at, and who cooked good and was one of nicest widow ladies I ever seen. And there was some other good fokes, like the family we seen who went to look at a purdy waterfall and they was all healthy but one of them was a crippled boy in a wheel chair, and they took him out of the car real gentle and put him in the chair and rolled him over to wear he could see the falls as good as them. Reel nice I call that.

I wish I could tell you everyone we seen was nice, but I wooden be tellin the trooth. There was one guy neerly run me off the road, and another who drove his car that was pullin his motor house down a mountin at maybe 100 and nearly kilt three people comin out of gettin gas, and then ther was a gravel truck that spillt a bunch of stones all over my new car. Then there was a restrant we et at where ther waz 4 negros (this is what they call Afro-Americans in North Carlina) and they was partyin it up and smokin and drinkin and makin noise like they all just wun the No Bell Prizes, and there was all the white folks sittin up near the far wall tryin to preten they couldn here the noise and didn really mind.

Peeple in the South are a little diffrent than usual. The boys all where ther hats with the brims pointed back, protectin ther necks, and makin their four heads look all slopey. And lots of the folks here are sur hevy. We seen one famly with a mother wayd over 300, her husband musta wayd much more, and the kids were all over 100 even the little girl who was bout four - hole family together musta been over half a ton, and grone.

We took a turist trane from Blue Hill Georga to another town about 10 miles away. Trip took ever an hour on this old trane. When we got there Dick C. and the rest of us went shoppin. Dick C. got a pear of genes for 25 cents and I got a Columbya Savings and Lone hat for 25 cents two. They fit reel good and we are werein them evry day goin home.

There aint a lot of news papers hear in the suthern cuntry, but we seen enuf to no whats' goin on. Seen somethin about how President Bush and his frends Freddy Mack and Fanny May are settin up a special program to give loans to Arabs so they can all get free homes. Gess he doesnt want anyone to think hes prejudice becuz of the little fight up in New York last yere.

We went from Georga to Carlina on the Blue Ridg Park Way. Very purdy. You could see all the mountins covered with all them trees. And up at bout 5000 feet in the air there was all kinds of purdy flowrs - "row d' denims" all purpl, orange flaming azalees, and Dick C.'s favrit, the mountin Laurel that her paw loved so much afor he dyed.

Anyway, I thunk you mite like to here from us and no what is goin on. Dick C. tells me I might not want to send this lettur since she sez it aint "politicly correct" but if you think it is you jus shouldn't reed it or send it to yur frends. Also, Dick C. beleves that since I re-tired last Septembr my spellin and grammur are gettin wurst. I don't agre, and if you think Im right pleeze let me no.

Your frend, Joe

Dad Comes to the Wedding

So there we are, just arrived at San Francisco International Airport for the wedding of my niece, Debbie to a sweet guy named Eric. It is about 6 PM on May 28, 1999, and I am near the baggage carousel in United area 5. All our luggage is piled on a cart over where Mom is resting, looking a little pale from her trip all the way from Florida via Chicago. Her vision is not so good any more, and her gaze appears more inward than outward. Dixie has gone to get our rental car from Hertz, and it is taking a while since this is the Memorial Day weekend (what a great time for a wedding!) Oddly, the area where we wait is not very congested or noisy.

I am standing near the carousel and Dad walks over. He is smiling broadly, his eyes are bright, and his face is ruddier and healthier than I remembered it. His hair is grey but fuller than before, his shoulders are a little broader, maybe he has added a few pounds but he is fit. He is wearing a blue blazer with the old school emblem of some college, perhaps NYU or Columbia. His slacks are tan, well pressed, comfortable, elegant. He looks great.

"Dad," I say, "I didn't expect to see you here. You died quite a while ago."

"They let you come back once in a while," he said. "So I decided to do it today."

"What is it like over there?"

"Well, it's hard to describe. Impossible really. But it's very nice. Actually, it's a lot better than it is down here."

I glance over at my mother about 50 feet away on the bench. She is looking calmly ahead, and sees nothing.

"I don't think it would be a good idea to tell your mother that I'm here," my father continued. "You know how easily she gets excited, and there are other times for me to talk with her."

I am amazed at how my father is speaking. His words are confident, delivered with a penetrating intelligence that I did not recall.

He asked many questions. Each reflected a deep insight, a mature wisdom as it sought to know more. "How is so-and-so, is she still focused on her career? And what about little X., is she still trying to show that she is smarter than her sister? Has Y. learned to be more respectful of her mother? Has A. gotten over the divorce and remarried happily?" I answered as well as I could, but what was remarkable was the insight, and the equanimity, the absolute gracious calm, with which he listened to each reply. It was as if these things mattered to him, he understood all that I said and more, and yet in another way none of it affected his poise and his inner peace. It was incredibly joyful to be talking to him. And I think he liked it too, since the smile never left his face as he looked at his only son.

After a while I said, "Dad, Dixie may be outside in the car. Let me see if she is waiting." And I walked through the glass doors but she had still not gotten back through the noisy traffic, and after a whiff of exhaust fumes I returned to the calm interior where my father waited.

"I don't have any more time right now", Dad explained. "But I will come back again. And someday we will have more time. It was good to see you, Joe."

Still smiling, he turned and slowly walked off into the crowd. I watched the dark blue of his jacket until I could see him no more. My eyes filled with tears.

Dixie had arrived with the car, and she helped my mother while I loaded the bags into the trunk, and we drove out of the airport toward Palo Alto.

The Diversity Thing

Few things are more politically incorrect than questioning the current cult of diversity. But why worry about popularity? Let's take a closer look at this subject anyway.

Diversity is universal. The galaxies, stars, planets, and asteroids are each unique. Diversity is evident in biology and in social organization. There are diverse animals, insects, and plants, some extant and probably many more extinct. Human beings come in various sizes, shapes, genders, hues. Human behavior varies from saintly to bestial, generous to selfish, kind to cruel, intelligent to stupid, heterosexual to homosexual. Men and women vary in their abilities and how they chose to utilize them; one becomes a mathematician, another a musician or a scientist, while yet another becomes a hired killer or drug dealer. Certain societies value personal freedom, in others "the nail that sticks out gets hammered," in others slavery is still legal. Some religions are monotheistic, others have multiple gods, some worship witch doctors. There are many languages. Examples of diversity are endless.

So *recognizing* diversity is merely acknowledging reality. But *recognizing* something, *tolerating* it, and *valuing* it are very different things.

Rational persons not only recognize diversity, but they have learned they must tolerate it in some measure. No democracy can work without peaceful acceptance of a range of different ideas, different degrees of human behavior, or varied religious preferences - a range but not an unlimited range.

Our tolerance is often tempered by preference and judgment, and basic common sense. Biological diversity means that mosquitos bite us at summer twilight, of which our acceptance is quite limited. We generally won't tolerate deer eating our gardens, unless the force of law compels us to leave them alone while they munch our daffodils and tulips. Most of us have sharply limited toleration for rapists, murderers, or drug pushers. An Inca-like religion which practices ripping the living heart from sacrificial virgins will not have its temple tolerated next to a church.

Most people choose to limit the diversity in their environment. We generally prefer beauty to ugliness, and would rather have the windows of our homes face toward snow-covered mountains or brilliant blue lakes rather than filthy alleys or garbage dumps. Dogs who destroy our sofas while expressing their diversity are replaced by more pacific canines. Among countless thousands of varieties of plants, we generally purchase only a limited range for our personal gardens or landscaping. We don't want random diversity when it comes to stocks and bonds. We seek friends whose values we appreciate, whose character we respect, whose intelligence or kindness inspire us. And most of us are highly discriminating in choosing spouses or lovers. The old song croons, "What's the use of wond'ring if he's good or if he's bad...." as long as you love him, but most of us know better.

The cult of valuing diversity for its own sake - with "diverse" being virtually synonymous with "good" - defies common sense and human reason, and causes profound difficulties. Many types of diversity are of insignificance, others are downright harmful. Stalin and Hitler were examples of human diversity, yet as one Russian said of

Stalin (after his death, when she could say it without being killed), "Better he had never been born." Should we prevent development of a town to save the shrike, a bird that butchers for pleasure? Should we block the use of insecticides to preserve some species of insect which feeds its larvae on the paralyzed and still living bodies of its prey? Or a more powerful example, should the use of DDT to prevent millions of deaths from malaria be stopped to limit damage to the eggs of certain avians?

Under the banner of a diversity valued because it is presumably worth protecting for its own sake, and hence "good," march countless causes. According to those who value diversity *per se*, every animal, plant, insect, religion, political faction, gender preference, moral system, person, or idea deserves to be equally appreciated, and valued because of its "uniqueness."

Yet few things would be more foolish, more downright dangerous, than widespread adoption of such a vision. The cult of diversity leads to fragmentation and absurdity. Mankind's progress has been due to never-ending selection in favor of sound ideas, decent values, better political and economic systems, improved technologies. The world is a far better place now than in the days of the caveman precisely because of our rejection of many forms of diversity. Some people thought the world was flat, others round; that variation in interpretation is over. We have eliminated the smallpox virus, a natural creation as surely as the snail darter, and we are much better off for doing so. Would the world be less good if some species of poisonous jellyfish, which kills many swimmers, were eliminated from the waters of Australia's Great Barrier Reef? Will our planet be harmed if some primitive society which practices human sacrifice and torture of its captives is suppressed? Will our cities be less desirable if criminals representing moral diversity are removed from its streets? Will our children be less happy if sexual perverts are prevented from playing with them? Would our schools be less effective were they to teach that good and evil are not just behavioral variants, that diligence and laziness are not mere equally valued alternatives, that becoming a physician or a murderer are not just different personal choices?

I raise my middle finger to diversity. The man (or woman) who created the Great Seal of the United States got it right. E Pluribus Unum.

Why Doctors Are Poor Investors

In the good old days when doctors had money, real estate developers and stockjobbers knew when they needed to find suckers for some dumb investment they could always go to their doctors. How true it is. I remember a hot tip from a friend. A family known for their real estate projects in southern Maryland were letting outsiders buy into their latest deal, conversion of a golf course to a mall in the outer suburbs. So I called one of the sons of the developer. He was willing to accept a minimum of $50,000 from me for a piece of the action. I asked him for a prospectus with more details. He said, "Doc, you can be in if you want. You can make a lot of money here." But there was no prospectus right now, there might be one later on. I asked about the degree of ownership that would be available for the 50K, whether or not my stake would be protected from dilution, how the company would be controlled, when and how I could sell. He said, "Doc, thanks for calling. We'll be here if you want to write a check. Trust me, this will be big. A lot of your colleagues are already in. Don't miss your chance."

Right.

Doctors could also be counted on to invest in startups, and not just in biotech - a field they might possibly have known something about. Standard operating procedure for raising money in new ventures involved blanket mailings to doctors. Almost always the proposed investments were dogs for which professional investors could not be found on agreeable terms, or found at all.

Now that most doctors are nearly broke from the combination of managed care, poor investments, and high

56

family expectations, it's tougher than ever for businessmen offering bad deals to raise money. Their capital source of last resort is gone. As one malpractice lawyer, who shifted from suing doctors to targeting corporate directors, so eloquently said, "The doctors have had their day."

Yes, doctors as a group are lousy investors. So are most lawyers, and most professors. But why? Surely they are not unintelligent. Many are very smart indeed, and a few are brilliant. They probably, almost surely, on average have higher IQs than the people who sucker them. Why do they get fooled so often?

There are all kinds of theories. One says that doctors make money easily, so they don't pay much attention to where it goes. Another view is that physicians feel it's better to invest badly than have their spouses spend it all. (A doctor whose credit card was stolen never reported it. The credit card company finally figured out something was wrong and called him. "Why didn't you tell us someone stole your card?", they asked. He replied, "The thief was spending less than my wife.") Still others guess that doctors are too busy taking care of patients to focus on investing. All these factors may be true to some degree. But I doubt they tell the main story.

Reading a book about construction of the first transcontinental railroad and thinking about Warren Buffett has stimulated a hypothesis which I believe represents the fundamental explanation of why most doctors are poor investors. Let's start with Buffett's brilliant summary, in one sentence, of investing: "Investing is spending money today in order to get more money back tomorrow." Period.

What does this have to do with the transcontinental railroad? The Big Four of the Central Pacific were Leland

Stanford, Collis P. Huntington, Charles Crocker, and Mark Hopkins. They got hugely rich from their investments in the Central, of course, but all were pretty prosperous before. Yet none was born wealthy, none had higher education. All were merchants. From the time they were teenagers, they were buying and selling things, saving their profits, and then using those profits to buy and sell more things. They did this at every opportunity.

Consider Huntington, who headed for California at the time of the Gold Rush. He was not dumb enough to want to become a miner, a high-risk personal investment with a very low probability of success. Many more people lost their lives in the Rush than got rich finding gold. Collis figured that the sure bet was to sell things to the miners, and he was right. To understand how his mind worked, note what he did on the way to California. There were three routes from the East Coast to the West. One was to take a wagon train across the continent; the second was to go by sea to the Panamanian isthmus, hike through the yellow-fever-ridden jungle, and then catch a boat to Frisco; and the third was to sail around Cape Horn. The fastest route, if you survived the jungle, was the second, and it was the one Huntington chose. But he arrived just after the only ship left Panama City, and he had to wait two months in that horrible place for the next boat. So did several hundred other persons. They waited, and while stuck there many died of the fever. Not Collis. Noting that conditions were terrible in Panama City and that decent supplies were needed by the many people there, he hiked through the jungle to the Atlantic port, loaded up, brought all kinds of supplies back with him, and sold them at a large profit. Then he went back and bought and sold again. He traversed the isthmus more than 20 times. And by the time he left Panama City, he had tripled his money.

Buy and sell, buy and sell. That's what merchants do. That's what investors do. It's the core activity of most businesses. But not of the doctoring business. Which is the main point. Doctors never have to buy anything and then sell it again at a profit. They have professional knowledge acquired with great effort, and they sell their skilled services to patients. Lawyers sell their expertise to their clients, ditto professors to their students and peers. So none of these folks has had to learn to turn a profit in a simple buy-sell transaction.

But investing is buying something now to get more money by selling it in the future. Doctors and other professionals are weak investors, as a group, because they have no practice, have acquired no skill, in buying things and then selling them profitably. Buying and selling sound simple. They aren't simple. Yet they're not frightfully difficult either. Surely investing is not more complex than brain surgery or quantum physics. The point is that, as with all things, practice makes perfect.

In a market economy, those who fail to learn how to competently buy and sell will be at a substantial economic disadvantage. When it comes to investing, "Physician, heal thyself".

Doing the Math - Contraception Part 2

A few days ago, law student Sandy Fluk_ , a name which reminds me of a good summer night on the beach, complained that she and her classmates at a law school in our nation's capital were being forced to pay $3,000 per law degree (over three years) out-of-pocket for contraceptives not covered by her Catholic school's health plan. Her complaint made it into the media, something obviously prearranged. Rushing to take the politically tainted bait was the ever-ready Rush Limba__, who on his nationally broadcast radio show called Ms. Fluk_ a "slut". The basis for Rush's slut label was presumably that he did the math. Mr. Limba might, for example, have logged on to Amazon.com and noted as I just did that a 48 pack of Durex Pleasure Pack condoms can be purchased for $16.07, which works out to about 33 cents per application. Thus Rush reasoned that a budding young attorney like Ms. Fluk_ would have to utilize about 3,000 condoms per year to expend $1,000 (assuming she was a member of Amazon Prime and that she took one day off from sex every two weeks). Further assuming that about half the time Ms. Fluk_'s sexual partners would cover the cost of condoms raises the number of her potential sexual partners to 6,000 per year, or 18,000 over the course of three years in law school. Even Wilt Chamberlain who claimed over 20,000 sexual partners in his athletic lifetime didn't reach Ms. Fluk_'s potential level of sexual activity while study law, thus calculated. The possibility that Ms. Fluk_ might, rather than being a slut, be setting him up, exaggerating, or might even be a monogamous nymphomaniac, seems not to have occurred to Rush. So thus misguided by his sophistication in mathematics, the commentator tumbled into the trap. Thereafter, the President of the Catholic school was forced to issue a statement defending Ms. Fluk_'s right to complain about paying for birth control, and the President of the United States found time in his arduous schedule to call Ms. Fluk_ and express his support for her while the media had a great time reporting it all.

I never complained about the cost of condoms when I was in school, but rather about the limited opportunities to use them. Times indeed have changed.

But there is more behind the story. And it has importance for what is going on in the field of health care today. Contraception has, for those who know a little history, always been controversial. According to Nobel laureate Robert Edwards, the inventor of the birth control pill, Gregory Pincus, was vilified by numerous churches for creating a devilish means to enhance trouble-free immorality. Unless the law has recently changed, in Connecticut it is technically illegal to *use* contraception, making Connecticut famous as the state whose laws are broken most often every night. There have always been folks who confound contraception with abortion. There have always been people misquoting the Bible about these two issues, none of which is in any way mentioned in either the Old or New Testaments (both of which I have read completely, not a minor task by the way). Furthermore, attempts to prohibit post-pubertal sex among the unmarried have never been successful and never will, and the Bible does recount stories of unmarried sexual encounters. Consider for example the heroic status of Esther, a beautiful young woman whose uncle obtained information from a source inside the King's harem about how best to please the King. Fortified with this data, Esther performed so well on her sexual audition with his Majesty that she was chosen to become his Queen. In this capacity, she was later able to save her religious compatriots from destruction. The Bible does not record the details of

Esther's use, if any, of contraception, nor more unfortunately about her sexual technique.

The problem is not contraception, it is politics. A large majority of Americans have long figured out that sex is a personal matter. But political activists on the left have argued it should be a government responsibility to facilitate "safe" premarital sex and abortion, while those on the right have argued the opposite. The problem is compounded by health insurance being provided by third parties like employers, or, for students, by their colleges, creating a further separation between the youth having sex and the obligation to pay for it on one's own. Thus a personal matter becomes a source of endless political conflict.

The Republican Party is committing suicide over these issues. Fanatics mostly associated with that party are trying to get laws passed to treat one-cell IVF embryos as "persons". In Delaware, one town council has recommended that sperm - I am not kidding - should be granted the legal protections of personhood. Most voters think this kind of stuff is crazy. As for abortion, it would be a waste of time to even try to review this well-known issue which every survey indicates most Americans feel should be a matter of personal choice.

Contraception, abortion, IVF, and pre-marital sex are among the items that should simply be off the agenda of government. But instead they have become yet another proof that people on the far left and people on the far right share the delusion that the powers of government should be utilized to influence people's sexual behavior. The debate between them is simply about in which direction the government should push.

One can only hope that most of us will continue to ignore the lunatics in both political factions, and not let the smoke and mirrors about human reproduction blind us to the significant other matters that government should and must address.

As for Sandy Fluk_, she has successfully launched her career as a birth control organizer. It would not surprise me to learn that she will be assisted by a former community organizer into future political office. But right now, anticipating fun on the beach while using up a few of those condoms as soon as the weather warms up in the northeast is doubtless under her more immediate consideration. No Rush. Go Fluk_.

Don't Know Much About History

Let's start with the following song and words, first recorded in 1959.

Wonderful World (aka Don't Know Much About History)
by Sam Cooke (1931-1964), Lou Adler, and Herb Alpert

"Don't know much about history
Don't know much biology
Don't know much about a science book
Don't know much about the French I took

But I do know that I love you
And I know that if you love me too
What a wonderful world this would be.

Don't know much about geography
Don't know much trigonometry
Don't know much about algebra
Don't know what a slide rule is for

But I know that one and one is two
And if this one could be with you
What a wonderful world this would be.

Now I don't claim to be an "A" student
But I'm trying to be for
Maybe my being an "A" student, baby
I can win your love for me

Don't know much about history
Don't know much biology

Don't know much about a science book
Don't know much about the French I took

But I do know that I love you
And I know that if you love me too
What a wonderful world this would be.

But I do know that I love you
and I know that if you love me too
what a wonderful world this would be."

Now let's check out where this message led. Sam Cooke who helped to compose and performed this popular tune and was a symbol of its message married his high school sweetheart, Barbara, who is considered to be the object of these verses. Here's what happened thereafter (more details are available online, what follows is primarily an extract from Wikipedia):

Four years after the first recording of this hit song, in 1963 Cooke's 18 month old son, Vincent, wandered away from his mother's supervision and drowned in their front yard pool while Sam was away from the home. With their marriage already in trouble largely due to extramarital affairs by both Sam and his wife, Barbara, the distance between them deepened as Sam blamed Barbara for their son's death. Cooke retreated into a deep depression, and asked that no one wear black to the child's funeral. He found his escape in out-of-town performances, which he agreed to at every opportunity.

Cooke died at the age of thirty-three on December 11, 1964, at the Hacienda Motel at 9137 South Figueroa Street in Los Angeles. Bertha Franklin, manager of the motel (or, as other stories differently claim, an unknown hooker or the CIA), shot and killed Cooke. According to what she told police he had attacked her, and she killed him in self-defense. Police found Cooke's body in Franklin's apartment-office, clad only in a sports jacket and shoes, but no shirt, pants or underwear. The shooting was ultimately ruled a justifiable homicide. Cooke's funeral was held in Chicago at A.R Leak Funeral Home, where thousands of fans had lined up for over four city blocks to view his body. Cooke was interred in the Forest Lawn Memorial Park Cemetery in Glendale, California.

It does not take a great deal of imagination to reflect on the combination of alcohol, drugs, too much money, disastrous judgment, and ignorance which led to this outcome for this performer. Cooke was black, poorly educated and, as the song implies, never acted as if learning was important. He didn't "know much about a science book" or pretty much any other school subject. To the extent the song says something about his personal attitudes, and I think it says a lot, he did not so much have difficulty with learning as a defective attitude toward the value of learning. His innate ability is obvious. He was not stupid. He pays lip service to the idea of being an A student so his girl might love him, but says nothing about all the other reasons.

Sadly for him and so many others, the views he articulated on education were dangerous, and such views are, unfortunately, all too common among other young American blacks today. And they are also common among many other students in our nation's schools. You have to work hard to learn. And to work hard to learn, you have to really want to learn. If you don't see the value of learning, why will you make the effort? And if you don't make that effort, how likely are you to succeed in a sensible and balanced manner in the world of the 21st century?

Eat Your Veggies?

Today's April 17, 2012 issue of the Wall Street
Journal has some articles about heart attacks - how to
prevent them and how to survive them. Some of what they
report is OK, and some of it is mere foolishness. Here is a
summary of what I think really matters.

Heart attacks are due to insufficient blood flow, and
sometimes total flow obstruction, to one or more branches
of the coronary arteries. This results in limited oxygenation
(ischemia) of the very active contracting muscle bundle we
call the heart. This can in turn cause irregularities of
cardiac action (arrhythmias) and/or death of heart muscle,
and, sometimes, death of the whole person. It has been
known for many years that one of the major predisposing
factors to heart attacks is damage to the inside surface of
the extremely important but narrow coronary arteries. The
damage can be due to the buildup of plaque-like
thickenings inside the arteries. Plaque accumulation is
facilitated in part by abnormal, or at least suboptimal, level
of certain types of cholesterol in the bloodstream -
particularly high levels of total cholesterol and LDL
cholesterol, and/or low levels of HDL cholesterol. Other
causes of damage to the inside, or intimal, surfaces of blood
vessels include diabetes, prior radiation therapy to the
chest, and other conditions. The damaged areas become a
focus for adherence of platelets, which are small cells in the
blood which are part of the clotting processes needed for
normal existence. The combination of damage + platelet
aggregation can result in clotting that blocks coronary
blood flow, causing the heart attack.

The progress over the last 50 years in preventing
and successfully treating heart attacks is almost

unbelievable. **There has been an approximately 75% reduction in the rate of U.S. deaths from coronary heart disease, adjusted for age, in the last 50 years.** That is truly amazing. Our population is, on average, older than it was 50 years ago, yet just in the last decade even admissions to hospitals for heart attacks have declined by about 25 %. Heart attack deaths in the U.S. last year were reported as between 500,000 and 600,000 (out of about 1.5 million heart attacks in a population of close to 312 million). It is no exaggeration to estimate that without the medical progress of the last half century, greater progress than has been made in all of human history, in treating and preventing many diseases, the U.S. death rates from heart attacks in 2011 would have been close to 3 million people, instead of 500,000. And that is just in this one year and in one country. The number of Americans whose lives were saved from heart attack deaths over the last 50 years surely can be conservatively estimated at not less than 50 million, in the same range as some estimates of worldwide deaths caused by World War II.

This extraordinary record of medical progress has real explanations, and many phony ones as well. The real ones mostly come from years of intensive medical research and billions of dollars of investment in such research from the National Institutes of Health and private industry, plus clues and ideas from alert medical practitioners. The key to medical progress is medical research at many levels. It is not a lot of other things, like scrimping on health care expenditures, having Uncle run our health care system out of Washington, DC., electronic medical records, dietary and exercise fads, and false promises of many kinds. Let's look at what really happened to cut the deaths from heart attacks.

Probably the single biggest factor in preventing heart attacks, surely one of the earliest, was the recognition that ordinary aspirin, acetylsalicylic acid, inhibits platelet aggregation and the triggering of blood clots. While confirmed by many scientific studies, interest in aspirin arose initially from clinical observation, things as simple as some smart people noticing that cuts from shaving bled more if you took an aspirin than if you didn't, or that simple tests showed that clotting times in response to a puncture of the skin got longer after taking aspirin. Daily aspirin use (either a single 300 mg. tablet or even the smaller "baby aspirin" containing one quarter of this dose) began to spread through the medical community in the late 1960s and early 1970s. Somewhere around 1980 some scientists at my alma mater, Harvard Medical School, belatedly dreamed up the idea of "proving" that aspirin reduces heart attacks by surveying the graduates of that medical school and comparing the rates of "coronaries" in the M.D.s who were taking aspirin to those who weren't. The study was abandoned when the scientists discovered that almost ALL graduates of HMS were already taking daily aspirins, and had been doing so for some years! Many of them took their daily aspirin with one or two Tums or a similar antacid to reduce the risk of gastric irritation or bleeding. Many studies have now shown that an aspirin a day keeps the cardiologist away.

A second factor was the greater understanding of the importance of cholesterol and cholesterol-related factors in causing heart attacks. The story here is a long one, and involved scientists in the U.S., Japan, and other countries, but the most important practical discovery to come out of it are the statins, a class of drugs which are easily administered and have large effects on reducing total serum cholesterol levels, reducing LDL cholesterol, and raising HDL cholesterol. It is possible by rigid dietary control to reduce circulating cholesterol levels by 10% or so in most people (there is a lot of variation here). But with generally well-tolerated doses of the modern statins like Crestor it is possible to reduce serum cholesterol levels by close to 50%. And while this extreme reduction is neither necessary nor even desirable for most people it shows the power of what can be done with these drugs. Not only can they greatly modify cholesterol levels, but alone or in combination with aspirin they make it possible to medically open or widen the lumens of already narrowed blood vessels. This has given realistic new hope to countless individuals who previously had no way to reverse widespread severe atherogenesis (plaque) within their hearts.

That said, nobody should conclude that *maximally* lowering cholesterol, with drugs or other means, is the right thing to do. Cholesterol and its derivatives are essential molecules in the body, necessary for health of all cells and particularly cells in the nervous system. Controlling excess cholesterol should be the goal. Statins are widely utilized at modest doses by doctors themselves, and millions of patients, to control elevated cholesterol levels and prevent plaque formation in coronary and other blood vessels even the absence of any history of coronary or cerebrovascular disease. It seems likely that doing this prudently is beneficial.

A third factor, which is still the subject of much speculation rather than proof, is the wider availability and use of antibiotics. These, of course, are utilized in the treatment of many infections ranging from earaches to pneumonia and sepsis. The great cardiac surgeon, Dr. Michael E. DeBakey, believed that the plaque-like changes in diseased coronary arteries represented infectious damage. There is interest in this topic among numerous medical investigators, and it is a difficult subject on which to gather conclusive data because, in part, of the already widespread consumption of antibiotics. Attention has focused particularly on organisms known as chlamydia, which are sensitive to many antibiotics, as playing a role in atherogenesis. The data from various studies so far are not definitive, but I tend to suspect that widespread use of antibiotics in the American population has played a meaningful contributing role in preventing coronary deaths.

In addition to preventive factors, survival from heart attacks which do occur has been greatly benefitted by progress in medical science and technology. Think of the complex advances needed to make possible coronary artery surgery, the almost miraculous ability to open occluded or partially occluded blood vessels with stents, improved and more widespread and inexpensive defibrillators, drugs that dissolve clots with the body, better electrocardiographic technology, improved imaging systems and dyes for examining coronary vessels for narrowing or flow reduction, the emergency medical teams and ambulance teams and their equipment available in many urban and suburban locations, and more. The benefits to mankind from these innovations are extraordinary, and the number of lives extended is in the millions each decade in our country alone.

The above benefits have, of course, been shared in whole or part by people in many countries. While the U.S. has the best, and most promptly and widely accessed, medical system in the world (misguided pundits not withstanding), what happens here in part, and sometimes in large measure, happens elsewhere. Multiply the U.S. data by some big factor, say 5-10, and you can make a crude estimate of what the advances described above have meant to the citizens of our world.

It is also worth mentioning that the types of things which facilitate maintaining healthy coronary arteries also help to keep other blood vessels healthy. Thus, prevention of heart attacks also favors prevention of the most common types of stokes and some other illnesses like vascular diseases of the legs.

In addition to the above factors, simple common sense can save many lives from heart attacks. If you are older, and if you can, choose to live in a community not far from a decent hospital with an emergency room staffed 24 hours per day every day of the year. If you have even a suspicion of a heart attack, get to that hospital as fast as possible; better to be safe than sorry, and communicate immediately upon arrival that you believe you may be having a heart attack - delay can be fatal, and minutes do matter. Keep aspirin in your car, pocket, or purse and take one immediately if you think you may be having a heart attack.

What about everything else one may read about? The Wall Street Journal articles noted earlier give the usual laundry list: work out aerobically with a meaningful increase in pulse rate at least 10 and perhaps up to 30 minutes per day; walk rather than sit; "don't worry, be happy"; "eat your veggies"; get a good night's sleep; avoiding salting of food; eat organically-grown produce; and more. (There are also people who feel that extreme vegan diets and major caloric restriction can extend the human lifespan, including reducing heart attack risk; a complicated subject we won't discuss here). The problem with these things is that the evidence they are really beneficial is weak to non-existent, tradeoffs are rarely considered, and anyone inclined to say otherwise is liable to be labeled politically incorrect if not downright stupid and therefore may prefer to remain silent.

Exercise can be fun, and may help to tune up your heart in modest amounts, but it can also kill you. Lots of people die from sudden exertion on tennis courts. Playing golf or swimming increases the risks of melanomas (nobody has yet figured out how to play golf in the shade), other skin cancers, and possibly of ultraviolet damage that could accelerate macular degeneration. Exercise also can cause injuries, including deaths from heads hitting walls or floors playing racquetball and accidents while cycling, and frequently damages cartilages of hips and knees leading to major surgeries and joint replacements, and these have complications and can also cause deaths. Jim Fixx, a leading sports writer in the 1970s, popularized the belief that if someone was healthy enough to complete a marathon (a 26 miles run) and maintained themselves in that state of conditioning they would never get a heart attack; regrettably, this was disproven when Fixx, a repetitive marathoner, himself died of a coronary. The data one reads on the benefits of exercise are heavily influenced by what geneticists call "selection bias" - people who tend to be more active are, on average, usually healthier to start with than people who are not - and it is almost impossible to correct for or eliminate this type of bias in human populations and critically examine long-term effects. Our claim here is not that moderate levels of exercise are bad. If a half-hour to 4-5 hours of your day can be enjoyably devoted to it, by all means do that and give up this fraction of your life of doing something else. But don't believe, really believe, that it is going to make you live longer. And, during those hours of exercise, do remember to keep an aspirin in your pocket and try hard to avoid serious injury.

Same goes for all the diet fads. Some years ago, there was a consensus that fat in food was bad for you, and it was better to shift your diet to more carbohydrates (after all, you have to get calories from somewhere, and foods that are largely protein are mostly expensive). But all that did was to make Americans fatter, and probably increase the frequency of diabetes. Alcohol, of course, was thought very bad for you until someone noticed that folks with moderate daily consumption of alcohol might be living a bit longer. Now one of the latest health dogmas advises consuming lots of organic veggies. Is that really going to make you get less sick? Maybe, maybe not. And of course poorer Americans, who have higher risks of numerous diseases, aren't going to pay up for expensive organics and, like the old joke about Chinese food, still feel hungry after eating. As for avoiding salt, actually salt is a necessary dietary element and, absent certain diseases, there is no good evidence that reducing intake of it will help you, though it probably will make your food taste worse and you might then eat less of it; especially in older people with subtle degrees of imperfect kidney function, low salt diets can make you very sick or even kill you (true confession: my own mother nearly died from the effects of gradual salt depletion due to avoiding dietary salt).

As for some of the other recommendations from the WSJ, like not worrying and getting a good night's sleep, who could say those are bad ideas? There is, of course, the unfortunate reality that a worry-free life is a rarity among even the luckiest and best-adjusted people, and rare too is the person whose every night's sleep is a good one. But presumably one should try.

Lastly, a disclaimer. Whether you agree with me or not, even though I'm a doctor I'm not YOUR doctor. Please see him about what ails you. I disclaim all responsibility for anyone who may find themselves influenced by any of the above opinions. I live part of the year in California, the world's most litigious location, so please note that I am not a licensed physician in that state and my thoughts therefore should be ignored by Californians. Finally, if you think what I am saying makes sense and you try it and it doesn't work and you get sick, if you sue me I'll never be your friend again.

As they say in Swahili, "Hakuna matata", there are no worries. Pretend that's true, and take someone you love out for a nice dinner.

Employing the Unemployable

I am becoming convinced that the genius of the American economic system is its apparently limitless ability to provide jobs to millions of people who are hopelessly incompetent. This is, in fact, a vital service without which our government's welfare and unemployment costs would be far higher than they are today. It also provides significant psychological advantages - dignity and a sense of self-worth - to the clueless many.

Allow me to describe three recent examples supporting this principle contention. These actually happened to me and my wife (so I have a witness) and I am not embellishing any of the details.

Example one occurred a few days ago when we stopped at a Friendly's restaurant. This company is well-known for its ice cream, has been acquired and turned over more often than a $50 dollar hooker, now has more debt that it can handle and thus is seeking bankruptcy protection. From the teenager behind the counter Dixie ordered a small cone, the kind that comes with a single ball of ice cream. She was given a cone piled so high with multiple balls of delightful product that she asked if this could possibly be just a small cone. This young man said that he was just giving her "the same amount of ice cream that he would want to get if he was paying three dollars."

Example two took place only yesterday, when we were driving back home from Philadelphia and decided to stop for coffee at a roadside McDonalds. I ordered a double espresso with two packets of artificial sweetener and one of sugar, and Dixie order a cup of regular coffee, black with nothing added. The young woman who took our order needed some help from the manager to enter our apparently complex order in the McDonald computer system. What thereafter arrived was a single cup of coffee, to which the shot of espresso had been added. At this point a third employee, the one who had made the coffee, appeared and was asked why she had put the espresso into the coffee and combined the two orders. She stated she had done this because the espresso by itself didn't nearly fill the cup. The order was processed again. This time two cups did arrive, one with coffee and one with a single espresso. I gave up trying to get the double espresso, and asked if the sweetener had been added. No, they had forgotten, what did I want? I explained again I wanted two artificial sweeteners and one sugar. One of the young ladies reached around, obtained some materials and handed me two little cups of half-and-half and an envelope with sugar. I then asked her to exchange the two creams for two packets of sweetener, and at last I could drink my coffee. Dixie was laughing so hard that she was almost unable to drink hers.

While all this was going on, a rather down-and-out old man shuffled up to the McDonalds counter and asked one of these same girls for "a cup". She gave it to him. He then proceeded to walk to the fountain bar and helped himself to serial free Coca-Colas. This guy got the best service in the whole place, and will probably become, if he is not already, a repeat customer.

The most recent illustration occurred just a couple of hours ago, and helped to inspire this little essay. Joseph S. Banks is a prominent clothier chain in the East, and has been in business since 1905. They offer rather good casual men's clothing at fair prices, and have periodic sales for their existing "corporate" and retail customers. Happening to need some tan cotton trousers, I drove by and took a look at what they were offering. They had a deal in which the first pair was 50% off normal price, the second 60% off, and any further pairs were 70% off. These casual slacks had a full retail price of $100 each (actually, for you, just $99.95). I decided to buy four pair. Simple mental math suggested that my order should come to about $50 + $40 + $30 + $30 = $150 plus tax. The order was processed at a computer by a middle-aged woman who seemed generally confused and took about 15 minutes to enter the necessary "data" including my credit card information. As she struggled with completing the order, a line of customers formed patiently behind me. The other salesman in the store gave her no help at all. Finally, she asked me to sign the receipt and I left. She had charged me a total of $115.26 including tax. I deemed it hopeless to try to fix the invoice and simply drove off with my 4 pairs of pants, having paid an average of about $26 per pair plus tax.

Now it is generally accepted that in an economic downturn, when there are more people looking for work than there are jobs available, the quality of those people still employed should rise. There is the famous example of the pioneering advertising agency, Benton and Bowles, starting up in the midst of the Great Depression after having figured out correctly that that was the time the best writers, illustrators, and photographers could be hired for *de minimus* wages. One possible conclusion from my recent experiences represented by the above, as well as other observations of what is going on with the American economy, is that the unemployment problem principally involves the construction and housing-related industries selectively. In many other industries, incompetents are simply continuing to be employed as usual.

Now, some of my highly ethical friends may say that Dixie and I have harmed the economy by getting more than we deserved in transactions one and three above, and by causing other customers to walk away while we insisted on getting our coffer order at least half-right in the second instance. With respect, I must disagree. We were innocent victims of the generalized incompetence embedded in our economy. And with the money saved in the above transactions, we have extra to spend on other things. I figure I have about forty bucks more from all this, and I plan to put it to good use buying Dixie two good vodka martinis and me a couple of drinks of Macallan at a nice restaurant. The profits lost by Friendly's, McDonalds, and J.S. Banks will simply be balanced by extra profits for other businesses. In fact, the net effect may well be to create more jobs.

It may be worth emphasizing that the three examples above were very recent, but are in no sense unrepresentative of many similar experiences over many years. One could fill a long book with nearly countless such real-life stories. Mostly they just cause delays or frustrations for us, the customers. One particularly amusing case involved a phone call Dixie made where which she was greeted by a recording saying "press 1 for English." She did so, and was then connected with an employee who began speaking in a language she could not understand. She then said, "I'm sorry, I thought I pressed 1 for English", when the voice said, barely recognizably, "I am speaking English." She simply gave up, and hung up.

Well now, some of you sophisticates may be inclined to think, "If Joe and Dixie didn't spend so much time in Cro-Magnon country, in backward locations like the Eastern Shore of Maryland, they wouldn't have these kinds of experiences." If any of you have that reaction and reside where the sorts of things described in this little rumination really don't happen, please let me know where you live and I will consider buying a home there. I will, at the very least, promise to check things out in person.

Meanwhile, God bless America and the absorptive capacity of the American economy.

Encomium on Henry Fielding

Notwithstanding what some might consider the futility of needless repetition, I reread Henry Fielding's "Tom Jones: The History of a Foundling" about once very ten years. This is done not to re-experience the almost overly contrived plot nor the unremarkable outcome of this lengthy work, in which the union of Tom and his beloved Sophia Western is anticipated from the outset by even the least perspicacious reader. Rather it is to know again the joy of receiving from one of the finest of all minds much of the wisdom which it took that mind a lifetime to acquire, and to be again inspired to internalize those maxims which can, it is hoped, be powerful guides to a worthy existence.

Fielding was a member of a noble family who was educated privately, at Eton and then at Leyden University in The Netherlands. He subsequently studied law and was admitted to the bar. From then on, his two passions were the law and literature. Ultimately, he found secure employment as a principal justice of the peace and was an advocate for various reforms in the English penal code. His first book was "Shamela", a parody of Richardson's "Pamela" which is sometimes considered the first English novel and frequently referenced as the longest ever published. "Joseph Andrews" and "Jonathan Wild", both very fine books, were followed by Fielding's masterpiece, "Tom Jones."

The structure of this classic is unusual and greatly enhances, for this reader, its surpassing value. For throughout the book, Fielding interrupts his narrative to provide chapters of commentary which are filled with genius. Far from constituting interruptions, these are the delicious fruits of a mature mind of the highest humanity and balance. An selection of these which seem of particular importance to this writer are collected below, and constitute the main body of this little communication, which it is hoped some will find edifying, or at least amusing.

It is time for a personal confession. Some years ago, yours truly was a physician-scientist engaged in genetics research at the National Institutes of Health. From time to time, I would discover literary pearls in my wide readings outside of science, transcribe these onto little pieces of paper, and affix them to the outer door of my office. Over the years this collection of aphorisms grew to encompass several score items, all of which were visible to anyone passing by that office. Some stopped to read, and a few to mutter - presumably about the rather odd mental state of someone apparently inclined to reveal so much of himself to others. For indeed what was posted on my door was also reflective of the direction I hoped to apply to my mind and my heart. The largest and most central of all the postings was a quotation from "Tom Jones." You will find it at the end of this essay. Fielding may or may not speak to you as powerfully he does to me, but I know of no wiser man, nor a better teacher for an enlightened life. With this preface, we begin our selections from "Tom Jones."

On charity: "There is one degree of generosity, of charity, which seems to have some show of merit, and that is where from a principle of benevolence, we bestow on another what we really want ourselves; where, in order to lessen the distresses of another, we condescend to share some part of them, by giving what even our own necessities cannot spare. This is, I think, meritorious; but to relieve our brethren only with our superfluities, to be charitable rather at the expense of our coffers rather than ourselves...this seems to be only being human creatures........As to the apprehension of bestowing bounty on such as may hereafter prove unworthy objects, because many have proved such, surely it can never deter a good man from generosity. I do not think a few or many examples of ingratitude can justify a man's hardening his heart against the distresses of his fellow creatures; nor do I believe it can ever have such effect on a truly benevolent mind."

Advice to the young (and the old): "We shall, if rightly understood, afford a very useful lesson to those well-disposed youths who shall hereafter be our readers; for they may here find, that goodness of heart and openness of temper, though these may give great comfort within, and administer to an honest pride in their own minds, will by no means, alas! do their business in the world. Prudence and circumspection are necessary even to the best of men. They are indeed, as it were, a guard to Virtue, without which she can never be safe. It is not enough that your designs, nay, that your actions, are intrinsically good; you must also take care they shall appear so. If your inside be never so beautiful, you must preserve a fair outside also. This must be constantly looked to, or malice and envy will take care to blacken it so, that sagacity and goodness of another will not be able to see through it, and to discern the beauties within. Let this be your constant maxim, that no man can be good enough to enable him to neglect the rules of prudence; nor will Virtue herself look beautiful unless she be bedecked with the outward ornaments of decency and decorum."

On a philosopher discovered in an embarrassing situation: "Philosophers are composed of flesh and blood as well as other human creatures; and however sublimated and refined the theory of these may be, a little practical frailty is as incident to them as to other mortals. It is indeed, in theory only and not in practice, as we have before hinted, that consists the difference: for though such great beings think much better and more wisely, they always act exactly like other men. They know very well how to subdue appetites and passions, and to despise both pain and pleasure; and this knowledge affords much delightful contemplation, and is easily acquired; but the practice would be vexatious and troublesome; and, therefore, the same wisdom which teaches them to know this, teaches them to avoid carrying it into execution."

On drink: "Nothing is more erroneous than the common observation, that men who are ill-natured and quarrelsome when they are drunk, are very worthy persons when they are sober; for drink, in reality, doth not reverse nature, or create passions in men which did not exist in them before. It takes away the guard of reason, and consequently forces us to produce those symptoms, which many, when sober, have art enough to conceal. It heightens and inflames our passions (generally, indeed, that passion which is uppermost in our mind), so that the angry temper, the amorous, the generous, the good-humoured, the avaricious, and all other dispositions of men, are in their cups heightened and exposed."

On taxes: "I am sure we are very good friends to the Government...for we pay a mint of money to them. And yet I often think to myself that the Government doth not imagine itself any more obliged to us than to those that don't pay them a farthing."

On the constancy of character: "It is admirably remarked by a most excellent writer, that zeal can no more hurry a man to act in direct opposition to itself, than a rapid stream can carry a boat against its own current.....For a man to act in direct contradiction to the dictates of his nature is, if not impossible, as improbable and miraculous as anything which can well be conceived.....Our modern authors of comedy have fallen almost universally into the error here hinted at; their heroes generally are notorious rogues, and their heroines abandoned jades, during the first four acts; but in the fifth, the former become very worthy gentlemen, and the latter women of virtue and discretion; nor is the writer often so kind as to give himself the least trouble to reconcile or account for this monstrous change and incongruity. There is, indeed, no other reason to be assigned for it, than because the play is drawing to a conclusion; as if it were no less natural in a rogue to repent in the last act of a play, than in the last of his life; which we perceive to be generally the case of Tyburn......as the heroes there are most commonly eminent for those very talents which not only bring men to the gallows, but enable them to make a heroic figure when there."

On credulousness: "Jones was well satisfied with the truth of what the other had asserted...[manifesting] a blamable want of caution and diffidence in the veracity of others, in which he was highly worthy of censure. To say the truth, there are but two ways in which men become possessed of this excellent quality. The one is from long experience, and the other is from nature; which last is often meant by genius, or great natural parts; and it is infinitely the better of the two, not only as we are masters of it much earlier in life, but it is much more infallible and conclusive......As Jones had not this gift from nature, he was too young to have gained it by experience; for at the diffident wisdom which is to be acquired this way, we seldom arrive till very late in life; which is perhaps the reason why some old men are apt to despise the understandings of those who are younger than themselves."

On choice of companions: "I believe I should not have erred so grossly in my choice if I had relied on my own judgment; but I trusted totally to the opinions of others, and very foolishly took the merit of a man for granted whom I saw so universally well received by the women. What is the reason, that we, who can have understandings equal to the wisest and greatest of the other sex, so often make choice of the silliest fellows for companions and favourites? It raises my indignation to the highest pitch to reflect on the numbers of women of sense who have been undone by fools."

On the impossible: "Jones now declared that they must certainly have lost their way; but this the guide insisted upon was impossible, - a word which, in common conversation, is often used to signify not only improbable, but often what is really very likely, and sometimes what hath certainly happened....And thus it is usual to assert the impossibility of losing what is already lost."

More on charity: "The world are in general divided into two opinions concerning charity, which are the very reverse of each other. One party seems to hold that all acts of this kind are to be esteemed as voluntary gifts, and however little you give, you acquire merit in so doing. Others, on the contrary, appear to be as firmly persuaded that beneficence is a positive duty, and that whenever the rich fall greatly short of their ability in relieving the distresses of the poor, their pitiful largesses are so far from being meritorious, that they have only performed their duties by halves, and are in some cases more contemptible than those who have entirely neglected it. To reconcile these different opinions is not in my power. I shall only add, that the givers are generally of the former sentiment, and the receivers are almost universally inclined to the latter."

On writing and reading: "As several gentlemen in these times, by the wonderful force of genius only, without the least assistance of learning, perhaps, without being well able to read, have made a considerable figure in the republic of letters, the modern critics, I am told, have lately begun to assert that all kind of learning is entirely useless to a writer; and, indeed, no other than a kind of fetters on the natural sprightliness and activity of the imagination, which is thus weighed down, and prevented from soaring to those high flights which otherwise it would be able to reach. This doctrine, I am afraid, is at present carried much too far; for why should writing differ so much from all other arts? The nimbleness of a dancing-master is not prejudiced by being taught to move......I cannot conceive that Homer or Virgil would have writ with more fire, if instead of being masters of all the learning of their times, they had been as ignorant as most of the authors of the present age.......I would not be understood to insist on the same fund of learning in any of my brethren as Cicero persuades us is necessary to the composition of an orator. On the contrary, very little reading is, I conceive, necessary to the poet, less to the critic, and least of all to the politician."

On pain: "This letter administered the same kind of consolation to poor Jones which Job formerly received from his friends." To which we add that timeless quotation from the same book of the Bible, in which God Himself silences those friends who impose upon the sufferer explanations for his suffering: "Who darkens my counsel with words without wisdom?"

On caring: "He had all that weakness which is called compassion, and which distinguishes this imperfect character from that noble firmness of mind which rolls a man, as were, within himself, and, like a polished bowl, enables him to run through the world without being once stopped by the calamities which happen to others."

On avarice: "This gentleman was what they call a man of the world; that is to say, a man who directs his conduct in this world as one who, being fully persuaded there is no other, is resolved to make the most of this. In his early years he had been bred to trade; but, having acquired a very good fortune, he had lately declined his business; or, to speak more properly, had changed it from dealing in goods to dealing only in money, of which he always had a plentiful fund at command, and of which he knew very well how to make a very plentiful advantage, sometimes of the necessities of private men, and sometimes of those of the public. He had indeed conversed so entirely with money, that it may almost be doubted whether he imagined there was any other thing really existing in the world; this at least may be certainly averred, that he firmly believed nothing else to have any real value."

On happiness and misery: "There are a set of religious, or rather moral writers, who teach that virtue is the certain road to happiness, and vice to misery, in this world. A very wholesome and comforting doctrine, and to which we have but one objection, namely, that it is not true.......and is indeed destructive to one of the noblest arguments that reason alone can furnish for the belief in immortality."

A quote by Fielding from Shakespeare on the "distracting anxiety" of the evildoer:

> "Between the acting of a dreadful thing,
> And the first motion, all the interim is,
> Like a phantasma, or a hideous dream;
> The genius and mortal instruments

Are then in council; and the state of man,
Like to a little kingdom, suffers then
The nature of an insurrection. -----

On parenting: "It is almost impossible for the best
parent to observe an exact impartiality to his children, even
though no superior merit should bias his affection; but sure
a parent can hardly be blamed when that superiority
determines his preference."

On affection biasing judgment: "Thus did his
affection for his nephew betray the superior understanding
to be triumphed over by the inferior; and thus is the
prudence of the best of heads often defeated by the
tenderness of the best of hearts."

On the wife (I hasten to add, lest I be
misunderstood, in the 18th century): "She always showed
the highest deference to the understandings of men; a
quality absolutely essential to the making a good wife. I
shall only add, that as she is most apparently void of all
affectation, this deference must certainly be real."

On marriage: "To discharge the matrimonial duties
in an adequate manner is no easy task."

On envy: "To say the truth, want of compassion is
not to be numbered among our general faults. The black
ingredient which fouls our disposition is envy. Hence our
eye is seldom, I am afraid, turned upward to those who are
manifestly greater, better, wiser, or happier than ourselves,
without some degree of malignity; while we commonly
look downwards on the mean and miserable with sufficient
benevolence and pity. In fact, I have remarked, that most
of the defects which have discovered themselves in the
friendships within my observation have arisen from envy

only: a hellish vice; and yet one from which I have known very few absolutely exempt."

On the devil: "I look upon the vulgar observation 'That the devil often deserts his friends, and leaves them in the lurch,' to be a great abuse on that gentleman's character. Perhaps he may sometimes desert those who are only his acquaintance; or who, at most, are but half his; but he generally stands by those who are thoroughly his servants, and helps them off in all extremities, till their bargain expires."

And lastly, dear friend, we come to offer what we consider one of the greatest of all quotations, which occupied the central panel on my door of yesteryear, and which along with the Golden Rule offers, we submit, a true guide to wisdom:

"True wisdom then, notwithstanding all which Mr. Hogarth's poor poet may have writ against riches, and in spite of all which any rich, well-fed divine may have preached against pleasure, consists not in the contempt of either of these. A man may have as much wisdom in the possession of an affluent fortune as any beggar in the streets; or may enjoy a handsome wife or a hearty friend, and still remain as wise as any sour religious recluse, who buries all his social faculties, and starves his belly while lashing his back.

To say the truth, the wisest man is the likeliest to possess all worldly blessings in an eminent degree; for as that moderation which wisdom prescribes is the surest way to useful wealth, so can it alone qualify us to taste many pleasures. The wise man gratifies every appetite and every passion, while the fool sacrifices all the rest to pall and satiate one.

It may be objected that very wise men have been notoriously avaricious. I answer, Not wise in that instance. It may likewise be said, That the wisest men have been in their youth immoderately fond of pleasure. I answer, They were not wise then.

Wisdom, in short, whose lessons have been represented as so hard to learn by those who never were at her school, only teaches us to extend a simple maxim universally known and followed even in the lowest life, a little farther than that life carries it. And this is, *not to buy at too high a price.*

Now, whoever takes this maxim abroad with him into the grand market of the world, and constantly applies it to honors, to riches, to pleasures, and to every other commodity which that market affords, is, I will venture to affirm, a wise man, and must be so acknowledged in the worldly sense of that word; for he makes the best of bargains, since in reality he purchases everything at the price only of a little trouble, and carries home all the good things I have mentioned, while he keeps his health, his innocence, and his good reputation, the common prices which are paid for them by others, entire and to himself.

From this moderation, likewise, he learns two other lessons which complete his character. First, never to be intoxicated when he hath made the best bargain, nor dejected when the market is empty, or when its commodities are too dear for his purchase."

The End of Gene-Driven Evolution

For hundred of millions of years, life on earth has evolved driven by the imperative for DNA, the genetic material, to replicate and expand its existence in future time. But DNA, the gene, cannot reproduce by itself. The double helix must split to allow each of its two strands to be copied accurately. This requires a complex supporting machinery of enzymes (generally proteins) and starting materials (the building blocks of DNA including the 4 bases adenine, guanine, cytosine, and thymine). And this machinery must not only allow DNA to replicate, but must ensure that it survives until it can replicate again. Hence the organism, the living entity that perpetuates DNA through time. The organism that can best perpetuate its DNA will overtake other organisms that are less efficient at doing so. The fittest survive better than the less fit. Through mutation, replicative error, recombination, shuffling of pieces of itself, and other mechanisms DNA can change over time to produce new organisms with enhanced selective advantages in the next generation. Viewed from this perspective, Professor Edward Wilson is correct to improve Samuel Butler's aphorism that the chicken is only an egg's way of making another egg by concluding that "the organism is only DNA's way of making more DNA".

Man is now by far the dominant species on earth. It was not so in prehistory. Two million years ago our early ancestors battled sabertooth cats and hyenas for food on the African savanna. At that time, man had a brain volume of about 500 cc., roughly comparable to the modern chimpanzee or gorilla. Over the past 2,000 millenia, the human brain grew at an extraordinary rate, achieving an average size nearly three times larger. This huge expansion produced a brain whose structural complexities are enormously increased, with a vastly greater capacity for thought and intentionality. The expanding brain was man's primary tool for evolutionary advantage. DNA, unthinking, made man who thought, so more human DNA could be made.

Not only could individual man outthink prey or predator, but the brain facilitated development of social systems which further enhanced man's ability to survive. Diverse species, including some insects, also cooperate to promote survival. The study of evolution in a social framework, sociobiology has provided important insights on the biological advantages of characteristics such as bonding, altruism, and communication. While these are not uniquely human traits, man's brain gives him extraordinary plasticity and adaptability in their application. Further, the large brain permitted man to develop language, complex tool manufacture and use, education, scientific method, capacity for worship, and unprecedented control of his environment. And the human brain now has come to comprehend something of its evolutionary history. DNA made the human brain, but now humans understand, and can even make, DNA. The brain, DNA's slave when present in other organisms, has now become DNA's master. For this fundamental reason, we live at an extraordinary inflection point in the history of our world.

To say that the brain is DNA's master does not mean that human beings are not genetically constrained by their DNA. But those constraints are, I believe, quite widely bounded. Man can be saint or a murderer, good or evil. He can organize societies based primarily on freedom or slavery, peace or war, love or violence. But he cannot choose to organize a society managed by the genetically programmed rules of insect groups. Man has many choices, but not all choices. Some scientists feel that with a deeper knowledge of human genetics, brain physiology, the detailed mechanisms of nerve cell interactions, and other phenomena we will be able to define the social and ethical framework optimally consistent with man's evolutionary legacy, in a sense the "ideal" society. I disagree. Man is bounded but plastic. The human brain permits innumerable but still limited options. Sociobiology helps us understand how we got where we are, and what we are, but I do not believe it will help us decide where we want to go.

The brain no longer is DNA's slave. For the first time in the history of this planet, an organism can choose, and is choosing, not to live by DNA alone. And the human brain is in the process of rapidly extending its control over the world by amplifying its awesome power with the development of computers that can "think" faster and deeper than man, assembly of vast databases of scientific and other information beyond the aggregate memory capacity of large numbers of individuals, and the knowledge to alter DNA itself.

The human species is thus the first to emerge from the constraints of classical evolution, although we bear and must understand our evolutionary and genetic legacy. But we can choose not to replicate without limitation, because we ("our brain") wants other things. And we do so choose. In nearly every society reaching the development of an advanced nation, the birth rate has fallen to limit population growth sharply, or even, as in modern Italy, to non-replacement levels. The further advance of modern civilization will produce a world with a more stable population. That is because the brain, and not our DNA, has taken control.

But we are still left with the great problem of what our brain will want to do after its triumph over DNA. We will certainly continue to strive to enhance living standards (create wealth) realizing that plenty reduces man's tendency, part of our DNA legacy, to aggressively compete for basic survival. The greater complexity and interdependency of advanced societies, and their great benefits, ensure that the relative value of peace will be enhanced compared to the vast destructiveness of war. And it is likely that our brains will continue to seek guideposts from the profound teachings of those who have been inspired to lead man away from the laws of the jungle toward a world in which the brain can achieve what it really wants, perhaps best embraced by the word "happiness".

"Love thy neighbor as thyself" and "Thou shalt not covet what belongs to thy neighbor" are likely to be much better guides to man's future happiness than clubbing thy neighbor, stealing his food, and raping his wife. Man's reaching for God, and his fear of our DNA-based heritage, are both part of the triumph of the brain.

Exercise and Longevity

I was recently asked by a medical colleague to analyze if there is convincing evidence that exercise promotes longevity or reduces age-related functional deterioration in human beings. Here is a summary of my attempt to do this after seeking data which might stand up to critical open-minded scientific scrutiny.

Before presenting my analysis, some disclaimers and background statements seem desirable.

I have no bias personally for or against exercise at my present, or indeed at any, age. In fact, there have been periods of my life when I hardly ever exercised, others when I did light aerobics, another when I tried weightlifting and rope climbing, a time when I ran extensively and even completed the Marine Corps marathon, and even intervals in which sex may have been my major sport.

I am not attempting here to assess the "subjective" benefits that some people experience before, during, or after exercise - anticipation of a good workout, the "runner's high", the enjoyment of the wind and speed of a bike ride, satisfaction from enlargement or altered shaping of certain muscle groups, the expectation or realization of a sexier or otherwise more "desirable" figure, the pleasure of playing golf in lovely surroundings, the joy of hitting a home run, the nice feelings some people have swimming in bright sunlight, the thrill of skiing at high speed, hang gliding, parachuting, wind surfing, or bungee jumping. For every person who feels good doing one, or several, of these things there are many who have an indifferent or even negative reaction to them. Personal preferences are subjectively important in affecting individual behavior, but they are not science.

Nor can I attempt to rationally weight the various tradeoffs associated with sports and exercise. I have personally suffered two injuries to my left knee and a tendon injury to my right foot from different engagements in sports. Friends and family have had a wide variety of non-lethal damage ranging from broken bones to serious head injuries while biking or riding horses, and almost all the men I know who were "jocks" when young have had knee and/or hip replacements when they got old. Even the most casual readers of the media know of the fatalities or quadriplegias of famous people from accidents related to horses, diving, skiing, mountain climbing, etc. As for near-misses barely avoiding injury or death during sports, they are abundant; on a single trip which I took with a group to fish in Alaska, one small aircraft incident nearly killed nine people, and a rafting accident nearly killed a tenth - and these really were close calls.

I also don't know how to weight such things as early deaths vs. later ones. One of my medical school classmates went back to Colorado to start his practice and died shortly thereafter while mountaineering. How can one compare this death at age 30 against the possible benefits to him or a group of people like him who were not killed but, say, lived 2 months longer on average because they were in "better shape" from climbing mountains, or simply because they "felt better" while they were alive but lived no longer than they would have without exercise? Another friend, a prominent geneticist in Pennsylvania, died in his forties after a head injury sustained on a racquetball court. Jim Fixx, the famous runner and exercise advocate-writer, died in the prime of life of a heart attack during a marathon. A few years ago, two young people died of heat exhaustion during a marathon in Virginia. I have had three acquaintances who actually dropped dead while playing tennis. Another acquaintance, the son-in-law of a good friend and a top surgeon, died suddenly from altitude sickness while taking a guided climb up Mt. Kilimanjaro. Several of my friends have developed melanomas, one metastatic to the brain, from sun exposure associated with swimming or surfing. And as for sexual exercise, another real cause of sudden death, one may recall the first, and perhaps most realistic part, of the movie, "Private Benjamin" in which Goldie Hawn's first husband dies just after their marriage, and his anguished mother pleads with Goldie, "Tell me, tell me, what were his last words?", the reluctant reply to which was, "I'm coming."

Because humans are so complicated, and health and longevity are influenced by so many factors, figuring out what really matters especially over long periods of time is exceptionally difficult. Just a few weeks ago I was at Ocean City, MD and saw a photograph of the boardwalk taken from a hotel window probably in the period around 1945-1950, maybe even earlier. The men are mostly wearing ties and jackets, the women dresses and sometimes a hat, during what was probably a Sunday promenade. The people in the photo are mostly thinner than the population today is on the boardwalk, also whiter and much better dressed, and they also look fitter - although they may not really have been. Of about 30 people in this image, nobody seemed to be obese, nor was anyone strikingly muscular either. Yet the obviously heavier boardwalk crowd of today, some of whom are walking along munching candy, ice cream, and French fries, will on average live about 20 years longer than those in the photo from 60 years ago. Of course, much of this is due to multiple improvements in medical care, disease prevention from less smoking, taking statins and aspirin, wearing seat belts, and other factors but who can say how much, if at all, the greater average weight of modern Americans lowers, or perhaps even raises, their average longevity compared to what it would be if they weighed 10-20 pounds less? This simple example illustrates why any *retrospective* comparisons of human longevity just cannot be helpful in assessing the kind of question we are asking with regard to the longevity and health effects of exercise or diet on humans today.

Then too it is very difficult to assess the combined influences of fashion, political correctness, and the self-interests of various businesses related to exercise. Models for women's clothes are almost always much thinner than average, they obviously limit carefully what they eat, presumably work out, and have genes for being innately tall and thin when young. As models they set a standard of good looks that influence many. But do they live longer? Do they stay smarter (or get dumber slower), compared to the general population, as they age? Do they even stay thin when older? The one woman I know who used to be one of Europe's top models when she was in her late teens is now, in her middle years, of average weight for her height, but fortunately remains healthy and plenty smart.

Political correctness is a far more serious issue that confounds analysis on exercise and longevity, as it does also on diet and exercise. Once some idea gets established as a current orthodoxy, it often becomes self-reinforcing to the point that contrary views simply never see the light of day, or at best emerge more slowly after passing over much greater hurdles. Imagine trying to publish in the medical literature an article that attempts to present evidence that exercise makes little or no difference in longevity or health. Anyone with experience of how medical journals and the peer-review process both work knows that data of this type will probably be close to impossible to publish in a major journal, while a similar difficulty will not apply for evidence reinforcing the current orthodoxy that exercise is good for you. Imagine the challenge of trying to publish an article claiming that 10-20 extra pounds makes no difference in how long you live, vs. one that concludes that losing 10-20 of those "extra pounds" helps you live longer. And as for the general non-scientific media, it is obvious that political correctness is an even more major determinate of what gets out before the readership.

And the problem is not limited to PC. There are intellectuals, both professional scientists and others like writers and reporters, who have large vested interests in exercise being a good thing; that is how they get grant money, or get their news stories and books published. They earn a living from spinning diet and exercise. They are a formidable opposition to scientific objectivity.

In addition, numerous business interests depend on the orthodoxy that exercise may help you live longer. Think of the manufacturers of running shoes, exercise clothes, bicycles, skis, tennis rackets, golf clubs, surfboards, rafts, mountaineering equipment, and so forth whose businesses in significant part depend on the dogmas about exercise. Consider the travel agencies, ski centers, golf clubs, gyms, bike stores, and countless other entities which benefit economically from the promotion of exercise. One should also include the major industries producing and promoting dietary supplements as well as ordinary vitamins as adjuncts to exercise. On top of that one finds less direct links subtly, even subconsciously, suggested between exercise and health reinforced by "running for breast cancer" or the "tour de cure" for diabetes or "walking for Alzheimer's". Can you imagine an event called "smoking cigars for the cure" or "boozing for liver cancer"?

And then one must consider too the statistical spinmeisters. By slicing and dicing data, aggregating data from many studies which failed to show significant differences, and so forth one may create "meta-analyses" which can produce virtually any outcome one wants. A recent article in the Wall Street Journal found at http://online.wsj.com/article/SB10001424052702303916904577377841427001840.html?KEYWORDS=analytical+studies has professional statisticians making precisely this point.

Examples of the types of foolishness an objective analysis should ignore are the pseudo-scientific studies done even by major institutions. Here is an illustration quoted from a recent New York Times article in which an inappropriate but commonly utilized control group makes the study useless:

"To see the results of such inactivity, scientists with the National Cancer Institute spent eight years following almost 250,000 American adults. The participants answered detailed questions about how much time they spent commuting, watching TV, sitting before a computer and exercising, as well as about their general health. At the start of the study, none suffered from heart disease, cancer or diabetes. But after eight years, many were ill and quite a few had died. The sick and deceased were also in most cases sedentary. Those who watched TV for seven or more hours a day proved to have a much higher risk of premature death than those who sat in front of the television less often. (Television viewing is a widely used measure of sedentary time.) Exercise only slightly lessened the health risks of sitting. People in the study who exercised for seven hours or more a week but spent at least seven hours a day in front of the television were more likely to die prematurely than the small group who worked out seven hours a week and watched less than an hour of TV a day."

For the moment, ignore the obvious biases in sentences like "the sick and deceased were also in most cases sedentary" - probably most of the healthy and alive were also. Now, think for a moment what it means to be an adult who watches TV an average of *7 or more hours per day*. I mean - really - anyone who actually does that has to be almost, or actually, a moron. Unintelligent people are of course at higher risk for all kinds of health problems compared to more intelligent folks, for reasons that will be obvious to anyone with medical experience. Thus comparing a group with average lower intelligence to one almost certain to be more intelligent invalidates the study. All the data really suggest is that stupidity kills, or TV kills, or both, as they seem associated with premature death with or without exercise. Exercise offers no cure for either of these problems. It may even be reasonable to extrapolate in the opposite direction and conclude that to become one of the longest surviving Americans one should aim to watch television little or not at all (which may also contribute to one's mental health). .

As a last preliminary comment, there is simple personal observation. The longest lived among my friends and family are my mother who is now 102, her aunt who died at about 100, my aunt by marriage who is now about 100, the grandmother of a doctor we employ who passed at 107 and could do the N.Y. Times crossword puzzles until she died, the mother of a friend doing remarkably well at age 105, and the father of a friend who died at 100. Of these, the only one who exercised regularly was the last, who played 18 holes of golf almost daily until his final moments on earth. But I now have scores of friends who have died. What did they die of? Most of them died from various cancers. Others died from neurological illnesses, acute mental deterioration sometimes of unknown causes, some related to Alzheimer's. Of those who have been disabled or made chronically ill, the causes have included neurological deterioration, strokes, hemorrhage from gastric ulcers, complications after joint surgeries, pneumonias, and automobile accidents. Amazingly perhaps, heart attacks and chronic pulmonary diseases have caused only very rare deaths if any in my population of friends, enriched in educated non-smokers. It seems most unlikely (though it is not completely impossible) that exercise would have extended the life-spans of some of my friends who died from the above causes. And among the healthy people 60 years and older whom I know, only a small minority exercise in the sense of regularly doing aerobics. Maybe half of the men play golf an average of once a week, and perhaps a quarter of the women do this. They engage in few other sports. With very rare exceptions, they are not grossly obese, but they are not notably thin either. In this group I am unable to observe any pattern of longevity or personal energy associated with presence or absence of regular exercise. As for mental vigor, the ten most energetic minds I can think of among my many very smart friends belong to men and women only two of whom exercise with daily regularity; most of the others exercise little or not at all although some may have done so when younger.

So now at last, how do I interpret the science? There is a vast literature on exercise effects and I can't pretend to have reviewed most of it. But what I have done, using primarily Google Scholar searches, is to try to find some key articles and reviews that seemed important to me. I read scores of abstracts and a sizeable group of full articles and spent quite a few hours doing this. Some items I found particularly helpful are available upon request, and you may wish to read them also. Basically it is possible to group the available data into that involving animal subjects, where better control (comparison) groups are usually possible, and that derived from humans.

The most frequently cited and important article on exercise and longevity in experimental animals appears to be the study done in the 1980s by Holloszy and associates. Holloszy has published other frequently cited articles on this general theme. It is particularly worthwhile to read his most important article carefully and in full, and I even paid $20 to the publisher to obtain it. The control group in his studies, also true of virtually all animal studies, is a group of rats who are forced to be extremely sedentary - they have been maintained in small cages from birth to death, and are thus less active than normal rats (and of course normal humans) would be. The controls are thus a group that, except when sleeping, could be regarded as being analogous to humans who watch television 16 hours a day. The exercise group is one where an exercise wheel is made available in the cage. Most young rats in Holloszy's study spontaneously ran on their wheels a lot initially, and then less and less as they aged. With careful reading one discovers that Holloszy removed from his "exercise group" several seemingly lazy rats that didn't use the wheels much on their own! This introduces a bias in the study. In addition, Holloszy also notes that many of the remaining exercise-group rats began to use their exercise wheels very little unless their caloric intake was "slightly" and chronically restricted to about 90% of what it otherwise would have been; this small food restriction appeared to make them more active. So the exercise group was really exercise plus mild caloric restriction when compared to the sedentary ad-lib fed controls, and they included an element of positive selection since the mice with little interest in spontaneous exercise had been excluded. This important investigation concluded that exercise did not increase survival in rats, it may have slightly increased (slightly altered the shape of) their longevity curve, but that the really clear effect was in yet a third study group - rats which were substantially *caloric restricted even though sedentary* lived longer on average than any of the other groups.

This same theme has been found over and over again in many studies before and after Holloszy's, namely that major degrees of caloric restriction do produce some extension of lifespan. Searches limited to more recent years, primarily since 2008, illustrate that far more convincing support has been found in animal studies, including more recently in primates, for the helpful effects on aging from substantial caloric restriction than for exercise, where the corresponding benefits are small or absent.

For humans, the data is almost impossible to interpret unambiguously. Exercise seems to promote a sense of psychic well-being in some individuals who are predisposed to mild degrees of depression. There are various studies which conclude that, as in animals, caloric restriction has substantial effects in circumstances where exercise may have small to absent ones. There is reported a weak suggestion of exercise benefits in one elderly institutionalized population. Very recently, Bouchard et al. published a fascinating, rather iconoclastic, study entitled "Adverse Metabolic Response to Regular Exercise: Is It a Rare or Common Occurrence?". Bouchard is professor of genetics and nutrition at Louisiana State University, and a prominent researcher. As predicted his study appeared not in one of the "top" medical journals but an open access free online scientific publishing vehicle known as PloS One (see www.plosone.org to find the article).

Bouchard's work attracted attention from one of the New York Times' leading science reporters, Gina Kolata, who has written on many scientific topics ranging from RSA encryption to assisted reproduction. Kolata's article appeared in the Times on May 30, 2012 under the headline "Can Exercise Be Bad for You?" and is available online. Kolata correctly summarizes the Bouchard group's conclusion (based on data from six rigorous studies of human exercise involving over 1,600 people): using analyses of several factors, like insulin levels and HDL cholesterol concentrations in blood, *about as many people showed potentially adverse changes in one or more factors after exercise as did those with potentially beneficial alternations.* "This is bizarre", said Bouchard, yet other experts agreed that the study was interesting and "well done" despite making them "worried about its consequences". Speaking for what I would call the PC opinion, William Haskell, emeritus professor at Stanford was concerned that "There are a lot of people out there looking for any excuse not to exercise" and "This might be an excuse for them" not to do so. Another expert, Dr. William Kraus from Duke, chose to look only at the subgroup with the possibly beneficial changes, ignoring the equal and opposite group completely!

The reporter correctly states that researchers in many human studies, by looking at blood changes associated with exercise, "infer that such changes lead to better outcomes - something that may or may not be true". She also states that "The national guidelines for exercise are based on such inferences and also on studies that compared the health of people who exercised with that of people who did not, a weak form of evidence often said to be hypothesis-generating rather than proof." Perhaps most significantly, Kolata obtained a quote from Dr. Michael Lauer, director of Cardiovascular Sciences at the National Heart, Lung, and Blood Institute of the NIH, which reinforces a conclusion close to my own view: "We do not know whether implementing exercise programs for unfit people assures better outcomes", said Dr. Lauer. He further said that "That has not been established", and "There is a lot of debate over how strong the [national] guidelines should be in light of weak evidence." Bouchard, Lauer, and other experts also agreed that it is currently impossible to identify in advance people who might have either beneficial or adverse effects from exercise.

So where do I finally come out on all this?

My current opinion is that caloric restriction of a major degree, maintained for years, seems to have longevity benefits and may slow the aging process somewhat. Most folks are not going to attempt to live like this, although there are some dedicated people doing exactly that today. This group of pioneers will have many "dropouts", but it will be interesting to study long-term those highly motivated beings who can and do hang in there for decades of semi-starvation.

The benefits of exercise both in animals and in humans seem much less clear-cut, and may be minimal or absent. Using extreme "control groups" such as rats in small cages and humans so constituted as to be able to watch television for at least 7 hours per day on average magnifies, and may to some extent create, the modest benefits of exercise in the studies that suggest they are there at all. Exercise takes time, and even if it may have some benefits those must be rationally traded off against the time consumed unless the chosen exercise produces its own near-term psychic or physical positives.

It seems common sense that exercise generally be done as safely and gently as possible. Treadmills are not only safe but have soft belt surface likely to minimize shocks to cartilage of knees, ankles, and hips, although treadmill use still involves weight-bearing and stress on joints. Distance walking seems safe and sensible, but over time could lead to cartilage wear especially if done on paved surfaces, in comparison to the same exercise done on a treadmill. As one gets older, it is important to preserve joint cartilage - which does not naturally regrow - and to avoid sports and other injuries. Swimming involves low joint stress, but is associated with exposure to direct sunlight, itself undesirable since ultraviolet light can facilitate mutations contributing to melanomas and other skin cancers and sun-protective garments and lotions provide only partial protection; much the same is true of golf, which nobody has yet figured out how to play well in the shade. And, like the rats smart enough to do so on their own, it may be wise to phase down on one's total amount of exercise as the years advance.

As for food, take supplementary vitamins, including D3 and E. Use of sweeteners other than sugar and avoidance of high carbohydrate loads may reduce blood vessel damage from glycosylation, and may possibly reduce the risk of developing diabetes. Keep your cholesterol in or near the normal range, with statins if necessary. An aspirin a day reduces the tendency for blood to clot in undesirable locations, like one's coronary arteries. "You are only as young as your blood vessels", as one of my medical school professors used to say. Eat a little less if you can do it without major difficulty; many older people manage well with just two meals per day.

Stay mentally active via reading, writing, developing new interests, and maybe - just maybe - it will help you stay a bit smarter a little longer. Don't waste your time on trivia, time is what everyone runs out of some day. Worry less, and don't sweat the small stuff. Take a drink if you enjoy it, since alcohol in moderation appears probably beneficial. Get a good night's sleep. Have fun and maintain as happy an attitude as you can. Avoid anger, defensiveness, and hatred. Laugh more. Enjoy your family and friends. Keep your integrity and maintain a clear conscience. These are the basic things we all know are worth doing to make life happier, and - maybe - healthier and longer.

Much of this is in Ecclesiastes. It repays repetitive reading. Live fully while you can "before the days of trouble come and years approach when you will say 'I find no pleasure in them' - before the sun and the light and the moon and the stars grow dim.....and strong men stoop.....when men rise up at the sound of birds but all their songs grow faint.......when desire is no longer stirred. Then man goes to his eternal home....the golden bowl is broken...and the dust returns to the ground it came from." Can it be said any better?

Functional IQ

In the 1930s, when some Okies left the dustbowl behind and migrated to California, the IQ of both states was simultaneously lowered. That is the California version. Oklahomans of course claim the migration raised the IQs of both states. Who's to be believed? And who ever bothered to do the IQ measurements? Are Californians dumber or smarter than Oklahomans today? Were they in the 1920s? It depends, I guess, who you ask.

Few subjects are more mired in controversy than IQ. We all know that the average IQ in any population is supposed to be 100 by definition. That implies that all populations are, on average, equally intelligent. But is that really true? Then there is the question of whether IQ is due to heredity, environment in its broadest sense, or both. Most scientists think heredity has a big role to play, but that non-genetic factors also are important. A few people, especially the real die-hards of the Left, believe that the famous "bell curve" of human intelligence is shaped entirely by inequalities in toilet training, schooling, sexual freedom, political involvement, family money, racial advantages, and so on independent of innate giftedness.

Let's admit that fundamental brainpower, "true IQ", is difficult to measure exactly and explain fully. But there remains for further examination the more easily observed phenomenon we choose to call "functional IQ".

Functional IQ is what the California - Okie debate is really all about. Who, on average, ACTS dumber? Smart people can do stupid things. Dumb people sometimes do smart things. But, on average, how people

110

BEHAVE says something important about them - it is the measure of their functional IQ.

In the brilliant writer John McPhee's non-fiction book, "Uncommon Carriers", a trucker drives across the border from Oklahoma into Nebraska and says to McPhee, "Intelligence goes up ten points when you cross that line. Back there you go barefoot, screw your cousin, and look for something to steal." He also tells McPhee about a public hearing in Wyoming, another neighbor of Nebraska, at which an official outlined a proposed program for the sterilization of coyotes. A rancher lifted his hand and said, "We don't want to f-ck the coyotes, we want to get rid of them." Now, the particular truck driver telling these stories, who is a plenty smart guy by the way, is from - you guessed it - Nebraska. Is there any substance behind his stories? Is he on to something that is maybe too politically incorrect for anyone not blue collar to say?

Now, my wife and I have traveled by car into all the states in the continental U.S. except Arkansas. (We missed that state on purpose because my wife is allergic to spinach dip, I've read Huckleberry Finn, and we both know Vince Foster's death was not a suicide.) We believe, from extensive personal observation, that the mean functional IQ of the various states of the U.S. is quite unequal. We can't say if those differences are permanent or transient, genetic or environmental, due to migratory selection, local culture, or other phenomena. But differences there are.

We hope that when you are done reading this, you will write to us and tell us your thoughts on the functional IQs of states you have visited. In particular, we are interested in knowing your candidate for "state with lowest functional IQ." But first, we'd like to be more precise about what we mean by this concept.

Consider age. Very, very old people - on average - act less smart than when they were in their prime. They have a perfectly good reason for that, namely that millions and millions of their once-active brain cells have died, and it's not their fault that they are old as Methusaleh. But when that neuronopenia (also known medically as oligosynapsia) leads them out on the highways to obstruct traffic, drive into people they can't see, hit the gas pedal instead of the brake, and so forth they are showing their age-related reduction in functional IQ.

Consider education. There is a neighborhood in Los Angeles where (and I am not making this up) only 1% of the high school students can read at or above grade level. I have no idea what their "true IQ" is, on average. Maybe they really are innately as smart as a bunch of kids at Andover or Exeter, but with much poorer mommies and mostly no daddies. But it's a pretty safe bet that the mean functional IQ in their ghetto is awfully low.

There could be countless other examples. Alcoholism lowers functional IQ, so does drug abuse. Ill health often messes up the mind. Driving way too fast is acting dangerously stupid. Motorcyclists sliding between lanes of cars on busy freeways are proving their functional IQs are almost immeasurably low.

SO ---- which state gets our vote for lowest FUNCTIONAL IQ? We think it's a slam dunk. It's Florida. Don't scream just yet, all you Floridians. Florida is loaded, just loaded with old, old people who went there to wait to die and are still waiting - mostly in their doctors' waiting rooms. The almost infinitely many of the almost infinitely aged include countless thousands driving with macular degeneration, cataracts, or deafness. They form an incendiary mixture with the angry blue collar types driving humungous pick-ups like police cars chasing crack dealers, kids who dropped out of school at age 13 using cell phones and bobbing to rap music while speeding, and other lunatics using ordinary streets as raceways while cutting in front of slow drivers who don't speak English or are on Island Time. Driving in Florida is proof positive, and a very danger-filled proof indeed, that there is a serious functional IQ problem in that state.

Now, there is plenty of room to disagree with our vote for Florida. Maybe you Nebraskans will agree with McPhee's truck driver that Oklahoma or Wyoming deserve special recognition. Perhaps some of you in the warm southern part of America will look at the people wintering over in North Dakota as functional idiots. Many folks in the spacious mid-west will believe that most residents of New York City are fundamentally demented.

So I'll wait to hear what you think. In what state is the average functionally lowest IQ to be found? I'm eager to get your vote. And, oh, please note that the District of Columbia doesn't count. It's not really a state, it's a district and an inner city, and including it wouldn't be fair, would it?

Please don't do one thing. Don't give me the politically correct response that all people are really functionally equal, have the same average functional IQs. Unless you can prove it, which I doubt, my wife and I won't believe you. IN FACT, I WON'T EVEN REMEMBER YOU SAID IT.

AND WHEN YOU WRITE TO ME, PLEASE USE LARGE LETTERS SO I CAN READ IT. IF YOU CALL ON THE PHONE SPEAK UP SO I CAN HEAR YOU.

AND IF YOU ASK FOR IT, I'LL GIVE YOU MY
FLORIDA ADDRESS SO YOU CAN DRIVE DOWN
HERE AND VISIT ME IF I'M NOT SEEING MY
DOCTOR THAT DAY.

Fossil Fuel

Not more than a month ago, my wife and I were in Tucson listening to lectures about such complex and arcane subjects as the birth of galaxies and the explosions of old stars. That same evening we met one of the speakers and his wife at a post-event party for the faculty and a group of fossils like me, politely misnamed the Astronomy Advisory Board, whose aging members actually provide little or no useful advice but generate financial and moral support for astronomy at the University of Arizona.

The lecturer we chatted with over drinks had given a fine talk earlier in the day. A Ph.D. astrophysicist about 35 years of age with 5 years of post-doctoral experience, he was now an assistant professor at the university. His wife was about the same age, and worked as a practicing attorney in some kind of do-good agency for "the poor." They were polite, friendly, and appealing young people, born and bred in America, recently married, and had met at "a bar", one of the surviving old-fashioned alternatives to modern internet date-matching.

The subject of World War II somehow arose. Neither of these bright young people, notably including the attorney, knew the dates when the United States had been involved in that war. They thought perhaps maybe sometime in the 1930s, but were not sure. As to why World War II started, the astrophysicist seemed to recall that it had something to do with the assassination of an arch*bishop.*

There is an Air Museum in Palm Springs, CA which is devoted primarily to events related to World War II and has a substantial display of historic aircraft. One day when my spouse was there a school group arrived, and Dixie actually heard the teacher explain to the children that "today you'll have a chance to learn about World War Eleven." A friend witnessed, at the same museum, another school group whose teacher informed them by way of historical clarification that Japan attacked Pearl Harbor because America dropped the atomic bomb on Japan.

I am not making any of this up.

And about two days ago, my bags were being brought up to my room in a hotel near Washington, DC by a friendly young man who noticed my "I LIKE IKE" luggage tag and asked if "Ike" referred to a rock star. I explained my tag replicated the famous campaign slogan of a man named Dwight Eisenhower, nicknamed "Ike", who had been a top general in World War II and then President of the United States for two terms starting in 1952. He said, "Wow! That was a long time ago. My father was born in 1956."

What is the significance, if any, of such gross ignorance of American history by many younger members of our populations? Of course one may not be surprised by unawareness from a bellboy, although this particular young man seemed reasonably intelligent and will almost surely not remain a bottom-level hotel employee for the rest of his life. He had curiosity too, and wanted to learn. But what about the school teachers, the Ph.D.s, the lawyers?

It would be easy to respond by bemoaning the state of our educational institutions, the declining quality of teachers, the lack of required core curricula, and so forth to explain this degree of ignorance. And all of that may be true. But young people have access to something called the internet, a form of educational supplementation not available to prior generations. They can, and do, use it abundantly, and the last time I checked major facts about World War II were available on the web. Sources of information include free online encyclopedias. Modern youths also have electronic devices that can receive wireless downloads of whole books, many at very low cost, in mere seconds. These same young people communicate verbally and in writing with one another, and older people also, with unprecedented ease via cell phones. They have many opportunities to learn and compensate for deficiencies in their formal "school" educational offerings. So why the ignorance?

Maybe the answer is that it's just mostly fossils like me and my elder contemporaries, plus a smattering of history buffs and professional historians, who have much interest in events that happened over half a century ago. My date of birth was close to the time of Pearl Harbor, and my early youth was filled with hearing about and reading accounts of the many horrors of World War II. I know people who nearly died in that war, who survived Hitler's death camps, and who lost first-degree relatives in it. How much should the details of that time matter - and is it realistic to expect that they should matter - to someone born in, say, 1980, let alone some little kid born in 2001. What will the Korean War, the Vietnam War, mean to them? As for things like World War I, the Great Depression, the Civil War - forget it! Literally.

It seems to have been a chronic complaint also in the past that youth is becoming more ignorant of history, but who really knows if that is true. Some surveys claim that half of American recent high school graduates, and most American youths finish high school, don't know what century World War I was fought in. Assuming that's true, it sounds terrible. But do we have comparative data on what proportion of our country's youths in 1911 knew what century included the Battle of Waterloo, or who was Ulysses S. Grant? Probably most of them couldn't even have told you when the War of 1812 was fought, and certainly not where it took place nor that Washington, DC was torched during it. How many of our young people, mostly living on family farms in, say, 1840 could tell you anything about the French Revolution or even the American Revolution or John Adams? And as for things like the Peloponnesian Wars, Alexander the Great, Genghis Khan, Julius Caesar, Socrates, the decline and fall of the Roman Empire - forget it! Literally. In evaluating today's educational level about history one is reminded of the old scientific saw, "Compared to what?"

So what I really think about all this, quite apart from amusing stories I shall continue to tell over drinks about the Ph.D. and the murder of the archbishop, is something like the following. My guess, and it is just a guess, is that the youth of America are, today, on average more knowledgeable that their predecessors. They are just interested in different things. And they have plenty to learn about life in the modern world that you didn't need to know in the world of the past, and they are mostly learning what they need to know. And like every generation, they will over time discover the timeless truths of history. They will experience booms and busts, success and failure, health and illness, war and peace, poverty and wealth, suffering and joy. They will survive political folly, and the stupidity, greed, and corruption of some of their contemporaries. They will witness bravery and cowardice, saints and tyrants, good and evil. They will defend themselves, their families, and their nation when danger threatens their survival and freedom. They will discover that unending change and problems are timeless elements of the human condition. They will, in short, grow up and work as well as they can with the hand that fate has dealt them.

And I predict too that when the fuel for fossils that is the current youthful generation starts to get old they shall - as my friends and I do now - regale each other at dinner parties with hilarious examples of the folly of youth, complain that education is getting worse, and tell other old farts how on a bad day it sure looks like the world is going straight to hell.

.

A Birthday Gift

December 19, 1999 was the eve of my 58th birthday. Dixie was trying to recover in Oxford from a bad cold, and I was amusing myself with various books on economics and history. It was a dark, wintry night and we were planning to dine at home.

For some reason, about 8 PM I said to Dixie, "You are not feeling well and perhaps it would be easier to just bundle up and let's go to dinner at 208." After some hesitation, she agreed and a few minutes later we were in our big BMW and headed for St. Michaels. Along the Oxford and St. Michaels roads we were cheered by the Christmas lights on many trees and houses, and on the main street of St. Michaels the shops were covered with colorful illumination.

208 Talbot is a small, high quality restaurant at the western edge of town. We dine there a few times a year. They have a dish of chicken, peas, and mashed potatoes which is a winter favorite of ours, and a nice assortment of red wines.

We were seated at a corner table near the window, our food was ordered, and we had begun working on a bottle of Beaujolais and an appetizer of fried Ipswich clams - not low fat, but you only have one birthday eve per year. There were few other couples in the room, and at one table were a group of three, a man in a camel's hair jacket with his back to us and two women in their middle years.

Suddenly Dixie and I looked up in response to some kind of soft noise and saw the man in the camel's hair jacket, now standing still facing away from us, and another, smaller man was grasping him around the waist. The taller man was choking, and the other was trying to apply a Heimlich maneuver to clear his airway. As I moved toward the men, Dixie said, "They need a doctor."

The man had tried the Heimlich unsuccessfully three times in the few moments it took me to get behind him. I tapped him and he made way for me to try. The choking man was large, and it was not easy to get around his girth. I applied the maneuver twice, but his abdominal wall resisted my efforts. 'Lean forward", I said to him, and tried again. Immediately afterward, and without turning around, he spoke. "You got it. I am alright." I said, "OK. Are you sure?" But I knew he was OK. He confirmed this, thanked me, and sat down.

I returned to my chair. My heart was pounding from the exertion and anxiety. After a few minutes, my emotions were under control.

I said to Dixie, "Now we know why God wanted us to be in this restaurant tonight." She nodded her agreement.

The manager came over and thanked us, then the chef. The wife of the man we had helped offered to the manager to pay for our bottle of wine, and he delivered this message to us but we declined. The restaurant said they would pick up the cost and take it off our bill. We accepted. The rest of the meal continued uneventfully.

The man we had helped and his wife got up to leave, and turned toward us. I will never forget the powerful, shocking moment when I noticed that he was holding a white cane. He was completely blind. Dixie was facing toward me and did not see this. I said to Dixie, "My

God, the man is blind." Momentarily puzzled, she replied, "What do you mean?"

They approached our table.

"My husband and I would like to thank you again," the woman said. The man held out his hand. His eyes moved whitely with the searching wanderings of the sightless. I shook his hand. We wished each other a happy holiday season. And then they slowly turned, and she led him carefully across the room and through the door that the manager held open for them, and then they were gone.

My eyes filled with tears. There was nothing I could find to say. Here was this man to whom everything in life was so difficult and laden with added risks. He could not see his food well, so even eating had some extra dangers as we had witnessed. No matter how talented he was, he could not ever do the type of work I did. And tonight, he had nearly died, in fact might well have died.

I told Dixie a story she had never heard about Paul Porter, a giant of man who had founded, with Thurmond Arnold, the DC law firm originally known are Arnold Porter. I had briefly met Porter in New York in the mid-1970s. One night he was dining at the Palm in DC with two other famous Washington lawyers Clark Clifford and Abe Fortas, whom Lyndon Johnson had unsuccessfully nominated to be Chief Justice of the U.S. Supreme Court. During the evening Porter suddenly turned red, and after a few moments collapsed. He had choked on some food. Nobody had thought to do a Heimlich, and he died. It is a story not to forget.

On the way home, I thought of Dr. Heimlich. An orthopedic surgeon. He never made any money from his discovery of this lifesaving technique. It must have taken tremendous determination and effort on his part just to educate people to start using it. I don't know how he did it or how long it took him. But it cannot have been easy. A great person.

As we arrived back into Oxford, we saw the beautiful lights on the boats and trees at the end of Town Creek. And Dixie said, "Joe, look at that!" Over the top of the Oxford Inn, were lights on a huge tree we had never seen before. We had to turn into a small side street to find it, a massive pine covered with hundreds of multicolored bulbs, higher than the three story white house whose entire front lawn it occupied. How had we never found this tree in other years? It was miraculously wonderful, the finest tree we had ever seen on the Eastern Shore. Seeing it was another birthday blessing.

Is it just a coincidence that we were in that restaurant that night to help save the life of a blind man? Did the cold white stars watch, or the universe care? Did God guide us there? How can we ever know? But I believe our presence there was not coincidental, and so does Dixie, and that belief will abide with us for the rest of our lives.

For the Highly Literate

It has been my *fortuitous* good fortune to be befriended by several first degree relatives of that *feisty* and occasionally *factious* observer of the world scene, Mr. William F. Buckley, Jr., although I have as yet to meet the master himself. The articulateness of this *inimitable* guru, his somewhat *haughty hermeneutic* abilities, might be thought *generic* or perhaps genetic, given the large number of his family members who are also skillful wordsmiths. But the secret of his success has now been discovered through my encountering one of the small books by Eugene Ehrlich which appear to have provided Mr. Buckley with much of his legendary vocabulary. In fact, Mr. Buckley once wrote a most *encomiastic* review of one of Mr. Ehrlich's *unimpeachable* volumes. It is also an encouraging observation about the *inordinate* if not always *intemerate* genius of the American heartland that I discovered Mr. Ehrlich's "Golden Adjectives of the Extraordinarily Literate" in *favonian* fashion in an *innocuous* book bin at a truck stop in Odessa, Texas.

As proof that I have discovered the true secret of Bill Buckley's *ineffable* skill with the English language, I have sprinkled throughout this short essay various italicized words from the above referenced book by Ehrlich. Should any of you be tempted to deny, especially in an *emunctory*, *flatulent* or *fecaloid* fashion, that I have now been able to outBuckley Buckley, I shall consider that *effulgently egregious, flatigious,* and *fescennine,* and it shall be resented with *febrifacient Falstaffian* haughter.

In pseudo-Buckley style, let us consider the life and times of that late murderous terrorist and assassin whom the New York Times and the BBC refer to with *fatuous fecklessness* as Mister Yassir Arafat.

A few days ago, upon the *tabescent* demise of this *anguine, effete* bloodstained *anaphrodisiac* barbarian, the headline in USA Today was "ARAB WORLD MOURNS", instead of the *ebullient, effusive,* and *effulgent* alternative "NON-MOSLEM WORLD REJOICES", or perhaps the more *eclectic* "ARABS MOURN, JEWS CONSIDER DEATH *THAUMATURGIC.* "

Arafat has been a major source of obstruction to the possibility of peace between Arabs and Jews. His *objurgatory* methods have included the systematic assassination of moderate Palestinians. The persona, life, and actions of this *gnathonic fribbler* can be defined by adjectives running from A to Z such as *abdominous, bilious, caprine, casuistic, dipsomaniacal, edacious, esurient, fastuous, fatuous, garrulous, heinous ,hircine, huffish, implausible, inapposite, inchoate, irascible, ithyphallic, Janus-faced, jiggered, Kafkaesque, lily-livered, louche, lubricious, lupine, Machievellian, malapropos, malevolent, mendacious, mephitic, meretricious, minacious, miscreant, nefarious, nettlesome, nocuous, noisome, nubilous, nugatory, oleaginous, oppugnant, ordurous, Paphian, peccant, Pecksniffian, pervicacious, pilose, plangent, predacious, querulous , rabid, rancorous, rebarbative, reprobate, salacious, sanguinary, scrofulous, sententious, sinistrous, specious, splenetic, steatopygic, sudorific, temerarious, tendentious, tenebrous, thersitical, thrasonical, troglodytic, ululant, umbrageous, unctuous, vacuous, vainglorious, ventricose, vespine, vituperative, vulpine, wrongheaded, xerothermic, yucky, and zymotic.* Otherwise, Mr. Arafat was a fine man, except when *crapulous.*

Now, at last he is gone. Hopefully, we shall never see his like again. His passing opens the door to potentially *salubrious, salutary,* and *sanguine* opportunities for progress in the Middle East. I very much hope that *festinate* opinion will prove *idoneous.*

The Poolesville Indians

It's about time that Poolesville made it into the major newspapers. I've been awaiting this for years. You may not have heard of Poolesville, a sleepy Maryland town just across the Potomac from Leesburg, Virginia. Leesburg is booming, and all the folks who were smart enough to buy investment property there 15 or 20 years ago are retired and flying around in their fractional-owned jets. People like me who bought investment properties in Poolesville are still trying to figure out how to unload them and pay off our debts. The difference between the poverty of Poolesville and the prosperity of Leesburg is due to the totally Neanderthal nature of local government and attitudes toward development in Poolesville. Almost nobody can extract water or sewer permits from a band of town commissioners determined to maintain Poolesville as the last bastion of rural reaction in Montgomery County.

So it is entirely appropriate that Poolesville's backwardness has at last been publicly exposed by a Maryland judge who ruled that Poolesville High School must change the name of its football team from the Poolesville Indians. The term "Indians" was deemed by His Honor to be insufficiently sensitive to the delicate feelings of Native Americans. The judge's decision has activated our tiny community even more than the granting of universal sewer and water permits could have done. Town meetings have denounced the Judge, T-shirts emblazoned "Poolesville Indians" are appearing everywhere, and shotguns are being cleaned and extra ammunition purchased. Poolesville also happens to be the residence of a disproportionate number of policemen, and even they may join the rebellion against state authority before all this is over. We'll see if the Judge gets his way after all. And he'd better not try to visit Poolesville for the rest of his life, unless he wants to attend his own hanging.

But let's leave the Judge to worry about forcing his personal opinion on thousands of angry rebels, and reflect on the general issue of naming sports teams. It's a hell of a problem, it's hard to think of anything more important to do right, and the more you think about it in the politically correct way the bigger the challenge seems.

Some of you may at first think that there's nothing wrong with naming teams after Native Americans. Such labels as Braves, Warriors, Chiefs, Indians, and Redskins (my favorite, because it really has *everything* wrong with it) could perhaps be viewed as complementary. You might imagine that sports teams were so often given Native American names because the Indians (if I may use that word without offense) were tough, determined, swift, courageous, never surrendered, fought to the last man, and often won when the odds were against them. Hence, you might be so misguided as to feel that Indian names actually reflect admiration for the sheer guts and skill of the outnumbered natives who resisted for decades the full force of the United States Army and an overwhelming number of tough pioneers. But the Judge has clarified for us that thinking this way is a grave error, and one that it takes the force of law to correct.

However, sports teams still need names. If you can't name them after Indians, you can't - for the same reason - name them after any group. I am reminded of the three misnamed professional baseball teams during my childhood in New York City. With the new insights that the Judge has provided, I can now see that the term Yankees is just as offensive to New Englanders as Indians is to Native Americans. Then there were the Giants, clearly a slur on tall people. Third was the Brooklyn Dodgers, a name obviously implying evasiveness, cowardice, and sly treachery. All of these names fail the test of modern correctness. The mind boggles as you start thinking of all the teams who need to change their names - the Patriots, the Pirates, the Browns, the Cowboys, the Harlem Globetrotters, etc. Why go on?

So naming teams after groups of people is out. What's left? At first glance, it may be thought suitable to name teams after certain animals - Lions, Tigers, Cheetahs, Wildcats, Bobcats, Sharks, Stallions, Broncos, Bulls, Blackhawks, Eagles, Falcons, and so forth. But that creates major animal rights issues. Nobody can be sure that there would not arise misunderstandings of the true nature of these peaceful and gentle creatures if their names were adopted by certain teams. Selected animals could come to be viewed as aggressive, destructive, wild, and the consequences could be devastating to their image and their habitats. They might even become the targets of hunters. They could become endangered. Clearly it's better to do away with animal names altogether, except perhaps for mythical animals. It might be OK to use such names as the Denver Dragons, the Phoenix Phoenixes, the United States Unicorns, the Washington Werewolves, the San Francisco Frankensteins - but even then one can't be sure, as it might still give all real animals a bad reputation. Better to stay away from animals completely.

The only living things left for naming teams seem to be insects or plants. There are not yet many insect advocacy groups, although this will be coming. Some of you may have already seen the bumper sticker, "I brake for insects." Perhaps such names as the Miami Mosquitoes, the Seattle Spiders, and the Dallas Dragonflies could prove acceptable. It will doubtless take time for the courts to review this set of possibilities, and it's hard to say how it will all turn out.

It may be safer to use plants. Here advocacy is still at a low level, except for genetically engineered plants (thereby ruling out a name like the Rochester Roundups or the Michigan Monsantos). I think there are many fine opportunities with plants: the Pittsburgh Primroses, the Denver Daffodils, the Los Angeles Lilies, the Milwaukee Mimosas, the Dallas Dahlias, the New York Narcissuses, the Miami Mangroves, the Wisconsin Wisterias, the Georgia Gladiolas, the Florida Forsythias, the Alabama Azaleas, the Oakland Oaks, the Kansas City Cactuses, the Palm Springs Palms, and so forth. Still, even here one must be careful, as attracting favorable or unfavorable attention to particular plants has political and economic implication for many persons in the gardening and horticultural industries, could affect the ecological balance of nature, and may have other unforeseen consequences. And, of course, such names as the Pansies would be out, and the use of any type of Fruit would be excluded for the same reason.

Given the problems with groups, animals, insects, and plants we retreat toward naming teams after inanimate objects. It's difficult to see how one could get in trouble using identifiers like the Stones, the Oceans, the Clouds, the Storms, the Hurricanes, the Deserts, the Mountains, the Rivers, and the Dunes, or such manmade inanimates as the Machines, the Rockets, the Irons, the Toasters, the Mixers, and so forth. On balance that seems the safest strategy for team naming as political correctness and sensitivity spread deeper into our national fabric - as I very much hope they will.

One thing is clear. The Washington Redskins have got to change their name, and fast, or the Judge will be after them. Inoffensive possibilities could include the Washington Wringers, the Capital Coralreefs, the D.C. Dryers, and others. I'd love to hear what names you like.

And no funny stuff, please, in your reply. Possibilities like the Washington Brownskins are just too offensive even for joking. The Judge doesn't like it when you make fun of him, e-mail is hardly a secure medium, and the arm of the law is long and strong. Be correct, or be silent.

Investment Returns

In May, 2011 my wife and I attended, as invited guests, the annual meeting of a well-known investment fund in New York City. We had been given the opportunity to attend by friends who were long-term investors in what we shall call simply the Fund which had been investing on their behalf. Their account was in fact supervised, at least in part, by the CEO of the enterprise, Mr. G. We stayed at the meeting for about half of its two hour planned duration, and then left to return home.

Much could be said about the people at the meeting, and the youthful self-confidence of many of the members of the firm's "research team" who spoke about the reasons for some of the firm's current investments.

This particular fund, started by a now-deceased "value" investor who knew Warren Buffett, collects annual fees of 1.05% of assets under management (ie., of "investors' money"). The fees of the Fund management company for managing assets of approximately $3 billion in 2010 totaled approximately $31 million plus another $545,000 collected as brokerage commissions for trades made on behalf of the Fund. The management firm has about 20 analysts most of whom appeared to be under the age of 40. It was announced that two of the senior staff could not attend the Fund's major annual meeting - one because his child was graduating the same day from the third grade, and another because of a Girl Scout meeting. There are three persons (one deceased) whose name is on the letterhead. The Fund may be assumed to have about 10-20 additional employees at most. Thus the *average* current annual compensation collected per employee is in the range of $750,000, and this is certain to be very unequally distributed. Most probably, Mr. G who seemed in his sixties and the other surviving principal, Mr. C likely in his eighties, are each compensated at about the $10M level for their yearly efforts.

A detailed analysis, involving some complex spreadsheet work taking many hours and supported by further analysis and input from a colleague who is an experienced investor, trustee, and expert on tax law, reveals some of the results of the efforts made by the advisors on behalf of their clients over the last 40 years based on the information and data tables in the Fund's 2010 Annual Report. The returns shown in the Annual Report assume that income, dividends, and capital gains distributions are fully reinvested in shares. However, such full reinvestment would require substantial annual tax payments caused by capital gains and dividends for a taxable investor unless the Fund shares were held in an IRA on which at terminal withdrawal income taxes would be due only at the end of 40 years. Over the years, the $3 billion Fund has paid out as capital gains plus dividend distributions a large fraction the total value of its monies currently under management. The tax effects on such distributions are very large and greatly affect the economic value of the investment. The returns implied by the dollar amounts shown in the Fund's Annual Report are not corrected for the ongoing tax payments required annually, and as much as 39 years earlier, by you or me as taxable investors. The implied rates of return of an investment in the Fund which, ignoring taxes, calculates to about 14% per annum, really apply only to a fully tax-exempt entity such as a foundation or university.

The Fund's model account illustration assumes an initial $10,000 investment made in 1970 at Fund inception. During its early years, the Fund had a large position in shares of Warren Buffett's Berkshire Hathaway company. As recently as a decade ago Berkshire constituted at least 30% of the Fund's portfolio. At end 2009 Berkshire was 20.3% of the Fund's investments, but after the recovery of stock prices in 2010 the Fund reduced its holding of Berkshire to 10.6%. It is virtually certain that Berkshire has been the Fund's best long term investment, and indeed that much of its return can be assumed to result from that single large holding. The Fund managers are hardly to be faulted for their judgment in making and retaining for most of the past 40 years their single largest investment, but future investors in the Fund will not be able to benefit to nearly the same degree from the exceptional past performance of Berkshire. Furthermore, a direct investment in Berkshire would have been far more profitable and tax efficient than an investment in the Fund as indicated below.

Using the internet as a source of data including changes in tax rates followed by a spreadsheet analysis involving calculating IRRs (internal rates of return) with and without tax effects, it was possible to compare the Fund and its tax effects to Berkshire and to a hypothetical S&P 500 Index fund (equivalent to a typical S&P index fund charging fees of about 0.15% annually) from 1970 to the present. In all cases, full reinvestment of taxable dividends and distributed capital gains into the Fund or the S&P index fund were assumed. Berkshire is highly tax efficient since it paid no dividends for the past 40 years, and only a final capital gains tax would be due to monetize it at the end of this period. The S&P Index fund normally would require a taxable investor to pay taxes only on dividends but has very little, if any, annual capital gains tax liabilities given the inherently low turnover of an index fund; it is thus more tax-efficient than the Fund but less so than an investment directly in Berkshire.

Now to the results of the spreadsheet analysis, which assume all taxes at the top federal rate for any applicable year. The calculations also assume that in any given year the average state adds a 5% income tax to any federal capital gains or dividends taxes (for example, the 2010 tax rate on a long-term capital gain would be 15% federal + 5% state = 20%). Let us compare the *net economic benefit (NEB)* taking the negative cash flows of taxes into account (including terminal capital gain taxes to convert each asset into cash at the end of 2010) for a taxable investor placing $10,000 in the Fund in 1970 with full reinvestment of annual proceeds vs. the alternatives of an investment in an S&P index account with full reinvestment or in Berkshire after 40 years:

	Initial investment 1970
NEB 12-31-2010	
Fund	$10,000
$215,642	
S&P Index	$10,000
$180,442	
Berkshire Class A	$10,000
$5,669,661	

Language can be tricky, so let's try to carefully define what is meant by *net economic benefit* in the above examples. I believe it is what really would matter to a rational investor. It is not just the nominal dollar amount upon exiting the investment and ignoring all associated prior and current tax payments. It means the equivalent economic advantage to placing $10,000 into a magic machine in 1970 which, at the end of 2010, gave a taxable individual with all taxes prepaid by the machine the indicated sum in cash. Thus defined, one can summarize the above results as saying that the net effective return in the Fund in nominal dollars is about 21-fold after paying any ongoing and terminal taxes and fees, about 18-fold in the S&P index fund, and about 567-fold in Berkshire.

The greater benefits of the direct investment in Berkshire are striking.

Note also that these results have not been adjusted for inflation. The purchasing power of $1.00 U.S. in 1970 is approximately equal to the purchasing power of $5.73 U.S. in 2010. The inflation rate averaged 4.46% during that time. Thus the inflation-adjusted net economic benefit for a fully taxable investor would be the equivalent of:

Fund $37,634 in 1970 dollars from
$10,000invested

S&P index fund $31,491 in 1970 dollars from
$10,000 invested

Berkshire $989,479 in 1970 dollars from
$10,000 invested

We add here the results from placing the identical initial investments in an IRA. The results include fees but assume taxes are deferred until 2010, and that a final tax has been paid of 35% federal + 5% state = 40%. Unadjusted for inflation we obtain NEBs of:

Fund $1,325,176

S&P index fund $264,497

Berkshire $4,253,746

And adjusting for inflation, the IRA investor's NEB would be:

Fund $ 231,270 in 1970 dollars from $10,000invested

S&P index fund $ 46,160 in 1970 dollars from $10,000 invested

Berkshire $742,364 in 1970 dollars from $10,000 invested

There are many fascinating aspects to these comparisons, including the following. The combined effect of the much larger annual fees and taxes on investors in the Fund almost eliminated the benefits of the above-average performance of the Fund compared to an index fund when held in a taxable account. There was a far greater comparative benefit to holding the Fund in a tax-deferred IRA than in a taxable account. Remarkably, a highly tax-efficient investment involving no annual tax obligations or fees, such as a straight common equity investment in Berkshire, is better held in a taxable account than a tax-deferred IRA. The value-shrinking effect of inflation since 1970 is dramatic for all investments. And the obvious advantages of a direct investment in Berkshire regardless of tax considerations are strikingly apparent, and especially so on a comparative basis for a typical taxable investor

Lastly, for achieving results which were largely due to the Fund's long-term position in Berkshire, the managers of the Fund may be estimated to have collected fees of not less than $400 million over the last 40 years (an average of $10 million per year), based on the assumption of an average Fund value over this period of $1 billion and a 1% annual fee. Over that 40 year period Mr. G, Mr. C, and their associates will have collected about 40% of everyone else's money, and the investors will have retained 60%. An interesting way to look at the benefits to the Fund managers from their seemingly low "only" 1% per annum fee can be derived by following the fate of the fees from the model initial $10,000 investment over 40 years. The fees collected over 40 years from a $10,000 investment of "other people's money" in the Fund total $270,328. If it is assumed that the managers managed to invest their annual fee stream from your initial $10,000 in investments which yielded them, after taxes, a 6% rate of return they would wind up with $466,880!

That is why and how many people get rich on Wall Street! Those of you who have read Fred Schwed's classic "Where Are the Customer's Yachts: A Good Hard Look at Wall Street" will not be surprised.

.

The Jewish Bond

It is estimated that monetary losses from the giant Ponzi scheme of Bernard Madoff ("Bernie" to his former friends) are approximately $50 billion. He fooled people by offering his investors a steady return of 10% to 12% per year, which became known to many in the Jewish country club and philanthropic set as the "Jewish bond." Bernie's "bonds" fooled many people, and more resembled Tosca's kiss than U.S. Treasury securities. According to an advocacy group for Holocaust survivors known as the "1939 Club", which has no reason to underestimate historic losses, in present value terms the total destruction to Jewish assets of all 6 million Holocaust victims may be as high as $230 billion, or about $40,000 for every Jewish man, woman, and child who died in or survived the Holocaust. Thus Bernie and the relatively small group of criminals who knowingly assisted him managed to scam Jewish friends and colleagues out of nearly ONE-QUARTER of the entire financial losses due to the worst disaster in Jewish history. Adolf Hitler would be pleased.

I fear we risk becoming corrupted by psychological adaptation to the scale of U.S. government financial shenanigens. In response to the recent economic downturn these have already totaled about 2 trillion dollars. Our federal government also finances a war that is costing about another trillion or so, and a Medicare prescription drug benefits program for rich and poor alike which will consume another trillion over the next few years. Those staggering costs will ultimately be borne by the American citizenry primarily through deprecation of our currency and higher taxes on anyone who has the resources left with which to pay up. In comparison to our government, Madoff wasted a good deal less of other people's money, but the magnitude of his accomplishment is nevertheless breathtaking as well as heartbreaking. Never have so many lost so much to so few.

Nobody can visualize what one trillion dollars represents in terms of real goods. Maybe we can come a little nearer the mark by offering some perspective on the Madoff-induced losses of $50 billion.

I spend my winters in the sunny and warm Coachella Valley, which includes well-known affluent communities like Palm Springs, Rancho Mirage, Indian Wells, Palm Desert, and La Quinta. The entire Valley is about 30 miles long and in it reside approximately 100,000 households. The median home price here, including small condominiums to large estates, is about $500,000 or less. Fifty billion dollars would buy ALL the homes of ALL the families (perhaps 300,000 people) in the entire Coachella Valley.

Here is another way to look at $50 billion. Bill Gates and Warren Buffett, the two richest men in America and arguably the richest honest people in the world, each have personal fortunes which would be almost wiped out by a loss of that magnitude.

Here's another glimpse. Childe Hassam is America's most famous impressionist painter, and his paintings are among the most expensive - on average - in the American art market. A typical Hassam might sell for about one million dollars. Fifty billion bucks is enough money to buy FIFTY THOUSAND Hassams. Of course, the artist probably did only a thousand or so in his lifetime. It is no exaggeration to claim that if all the works of art of all types in the National Gallery of Art in Washington, or the Metropolitan Museum in New York, or Chicago's Art

Institute were to appear on the auction block, the total hammer price of these items - many of which are sometimes inaccurately referred to as "priceless" - would likely not exceed $50 billion.

Many other ideas could be proposed to help one understand how much money $50 billion really is. But it is the Holocaust comparison which I find most profoundly horrible. "Bernie" Madoff didn't kill anyone in death camps or warfare, although some suicides will surely be among the damage he caused indirectly, but he destroyed the wealth of his investors - mostly fellow Jews - at nearly the same level as the vast horde of Nazis led by Herr Hitler. Hitler never pretended to be a friend of the Jews. Madoff claimed he was, and many who believed him are now ruined. Good old "Bernie" was the supreme financial con man of our era, who put into practice in a totally immoral framework the oft-quoted advice of financier Michael Milken, "If we can't make money from our friends, who can we make money from?"

My Yiddish-speaking grandmother would have exclaimed "Oy vay!" had she lived to hear about Madoff's crimes. And so say I. And I'd like to add as well, despite everything recounted above, "Happy Chanukah to each of you."

.

Mason and More

So here I am in Florida, and I visited my mother who is a hundred and one God bless her, and what is there to do in Florida?, nothing really, you walk north on the beach, you walk south, you walk west on Worth Avenue, you walk east, and you get tired of dover sole every night, but then I saw Jacky Mason was performing at the Kravis Center in West Palm and he was supposed to be funny and I had never seen him and I remembered that my wife once got a book on Jewish humor by Mason, whose name didn't sound Jewish to me (does it sound Jewish to you?), and so I went online and reserved two seats and it was amazing because he was nearly sold out and that night we skipped the sole and went to hear Mason, and I got to one Will Call window and stood in line and my wife stood in the other Will Call line and we both found ourselves behind somebody hogging each window who was so drunk, stupid, or both that it took about 15 minutes to give them their tickets, they must have forgotten their passports or their photo IDs because God forbid you should steal a ticket and they also didn't know their reservation numbers, and then someone opened up a third window and we finally got in, and we passed a man with a black cap sitting at a table selling tickets for breast cancer, then we climbed up four flights of stairs because the elevator wouldn't come, and arrived in the stratosphere of the loge, top row, end seats but still had time to go, you should excuse the expression, to the toilet before, then the lights went out and Mason shuffled onto the stage all alone, and I'm thinking he's a brave little man to come out by himself before this crowd, so he started by speaking in English mixed with what sounded like Yiddish, a language I know like I know Kenyan or Nepalese, and his idea was to show the crowd

that they could relax, that he was *one of them*, so that now
he could insult them and they wouldn't feel the pain when
the knife went in and it worked, he insulted the 800 or so
Jews in the audience over and over again and they laughed
or smiled or sat silent, and only one booed him but that was
later when he talked about Obama (and I'll tell you about
that soon), so he started on how crazy rich Jews really are,
how they all want to have a pool or a boat that they never
use, did you ever hear of a Jew who actually *used* his boat?,
who even *moved* it?, some goy would sell a boat to a Jew
without a motor and he wouldn't even notice it was
missing, and this guy with the boat and the pool and the
300 million dollar house and the Mercedes which was
better than the Chevy he despised because he maybe could
hear the motor running, this guy wouldn't give a two dollar
tip to a kid waiting table in a restaurant because nobody
would know he hadn't given it but he'd give to charity to
get his name on some wing of the hospital and everyone
could see that, and if he's married and you ask him, "You're
married, are you happy?" he gives you a *number* as an
answer, 29 years, 43 years, but if you ask him again are you
happy? now every Jew becomes a philosopher - what is
happiness?, who is really happy?, how would I know if I'm
happy? - and then Mason went on about Jewish diets and
how Jewish scales lie so that couldn't really be my right
weight, and about how you can't find a Jewish doctor
anymore, it used to be that if you went to a hospital the
doctors were Jewish and the patients were Indian but now
the patients are Jewish and all the doctors are Indians and
you can't understand what the Indian doctors are saying,
and they don't care if you live or die anyway, if you're 40
you can get surgery, at 65 maybe and maybe not, and if
you're 90 Medicare only pays funeral expenses, and that
reminds him about how in New York (he asked if anyone
in the audience was from New York and they were) all the
cab drivers are Indians or maybe from Pakistan or

Bangladesh which he called the three Indian countries and they're playing this shrieking Indian music on the radio, and they speak so you can't understand them and wherever you want to go they take you to Newark airport, which Mason said he had been driven to by Indian cab drivers 32 times and the last time it happened he got out and found himself in a crowd of 3,000 Jews all of whom had been deposited at Newark airport by Indian cabdrivers, and he never wanted to go to Newark ever, did you? did you ever even *hear* of a Jew who wanted to go to Newark?, and then he got into politics, Jewish politics, and how the Jews were out in the streets campaigning for Barack Obama but did you ever see a black person out in the streets campaigning to make a Jew President, how it wasn't just blacks that had been discriminated against that it was Jews too almost as much but not quite, and how Mason had been called a dirty Jew more times than he could remember, and did you need reminding that in 1960 in the New York Times there were advertisements for executive positions in the big companies saying that only white Christians should apply, so when did you ever see a person who became President of the United States who had never done anything at all?, had accomplished nothing except becoming President, who didn't do any job right but could talk good, who had no experience, imagine you call a plumber and then someone asks, "Did he fix your toilet? and you say, "Yes, but I wouldn't use him again he didn't speak good", or maybe your doctor who speaks good says you need heart surgery and you ask him "Have you ever done this operation before?" and he says, "No but I have enthusiasm and I speak good", and you're going to say, "Go ahead, doc, cut away"?, and he told how Obama had the worse attendance record in the U.S. Senate and never sponsored even a single bill, and of course who heard of his mother who was white? but if all our previous Presidents had been black he would be calling himself white, and nobody really knew who his

144

father was - a mother you know but a father maybe you don't know - and he didn't look black but more like a well-tanned Jew, if you ordered a black sofa and you got one his color would you keep it or send it back?, and how the job of the President is to fix the economy and work hard as President instead of flying off to three different countries every day and just working on his next job - getting re-elected, how would it go for you if you told your boss "I'm not working much today because I got to plan for my next job"?, and how he couldn't speak without two teleprompters - one on each side - and Mason imitated Obama swiveling from teleprompter to teleprompter with his head twisting in the air and the people laughed, and he talked about how this man had sat with his mentor and minister for twenty years and then claimed he didn't really hear what he said, maybe he said it on Tuesdays but I used to go there on Thursdays, and then he compared him to McCain who had actually done something in his life and he didn't even mention that he was a war hero, and Sarah Palin whom the Jews loved to hate because who was she? what had she ever done? she was only the governor of Alaska, so what kind of state was that? but why was it worse than Arkansas where Bill Clinton came from? and did you ever hear a Jew say, "Ah, Arkansas, now that is a great state!", why they can't even read and write down there, did you ever hear of a Jew that wanted to go to Arkansas?, but Arkansas was OK and Alaska was not if you were Jewish, and Mason never mentioned - didn't even have to mention - the word Israel or how Obama had insulted Netanyahu who is ten times smarter and tougher and more dedicated to his country that Obama is to his, and while Mason went on about Obama many of the Jews were applauding so maybe there is hope, although one of them stood up and bellowed boos at him and stalked out but nobody else did so maybe there is hope. Maybe. And if you don't believe all this really happened, it happened anyway on the last day of January 2012 (using the goyish calendar).

Why College Can Be Dangerous to Your Health

Talk delivered June 1, 2001 as commencement address
at Lee Academy in Tampa, Florida

I am delighted to be here to talk to you today. This
a very small graduating class, but your graduation today is
just as significant for you as it would be if you were in a
class of thousands. Each of you is an important person, and
I am going to try to communicate some correspondingly
important ideas. And since you are now finished with high
school and moving forward to college - and also headed
toward adulthood with all its complexities and
responsibilities - I should like to talk to you about serious
things, and speak to you as adults.

Let me start with some observations about the
century just ended, the 20th century. You all know that this
century witnessed the two most destructive wars in the
history of mankind. World War I and World War II
resulted in the deaths of close to 50 million people, and
devastated the lives of further countless millions. Even
more costly in human lives and misery was the ascendency
of communism in many countries, most prominently in the
Soviet Union and in China. Mass exterminations,
persecutions, starvations, and imprisonments in communist
nations caused over 100 million deaths. That is hardly the
whole story of the 20th century, in which great human
advances were also made. Nevertheless, the suffering and
destructiveness in this century exceed our comprehension.

Why did such terrible things happen? A few cynics
appear satisfied to merely state that man is capable of good

and evil, so sometimes evil things will occur. Even if true, that does not take us very far in our understanding, nor does it help us try to prevent future disasters. The historical lessons of the past century are many, but among them is the following crucial insight: The events I have described were due to the ascendancy of wrong and dangerous ideas, which were widely believed to be true by large numbers of people, and particularly by many intellectuals. The spread of bad ideas was followed by their exploitation by bad people.

Socialist ideology partly originated in Prussia, precursor of modern Germany, and in the late 19th century socialism was incorporated into the Prussian and then the unified German state by Otto von Bismarck. And there was also a long tradition in Germany and in some other European nations of militarism, nationalist triumphalism, and race hatred which were common orthodoxies in that era. We may be horrified, but should not be surprised, that these bad ideas gave birth to National Socialism, and led its charismatic leader, Hitler, to power with all the consequences which followed.

Communism also arose in Europe. Karl Marx, one of its originators, was a German economist and philosopher. Communism became very widely admired by leading intellectuals in many countries during the late 19th and throughout the 20th centuries. Communism was considered the irresistible ideological wave of the future by countless prominent people ranging from Thomas Mann and George Bernard Shaw to Jean Paul Satre and our home grown traitor, "Hanoi" Jane Fonda. That communism, which like Nazism was thus an offspring of European socialism, was hopelessly flawed in both economic theory and in its representation of human nature did not prevent it from being exploited and organized by such evil men as

V.I. Lenin, Josef Stalin, Mao Tse-tung, Fidel Castro, Ho Chi-minh, Kim Il Sung, and Pol Pot. And the deaths followed.

Ladies and gentlemen, ideas do matter. Bad ideas have bad consequences. Widely believed bad ideas can be extremely dangerous. And they do not necessarily produce all their damage immediately, but may have very long term effects. Karl Marx was writing the Communist Manifesto in 1847, over a century before Mao was exterminating many of China's finest people during the "Cultural Revolution".

Why am I speaking to you today about the dangers of bad ideas? Because as you embark upon your journey into a more independent and adult life, you will be leaving home and living for several years in one of the most ideologically dangerous places on earth - the modern American undergraduate college.

Now, of course many university faculty would be horrified to hear me speak of their university as dangerous. Such an opinion would hardly be considered to be politically correct. But I am not here to be politically correct, but rather to tell you the truth.

In expressing the view that colleges may be dangerous to your moral, mental, and physical health, and that the bad ideas so concentrated there and disseminated from campuses to the rest of the world may be very harmful, I do not mean to imply that going to college is the wrong thing to do, nor that universities are inherently bad, nor that universities promote only bad ideas. My own college years, at a commuter school called Brooklyn College, and later at Harvard Medical School, Cambridge University in England, and Harvard Business School were outstanding personal experiences of great intellectual and practical value. Many of my professors were fine scholars and excellent human beings. I have served on the faculties of several universities. My only sister, her husband, and both of her husband's parents are or were university professors. My older daughter has a Ph.D. in physics. Most of my closest friends are members of the learned professions like science, medicine, and law. Colleges and universities offer tremendous opportunities for the acquisition of knowledge, and permit necessary training for careers of considerable value to you and to our society.

So I am not anti-college or anti-university. Nor am I anti-intellectual, since I am not into self-hate and most people who know me look upon me as an intellectual, albeit one with more experience in the non-academic world and the world of business than most intellectuals have.

But colleges are dangerous places nevertheless. Let me illustrate with a few examples. The first concerns a college classmate. Let's call him Mike. Mike and I became good friends during our first year at Brooklyn College. He was an outstandingly bright, charming, and gregarious fellow. His academic performance was at the highest level. Like myself, Mike was headed for a career in medicine, and he was obviously very gifted and going to be a star as a doctor. But Mike had weaknesses - he was naive, and was susceptible to believing what he was told. With his heart of gold, he thought everyone had one also. He was honest and utterly devoid of deviousness, and believed that everyone else was like that too. He started out with sound values, and assumed that everyone else had them.

During his very first college semester, Mike fell under the influence of a charismatic professor of education, who had also tried - unsuccessfully - to befriend me. I thought that professor fascinating and brilliant, but also weird, and I kept my distance. But Mike did not. And that man messed up Mike's head. This professor was anti-establishment, anti-capitalist, anti-American, and opposed to conventional sexual mores. Soon Mike began complaining to me about the "ugliness" and "commercialism" and "emptiness" of American life. Almost at the onset of college, Mike had fallen in love with and became engaged to a fine young woman. But then Mike started to hang around with counter-cultural types, both faculty and students, early hippies who were always complaining about "the system". After three years at college, Mike decided go to Europe for the summer. His mind was now prepared to "see what the rest of the world was like". He bummed around in Sweden, and fell in with a group of anti-American university students, many of them appealingly blonde and sexually liberated. When Mike returned to the U.S., he immediately broke his engagement (and the heart of the lovely young woman who had been waiting for him) and told me he had "had enough with America". His original plans to finish college in America and then go to an American medical school and to get married had all become distasteful to him.

Mike dropped out of college after his junior year. He found one medical school in Scotland which would accept him even without a bachelor's degree. He spent four years at that mediocre school, freezing every night in a coal-heated flat, sleeping with a lot of nurses, and feeling proudly anti-American. Discovering upon graduation that health care in Europe was socialized, and that as an American graduating from a Scottish medical school there were no opportunities anywhere in Europe for him, he tried to return to the States. But good training opportunities were unavailable to him as a foreign medical graduate.

151

Eventually he returned to the U.S. and became further embittered by a bad job at a bad hospital.

The last time I saw Mike, during this hospital job, he was accompanied by a female companion who seemed, to me, most unsuitable. He told me he hated America, and was thinking of emigrating to Israel. Thereafter, he disappeared. Some years later, I tried to locate Mike, but he has been untraceable both in Israel and in the U.S. I hope God is watching over him somewhere.

Mike had the potential and ability to become an outstanding physician, a loving husband, and contributing citizen. His decline dates from his freshman year at college, and his seduction by the wrong ideas and by the wrong so-called "friends" on campus. Bad ideas promoted by one of Mike's professors had very bad consequences for Mike. And I could relate many other cases like this, from my own personal experiences.

And permit me one last story. In 1964, I had a discussion with a classmate at Harvard Medical School. He revealed that he was from a rich, New York banking family. To my amazement, he told me he hated banking, bankers, capitalism, wealth (of which he had so much), and looked forward to the triumph of socialized medicine in America and of communism around the world. His subsequent career has been such as to indicate no change in his views. Yet this very man - I kid you not - is today about to be elected to the Board of Governors of Harvard University!

As author Kurt Vonnegut would say, "And so it goes". College campuses are centers of a high concentration of activism, both overt and covert, of many dangerous ideas. Furthermore, many highly questionable and debatable ideas are treated on campuses as undeniably true, correct, and beyond debate. Where more than on our campuses will you find such overwhelming acceptance of promoting the interests of certain groups while ignoring the costs imposed upon other groups? (the politically correct name for this is "affirmative action"). Where else has the idea that all cultures are equally valid and equally valuable gained such a strong and unambiguous hold? (the politically correct name here is "diversity"). Where else has the view that all men are pigs been so widely touted? (this is called "feminism"). Where else are capitalism, consumerism, and the ghost of Ronald Reagan so widely cursed? Where else is envy of "the rich" and the cult of equality more orthodox? Where else is bigger government more worshipped? Where else will you more frequently hear that George W. Bush is "stupid"? My point is not that affirmative action, diversity, and feminism are necessarily bad, nor that capitalism, consumerism, Ronald Reagan, and getting rich are necessarily good, nor that George W. Bush is a genius. It is that on college campuses certain orthodox viewpoints on these and other subjects have been enshrined as so obviously true and correct that they are deemed beyond debate, and constitute the only "correct" intellectual and moral positions. And to oppose these ideas on many campuses can be difficult and uncomfortable, and may even result in damage to one's grades, one's career, and worse.

So be warned. By all means go to college. By all means go there to acquire useful, accurate, and important knowledge. By all means, begin to prepare yourself there for a career that will utilize your talents. By all means, study as long and hard as you can. By all means, become friends with the best of the students and faculty. And by all means, have fun - college can be a wonderful, joyous, and challenging experience.

But do not go to college and get caught up in political activism, student protests, and campus unrest. Do not unthinkingly believe everything you are told. Do not readily buy in to the orthodoxies that will surround you. Do not fail to maintain a thoughtful degree of prudence, and to think carefully and critically about all things. Do not abandon your values. Do not forget your family or your God.

And at least as much as any of these things, do not forget to choose your friends wisely Stay away from the wrong types of people. There are plenty of these folks on every campus. Leave them at a distance.

It may seem that I have said more about what NOT to do at college than about what you should do. That strategy is not original with me. It is also evident in the Ten Commandments, most of which are warnings about what Thou Shalt NOT do. It's in the nature of man to be easily led astray by his own desires and by bad examples and bad ideas. Don't let it happen to you in the next four years, nor during the rest of your life.

I wish all of you well, and congratulate you upon your graduation. And I thank you again for the opportunity to speak with you today.

Let Us Call Him Morilenes

His real name perhaps does not matter for our purposes. But this is a true story, a sketch of the life of one of Spain's most famous bullfighters.

He grew up in poverty. In childhood, he determined that he would do what he could to end the poverty of his family, to allow his parents to finish their lives in comfort and dignity. After many false starts, he discovered a talent for fighting bulls, a cool courage in the face of danger, a way to get rich. He developed a special way of engaging the bull which fitted his brave natural temperament. Standing motionless, feet together, perfectly poised, he would allow the beast to rush at the cape with its right horn passing within an inch of his abdomen or chest. There exist almost unbelievable photographs of him doing this. In the ring, he would do such passes again and again and again until the bull tired. At each lunge of the bull, the crowd went wild. Then Morilenes would kill the bull with a sword plunge over the horns into the heart. If the animal did not drop immediately, Morilenes would end its misery with a knife cut to the base of the skull. He did not like killing bulls; he did not like suffering. He did not, in fact, like bullfighting at all.

For 5 years he fought, about 50 fights a year. He was gored several times, but never severely. He earned over $1 million per year, was driven around Spain from fight to fight in his Roll Royce. Women tried to seduce him, but he would resist. He once discovered two American women in his hotel room, hiding under the bed, waiting for him to undress; he gravely escorted them away. He was said always to be thinking, never celebrating. He bought for his parents a large home and took care that their finances were secured for life. He built an institution for the care of 200 indigent children. Then he gave away his Rolls and the rest of his money, and entered a Dominican monastery.

A few years later, another famous bullfighter came to visit Fra Juan. He had had no other visitors from the world of bullfighting. He told his friend that he was no longer able to read magazines, as this was not permitted, and so he could not stay in touch with the events in the sport. He wished he could have done so, but he found that he could accept this restriction. So too with his cell, small and sparely furnished; he had learned to adapt. And the monastery food he had learned to accept also was not what he would have liked. But Fra Juan told his friend that he would not trade the cassock for any other life. He was now free to think, to pray, to live as he had wanted to do since he was a child. As it had been with bullfighting, all this was part of his life plan. He was where he knew he should be.

What a wonderful man! A monastic ascetic, a person of faith, a man of courage, of intense discipline, of responsibility to family, of selflessness, of unwavering dedication to an inner vision of how to live and how to sacrifice. Perhaps, even, a saint. Our hearts reach out to him, spanning time and oceans.

And yet, and yet........ What is going on here? A life of a talented man is being lived out based on a plan developed in the mind of an 8 or 10 year old boy. This boy would save his parents from the indignity of poverty, feed his hungry sisters and brothers, do work he did not like to make this possible, sacrifice himself, and then withdraw from a the world into a monkish cell, a good son, serving what he interpreted as God's will. Gifted with exceptional discipline and courage, Fra Juan was able to carry out his plan despite many obstacles, physical pain and injury, unimaginable temptations. And yet, and yet....... the psychologist asks, "It is sensible, is it desirable, for a man of vast gifts to live his life based on an emotional program decided upon by a 9 year old child?"

It would seem perhaps that cannot, should not, make sense. Yet here it is in almost pure form in the life of Morilenes. One feels an admiration for him, a respect, even a kind of love. Why? He could have found a job he liked better than killing bulls, he could still have helped his parents avoid poverty when old, he might have passed on his intelligence and iron will and courage to his sons, he could have loved a woman with the fidelity and intensity of his pursuit of the monkish cloister. Was he the "victim", to use modern psycho babble, of his own childhood shame and guilt? Was he a fool or a genius, an ignoramus or a man of deep wisdom? We must go further. Do we admire him in part because we empathize, because we sense that we too are living as extensions of our childhood selves, never freeing our inner hearts from the adaptations and visions of our remembered and unremembered youth, of the early events that contributed to the creation of our dreams, our ambitions, our feelings, our loves, our choices? Do we respect him because we also must respect our own suffering selves? Is he a model of how we should live, or an example of how we should not live? What do we tell our children if they ask us this question, and what do we - dare we - tell ourselves?

In Praise of Lettuce - and Lots of It

I'm old enough to remember when a salad was something that a man could eat and sink his teeth into. (And forgive me for ending that sentence with a preposition, something that Winston Churchill once said "up with which he would not put.") Yes, in ordering a salad in a good restaurant one used to be able to count on a good substantial portion of crispy lettuce, pale green and crunchy, large segments of juicy red tomato, thick slabs of cucumber, corrugated rings of succulent green pepper, and more. Not so today. At your usual high-end dining experience now, the salad has been redefined into a minuscule offering of wilted, soft leaves of colors varying from dark green to purple and brown, topped with cubes of pepper a few microns on each side, and placed in a two inch wide aggregation over near the side of a plate about a foot and a half in diameter. The rest of the platter is covered with a "drizzle" of sauce, or some paper-thin segments of possible cucumber or some pale, translucent root. The salad leaves themselves always taste limp and bitter, appear to include everything from radicchio to oak and maple leaves, which are particularly abundant and colorful on forest floors in the autumn, but the one thing you never find there is good-old iceberg lettuce - which has apparently become the salad base of the lower middle classes. Red tomatoes also are gone, unless they are shrunken to tiny ruby balls about the size of currants. Tomatoes at the high end, though usually absent from salads, when present are yellow, or green, or (as just stated) deformed mutants of diminutive size.

I can remember also when breakfast cereals meant Cheerios, or Corn Flakes, or cream of wheat or real oatmeal. Not today at a fancy country inn in New England.

Cereal is a mixture of dense bird foods, grains and seeds of all types, mixed with alpine nuts from the slopes of the Matterhorn. The expanded human consumption of millet, sunflower seeds, and other such ingredients has driven up the price of birdseed, likely indirectly causing the starvation of innumerable sparrows and songbirds. It has doubtless also increased the prosperity of gastroenterologists caring for patients with gastric irritation, and raised profits for the little drug stores in every tourist town that sell PeptoBismol.

It seems that some grand restauranteurs have determined that their biggest cost is food, and so the fancier the restaurant the higher the prices and the smaller the portion.

A Modest Proposal to Rapidly Create New Jobs, Increase the Gross National Product, and Decrease the Federal Debt

Nobel laureate economist Gary Becker has pointed out that household production in one's own home, performed largely by women, is not recognized when measuring the goods and services that are included in the calculating of U.S. gross national product (GNP). The largest share of this productive labor includes the rearing of children and preparing of family meals. According to a study by Robert Eisner of Northwestern University, *The Total Income Systems of Accounts*, from the years 1940-80 the approximate value of such labor, estimated from salaries of persons hired to perform similar work, is about 20% of GNP.

We offer the following modest proposal, which should find widespread acceptability since so many Americans now recognize that children may effectively be raised by substitutes for their own mothers. The proposal will increase the ability of government to add to tax revenue without raising tax rates or creating new classes of taxation, thus simultaneously accelerating retirement of the federal debt and enhancing federal and state programs of income redistribution. It will also appeal to advocates of fairness in taxation, since it closes one of the biggest of all tax loopholes, the untaxed labor of a woman working in her own home.

All that is needed is a Federal law prohibiting any woman from performing domestic chores in her own home. Instead, she would simply hire another person to work in her home, while she works in a similar role for a different family. In effect, many women would now just exchange jobs with one another. The benefits associated with this easy change would be remarkable.

As the new program takes effect, the U.S. would record a very rapid increase in GNP, perhaps on the order of an additional 20% in a single year. This would be the largest annual U.S. GNP rise in this century, and politicians could correctly claim credit for this huge acceleration of economic growth. They could also justly be proud of the creation of millions of new jobs which would be occupied disproportionately by women, and would include wide representation from minorities and even the partially disabled. Furthermore, through closing the huge tax loophole noted above, there would be a related large increase in both federal and state taxes derived from the additional millions of newly employed wage earners. And since most of those in the new jobs would be relatively young, the new program would also ameliorate the current Social Security crisis by substantially increasing payments into that system with little immediate impact on payouts by the program.

Other benefits that would result from action upon this modest proposal will be apparent to those with skill and sophistication in transferring tax revenues to wherever the need seems greatest. The added monetary inflows and corresponding expenditures would doubtless lead to wonderful, new government programs and expansion of existing ones. Many additional jobs will thus be created, one beneficial ripple effect of the innovation. Other secondary effects will include benefits to various businesses, such as the auto industry which will receive a boost from purchases of the large numbers of cars for commuting between home and workplace by the newly employed women. The hard-pressed health care industry will also benefit from moving additional uninsured women into the system of employer-paid health insurance.

About the only thing we can see wrong with this idea is that it would make it very difficult for mothers to spend time during business hours with their own kids, unless they worked close to home. But that is already a widely accepted practice in many families. Furthermore, women affected by the new law would be working with other people's children all day long; they would become better attuned to the diverse needs of different children, and these added skills could be quite helpful in raising their own during the ample evening, weekend, and holiday hours that would still be available for this purpose. Women in these new jobs would also experience the pride of being wage earners, less dependent upon their husbands, and thus become better and more independent role models for their own offspring.

One can only hope that Congress and the President will quickly act upon this idea. It's a terrific way to strengthen our country and better prepare America for the 21st century.

On Being An Optimist

On September 11, 2001 terrorists killed about 4,000 persons, mostly in the collapse of the two giant World Trade Center towers after airplanes were intentionally flown into them. This tragedy has driven some people to despair about the future of our country, and even the future of civilization. It may be helpful to keep our balance, and remember other things that happened that same week and which are of types recurring week after week. Good things.

Here's just one example. A day after the terrorists struck, on Sept. 12, the New England Journal of Medicine published a study by medical scientists which strongly indicates that gastric cancer - cancer of the stomach - can be prevented by the administration of two common antibiotics (amoxicillin and metranidazole) for a period of two weeks. This is because infection with a bacterium called *Helicobacter pylori* - which is killed by these antibiotics - is present in nearly everyone who later gets stomach cancer, and people harboring this organism develop gastric cancer at the rate of about 5% every ten years. Stomach cancer is often incurable when diagnosed, kills some 15,000 Americans each year, and annually causes hundreds of thousands of deaths worldwide particularly in Japan and other Eastern countries. Gastric cancer is particularly frequent in persons of Oriental ancestry, but is hardly limited to such ethnic groups. The report in the NEJM attracted almost no press attention. It will take time for the implications of this discovery to make its way through the conservatism of the medical community and out into practice. But the lives saved *each year* from this single medical advance will exceed the deaths from the WTC catastrophe by a very large factor.

Meanwhile, other good things were quietly occurring. Heart attacks kill millions of persons annually. Yet, due to multiple medical advances the U.S. death rate from myocardial infarctions has been approximately halved over the last 40 years. And this was before the new statin drugs, which dramatically lower cholesterol levels, came along to further reduce future cardiovascular deaths. One may estimate that the deaths from cardiovascular disease in the U.S. alone during the month of September, 1961 probably exceeded the number of deaths from cardiovascular disease plus the 4,000 dead from terrorism during the same month in 2001.

And there is more. Professor Robert Edwards (a personal mentor and friend) just won the Lasker Award for medical research because of his development of in-vitro fertilization. Since 1980, it is estimated that over one *million* children have been born throughout the world because of IVF. Most of them would never have existed without this breakthrough. It will take some time for terrorists to kill babies faster than the IVF doctors are making them - in fact, they likely will never manage to do this.

There were few survivors, and hence few maimed persons, as a result of the events of Sept. 11. In other terrorist attacks involving bombs and grenades, survivors often lose arms and legs or are permanently paralyzed. Let's give terrorists credit - if that is the right word - for crippling a few hundred people a year. Meanwhile, let us also recall that in the 1970s a British physician named Smithells discovered that dietary supplements of folic acid sharply decrease the frequency of spina bifida, a common, crippling birth defect. Public health authorities and the medical profession were slow to recognize the importance of this crucial insight, but eventually folic acid supplementation during pregnancy spread around the world. And each year some tens of thousands of healthy children are now born who otherwise would have been paralyzed and incontinent for their entire lives. Beat that, you terrorists, if you can!

Even the risk of violent death is falling. Rudy Giuliani and his associates managed to lower the number of crimes, including murder and other violent crimes, by approximately 60% in New York City during the past 8 years. Many people are alive today because of that, and replication of these advances in crime prevention in other major cities will save thousands of people - far more people than the terrorists destroyed. Automobile accidents annually kill approximately 50,000 Americans, but seat belts, air bags, improved automobile construction, better roads, and other technological advances have reduced deaths per mile traveled by many thousands each year in the U.S. alone. Rapists and murderers are now being locked away and prevented from committing future atrocities by new technologies using evidence from the DNA in their semen, hair, skin, or blood. And few of us who saw the desperate people trapped above flames in both WTC towers and then watched in horror as *both* these towers collapsed like a house of cards after different interactions with flying planes will doubt that architectural standards and building construction will be modified to reduce the risk of similar consequences from future airline accidents, explosions, or fires - and that this will save many other lives.

Terrorists will never be able to stop human progress, and they will never be able to do harm faster than so many of us are doing good. Theirs is the losing side. Man is capable of evil, but the history of mankind proves that there is much more good than evil in most of us and there are many more good than evil people. Progress from the relentless efforts of all the decent people in the world will overwhelm the harm done by the terrorist few. It has to be true. Just look at the numbers. And be optimistic.

Grapefruit and Oranges

The famous Yiddish writer, Shalom Alechem, tells of a family of poor Eastern European Jews who come to possess a fresh orange, an almost unknown rarity. They gaze at the beautiful fruit, and its magnificent color. They smell it, and touch the bitter rind with their tongues. The consumption of the treasure is intentionally delayed. After a few days, the golden fruit is lovingly peeled. A marvelous aroma fills the tiny room. The hungry family taste the granular flesh of the orange, and its sweet, delightful juice. Their experience is transcendent. That is the whole story, and it is unforgettable - a work of genius - about eating an orange!

But, of course, it's not just about eating an orange, any more than Marcel Proust's famous description in "Swann's Way" of memories stimulated in him by a taste of cake and tea is merely about food. Alechem's story captures the power of fresh experience to the human mind and soul, and helps us realize - like that poor family - what a miracle an orange really is. Only an orange can be an orange, and there is nothing like it in the whole world. As Gertrude Stein said, "A rose is a rose is a rose". So too for an orange.

In our new home in Palm Springs I am powerfully reminded of the Alechem tale. On the property are mature grapefruit and orange trees which bear abundant fruit all winter, and particularly in February. (There are also some olive trees as large as those in Gethsemane). Today,

Dixie climbed a ladder and cut down grapefruit
which filled three large buckets - and that was just
today. We have peeled and eaten grapefruit (both
yellow and pink) and oranges and tangerines from
our garden almost daily for the last month. Slices
of our own lemons are in our water glasses. This is
not just food, but a profound experience.

There were no citrus trees in Brooklyn.
When I was a child, my parents, little sister, and I
lived in an apartment occupying less space than
three of these trees in Palm Springs. The backyard
was a tiny concrete rectangle enclosed by walls and
iron grates. Dixie's family also was not wealthy,
and there is a childhood picture of her bravely
smiling bundled up in snowy Pennsylvania.

The purpose of this little essay is not to
enlist your sympathy for the young Dixie or Joe.
Like all children, we had a childhood chosen for us
by fate, and we have no complaints. But if you do
visit with us here, we will offer you some grapefruit
and oranges, and you will understand.

Playing Pool

When I was growing up in Brooklyn, "pool" meant a game played with wooden spheres on a table with pockets around the edges, and the object was to knock some of the balls into the pockets using a straight wooden cue. Pool was accompanied by gambling and drinking in dark, smoky rooms, and was mostly played by school dropouts of non-Semitic ancestry. With this background, I had no trouble understanding George Burns' famous quip that sex at 100 is like playing pool with a rope.

Here in the Southern California desert, the noun "pool" has an entirely different meaning. It refers to an inordinately expensive and rarely utilized artificial body of water created on one's property. While it was possible for a skillful player to make a little money on the Brooklyn type of pool, the California type can only be a source of monetary loss. In return for this loss, one obtains a conversation piece around which to hold outdoor parties, and can exercise swimming back and forth reversing direction every 50 or 75 feet, which gets pretty boring after a few minutes. A California pool can also be used by one's children, grandchildren, nieces, nephews, and their friends to splash noisily around in for a few minutes during holiday trips to visit old farts like me.

Those of you who don't have one might think that a pool is a simple thing, rather like a small natural pond or swimming hole. Nothing could be more wrong. Having a pool is far more complex, and infinitely more costly.

First of all, a pool has to be designed and built. For this purpose, after the layout is selected huge gobs of earth must be removed from your backyard with back hoes and other machinery which I don't know the names of. This heavy machinery churns up your property pretty bad. The big hole thus created is then lined with a steel meshwork and a layer of gunite many inches thick. What is gunite you may ask? It is mortar sprayed from a hose, and used in a variety of construction projects including making pools. The inside of the gunite is then lined with surfaces ranging from paint to tiling to plastics. Finished? Are we kidding? You can't just run water into a pool with a hose and walk away. A pool requires circulation, filtration, and heating systems, as well as some kind of method to keep the water level where you want it as evaporation proceeds.

Now the circulation, filtration, and heating systems are pretty complicated and require special equipment which must be housed separately from the pool itself. This requires extra space, and construction of an alcove or shed above ground, or a subterranean well. Since the equipment is noisy, it is often necessary to add sound insulation when creating this structure.

The water coming into a pool doesn't just get there by turning on a tap or pump. If you just filled the pool like this and left it alone, it would turn green and brown from algae and bacteria in no time, especially when heated or exposed to bright sunlight (and who wants a pool in the shade?). The water must be recirculated for some hours each day through a pump and filter system. The filters for this purpose are large - they can stand four feet tall or so - and are filled with an absorbant called diatomaceous earth (DE). This traps the little contaminants which would otherwise cloud the water. However, this filter must be periodically recharged with fresh DE, and that isn't so easy to do. It must also be backflushed and drained once in a while to prevent clogging. Even then, your pool will get dirty from bougainvillea blossoms, sand, grass cuttings, and other crap which blow into it daily. Now, most people who have enough money to have a pool don't want to do their own filter cleaning, repacking of the DE, backflushing, and skimming the crud off the surface of the water; hence there is a need to find someone called a "pool man" to carry out these functions. More about this later.

But even with the best filtration system, algae and their like will still emerge absent some kind of chemical treatment of the water. The "pool man" has to add various oxidizing agents or other poisons to the pool every few days, or one can substitute special equipment to make a "salt water" pool. This last term is misleading. What really happens is that a small and barely tasteable amount of salt is added to the pool and a special electric cell then keeps converting the chloride ions to chlorine, which kills the little buggers.

But there is more. Mere circulation, filtration, chemicals, and cleaning of the surface are not enough. There is the issue of temperature. A pool in California left at ambient temperature will never be utilized except in the height of the summer by a female of any age, nor by most males over the age of 10. So the pool must have a heater. These heaters mostly utilize gas, which costs in California about three times per British Thermal Unit (BTU) what it does back East. Don't think these are anything like little gas burners. They are mammoth devices standing several feet tall, and burning up to 400,000 BTU of gas per hour. Pools hold a lot of water, and water is hard to heat up. The amount of gas used of course depends on the temperature desired. Most folks aim to keep the pool at about 85 degrees, but there are many females including the one in my household who won't dream of getting into a pool unless it is close to body temperature (say about 95 degrees or above). The heating cost rises steeply with the temperature gradient between the pool and its surrounding. Here in Palm Springs, the cost of heating an average size pool to a mere 85 degrees can approximate $1,000 per month in the winter, and the cost can be much more if females or guests are present.

Pools also lose water by evaporation, and thus require some sort of auto-fill system to maintain the right water level. This sounds simple, but these things frequently need to be adjusted, repaired, or replaced.

I should also mention that a pool does not mean a hot tub. If you want one of those for soaking and drinking in at higher than body temperature, this needs to be separately constructed and maintained - basically, it is a second smaller pool with all the same problems.

Well, now let's say you've gone ahead and spent tens of thousands of dollars to build your pool and hot tub and get all the equipment installed and functioning, and you are keeping up with the bills from the gas company and the water company too. I didn't mention it before, but water for a typical pool can cost about $100 per month in southern California, and significantly more in the heat of the summer. The biggest problem is still ahead of you - you've got to find and employ a "pool man".

Sounds easy, but just give it a try. In the past 5 years, we've had several of these people, and none of them have been satisfactory. This is the almost universal experience. Running around from house to house cleaning filters, skimming filth off the water, and dumping harsh chemicals into pools is not a glamorous occupation. In fact, it's a pretty dull and dirty job, and any otherwise unemployable person in the great state of California can and often does try his hand at being a "pool man". Our experiences with these types of folks are typical - they periodically fail to show up at all, generally neglect routine maintenance functions, don't understand or actually do what you ask them to, get drunk, make false excuses, drop suddenly out of sight, and so forth. So even while paying ongoing wages to a pool man, your pool is still going to develop periodic problems from his neglect. (For example, right now our pool is a rich green color because our pool man said he's been "having problems with his kids".) This means that you must identify and utilize a pool repair service to fix what has been neglected, or has become non-functional through ordinary use and age. We have at long last found a pool repair service which actually seems competent - but, no, I won't give you the name since if they are working on your pool they won't be available to work on mine. On second thought, I might trade you the name of a reliable pool repair service if you can give me the name of a competent "pool man".

If you put all the numbers together, assuming average lifetimes for the pool, hot tub, and associated equipment, add in the costs of repairs, pool maintenance, heating, and so forth having this stuff in your backyard might cost $10,000 or so per year. If you like to swim in cold water and do your own pool servicing, it can of course be made a lot cheaper. On the other hand, it is also possible to spend far more if you construct a really big, fancy pool with water flowing over its edges, marble elements, and the like, if you are a perfectionist about keeping the pool in ideal condition at all times, and if you want to keep the temperature warm enough for your wife or girlfriend to be really happy bouncing around in the water. But let's take the $10,000 per year number and assume that you use the pool 200 times each year for an average of 15 minutes each time. That 50 hours of total use is costing you about $200 per hour! And that does not even count the added non-cash cost of the many hours of frustration you will experience managing the people who are supposedly managing your pool for you.

Having a pool is wonderful nevertheless. Just think of all the advantages. You can pretend you use it to stay in shape. It proves that you are one of the successful many who can symbolically proclaim that "poverty sucks". Your pool expenses will surely, over an average lifetime, materially reduce estate taxes you otherwise would have to pay. It's great to have parties around the pool, provided nobody gets too drunk and falls in. And your grandchildren might keep on visiting you if they can get to play in your pool.

But still, pools have become so drearily commonplace in places like Palm Springs. There's too much affluence around, and a pool hardly makes one's home sufficiently distinctive any more. I'm trying to think of what else I can waste money on that will really add to my status around here. Big parties, overly elaborate gardens, political or not-for-profit activities, flaunting a Rolls Royce or Bentley or Maybach, whispering about a private jet - heck, there are thousands of people doing this kind of thing here in the desert. There are even reported to be scores of people buying multimillion dollar homes, tearing them down, and replacing them with houses costing two or three times as much. Alas, how unremarkable all these things seem now that so many people are doing them.

I want to be admired for something really unique. Maybe I'll just fill in the damn pool with earth, top it off with grass, and recline over it in a lawn chair nursing a drink while saving 10Gs per annum. Come to think of it, that's not only a fresh idea but it might even be smart. Now that would certainly make it different, wouldn't it?

P.S. When I showed this bit of scribbling to Dixie, she said, "Joe, regarding keeping the pool going you don't know the half of it." So there we are. As

Charlie Munger often says when invited to comment at the Berkshire Hathaway annual meetings, "I have nothing to add."

Raymond Allen Weinstein c. 1941 - ?

In my adolescence, I discovered two interests while continuing my fascination with science. Actually, girls were a third new focus, but we're not going to discuss that here.

I became an active percussionist, taking lessons on jazz drumming and also on tympani. My tympani teacher, Alfred Frieze, had been the tympanist for the New York Philharmonic until one arm was crippled in an auto accident in Italy. Thereafter his best pupil, Saul Goodman, dropped out of medical school and took his place at the Philharmonic, remaining there for about 50 years. Frieze became a full time tympani teacher, and was considered to be the best in the world at the time I was privileged to become his pupil. I traveled by subway from our apartment in Flatbush to Frieze's small studio on the second floor of a run-down building just east of Times Square. Frieze was a slender old Viennese with a marked Germanic accent. He was a superb teacher. He believed I had the talent to become a professional musician and hoped I would do so, but while I flirted with that idea for a while, my fundamental enthusiasm for science and a career in medical research was too strong for me to take the bait. I was also discouraged by the leaders of my high school band and orchestra, Mr. Raphael and Mr. Rattner, from going into a musical career as they believed my abilities would better serve others as well as myself if I continued to direct my primary attention to science. Thereafter, tympani playing became nothing more than a hobby, which I enjoyed in various amateur orchestras until I got into my 40s.

Sadly, Alfred Frieze's personal story did not have a happy ending. Frieze had long been widowed, and lived with his only child, a daughter. During our lessons, he often lovingly referred to his daughter. When Frieze was in his eighties, and I was already in medical school in Boston, I happened to see a newspaper from New York - I believe it was the New York Post - with a front page story about the Friezes. His daughter and her lover had emptied Alfred's safe, taken all the funds from his bank accounts, and fled. I believe they were subsequently apprehended, but the money was gone. Mr. Frieze died shortly thereafter.

My second new interest was in chess. I had been taught the game by my father, Max, and was initially no more interested in it than checkers or Monopoly. But as childhood advanced, I somehow became more fascinated by chess. I acquired a few chess books, learned some of the openings, and practiced middle and end game play. Some years later I actually joined the famous Marshall Chess Club, located in the former Greenwich Village townhouse of chess master, Frank Marshall. As with the tympani, I spent many hours on chess, but I never took it really seriously and thus was never more than a better-than-average player. But my interest in the game led to close contact with some serious chess players about the time I entered Brooklyn College at age 16.

I first met Ray Weinstein while we were fellow students at Brooklyn College. Ray was not a very good scholar, but he was a hero at the Marshall Chess Club. We became friends, and sometimes spent time on weekends playing chess amidst the Club's darkly wooded, high-ceilinged, faded elegance. Ray was about my age, with penetrating grey eyes, thick glasses, and a round face with very full lips. He was an absolutely amazing chess player, had been a U.S. junior champion in the 1950s, and was ranked just below grandmaster internationally. During the years I knew him, roughly from 1959 to about 1962, he was a regular participant in the U.S. Open chess championship, which involved the top 10 or 12 players in the entire country.

I am not sure what initially attracted Ray and me to each other. We were both considered exceptional in our own ways, I as a student of science and Ray as a student of chess. These abilities separated us from most of our more ordinary contemporaries, and contributed something to feelings of isolation and differentness. I speculate these emotions contributed to our desire for friendship and our appreciation of one another. In any case, we started to spend a lot of time together during our college years. Sometimes, I would teach Ray about math or chemistry. He had surprising trouble, for example, understanding how a storage battery worked.

Ray was a loner. He had very few other friends, and I believe I became his best friend at this time of his life.

Ray and I played many casual games of chess together, some on campus, or at the Marshall, or at my home, and sometimes in his family's small apartment in Brooklyn. I never, ever, won a single one of these games, but my chess playing improved from watching his brilliant examples and from his teaching. At his apartment, I met his family - an authoritarian, sarcastic father who had a serious interest in chess but to whom Ray did not feel close; a quiet mother who was mostly in the background; and his only sibling, Joe, a rather fat, friendly kid who was getting all "A"s in high school and had absolutely no interest in chess.

Ray and I spent a lot of time together. Much of this involved chess in some way, but not always. I was in the audience on multiple occasions when Ray played in the

U.S. Championships at the old Empire Hotel in Manhattan. The best players in those years included William Lombardy (a priest), Larry Evans, Alfred Calme, Herbert Seidman (an American Cancer Society statistician who designed the study proving that cigarette smoking causes lung cancer, and who gave me my first summer job as a code clerk for this project), Samuel Reshevsky, Donald and Robert Byrne, and of course Bobby Fischer. I met all of these men except Reshevsky, who had dropped out of tournament play and quietly pursued an accounting career, via introductions from Ray. The only player Ray was really afraid of encountering over the board was Fischer - he said he had always lost to Fischer, and I believe he never did manage to win any game against him. Of course, Fischer was then the U.S. champion, and a few years later beat Tigran Petrosian and then Boris Spassky of the Soviet Union to become the world champion. Nobody could beat Fischer in those days.

Fischer's mastery of chess was unimaginably brilliant. One day, Ray and I went together to a "chess party" at the home of Harold Sussman, a Brooklyn dentist who was one of the strongest players in the country. A group of very strong amateurs, almost all at the master level, were playing lightening chess at about a dozen chess tables. In each game, the double chess clocks were set to three minutes each. Each player moved as fast as possible, and then using the same hand that moved the piece would hit the button which started his opponent's clock and stopped his own. The loser lost by either running out of time, when the little red flag on his side of the chess clock would fall, or he would be checkmated or resign in a hopeless position. The loser would then give up his seat to a waiting spectator, the clocks would be reset, and the next game would start. The scene was extremely animated, with very rapid movement, slamming of the weighted chess pieces on the wooden boards, and occasional cries of "potzer" (weak player), "take that", "weaky", and various other insults. I just watched, as my level of play did not justify wasting the time of these terrific people. Ray played a few games, and won nearly all of them. Then a buzz went through the house - Fischer had arrived.

Bobby Fischer was a blonde, crew cut teenager, tall and slender. He had a long, thin face and prominent, aquiline nose. Sussman's wife handed him a box with a dozen sugar doughnuts inside, and this he set beside a chess board on her kitchen table. Fischer said he would give challengers 6 to 1 odds. What this meant was that the opponent's clock would be set for three minutes of play, while Fischer's would be set for only 30 seconds! That was the full time allowed for all moves. And this was against some of the best players in New York, and in the whole country. If I had not seen what then happened, I would not have believed it possible. Fischer responded to each move of his opponents so fast that his moves and the subsequent hitting of the clock button were virtually instantaneous. His clock never seemed to advance at all. While playing, he would periodically grab a doughnut from the box and gobble it down. He talked and "kibbitzed" (made sarcastic comments about his opponent's moves) continuously playing like this for over an hour. He won every single game! It was the most amazing display of chess supremacy imaginable. Then, suddenly, he just stood up and left. All the doughnuts were gone. Fischer had never greeted the host, Sussman, nor did he say goodbye to him.

Through Ray, I met another student at Brooklyn College, who happened to be one of Fischer's victims at this chess party. His name was Bernie Zuckerman. Like Ray he was an undistinguished student, but a very fine chess player - a highly ranked master. A light bulb went on one day inside my head. Brooklyn College had no chess team, and yet here we were with Ray and Bernie who would be almost unbeatable by other college players. So with their permission, I organized and became captain of the new Brooklyn College Chess Team. Intercollegiate chess matches are played on four boards. A win gets one point, a draw 1/2 point each side, a lost game is a zero. Highest score on four boards is the winning team. I sometimes played fourth board, Ray always played first board, and Bernie second. I remember losing my game in our encounter with Harvard. But we still won that match, because nobody could beat Ray or Bernie. The team I had organized became the U.S. Collegiate Chess Champions in its first year of play.

I was accepted to Harvard Medical School early in 1961 and that summer, before I left Brooklyn to go to Boston, Ray and I decided to go to Europe together. I was able to go for two months with support from my parents; he scraped together enough dough to be with me for the first month only, flew over and met me in Copenhagen. He was a fine traveling companion. In meeting people who were not chess acquaintances, he was usually shy and uncomfortable, but during that summer he seemed to emerge a bit from his shell. In Denmark, we picked up girls together in Tivoli Park. In Amsterdam, we spent time with some of Ray's chess friends, who in their private club induced me in my naivety to drink strong "elephant" beer followed by a few chasers of gin "to clear my head", after which I passed out drunk for the only time in my life; I then, according to Ray, got sick in the lobby of the bed-and-breakfast place we were staying in. I have no personal recollection of this last event, which despite my profuse apologies to the landlady resulted in our expulsion the next afternoon, after I finally had awakened. Ray and I went to the museums together, ate three meals a day together, drank together, and had the best of times. When in the middle of summer he left to go back to Brooklyn, we were both sad to be separated.

Such are the memories of happy times. In September, I immediately left Brooklyn to start medical school. In Boston, I worked very hard at medicine and research, and began to court the Radcliffe student who would soon become my wife. Chess and music moved into the background. Ray and I stayed in touch by mail.

Sometime in 1962, less than a year after our trip to Europe, I received a strange letter from Ray. I no longer can locate it, but it went something like this:

> *Joe,*
> *I am sitting here watching the ice floating in a glass of water, and realize that I can't write to you again. You are enjoying life, and are headed somewhere. I am not.*
> *Ray*

I was quite upset by this. I wrote to Ray several times, but never got a reply. I called him repeatedly, but nobody ever answered the phone. In this manner, our friendship came to an end. For reasons I could not comprehend, I had lost one of my best friends. Furthermore, I believed that Ray had felt closer to me than to anyone else. I just could not understand his recent letter and behavior.

It is now more than 40 years later. I had tried a few times in the past to contact or locate Ray without success. On Thanksgiving Day, 2006 I began to read a book about chess, "The Immortal Game" by David Shenk, which had been given me as a gift. A chapter in that book is devoted to the apparently high frequency of mental illness in great chess players. Fischer later became, for example, a well known example of paranoid psychopathology, dropping chess and wandering the world as a fugitive from the American legal system while ranting anti-Jewish and anti-American babble. But it was with horror that I read the following as one of Shenk's examples:

"American Raymond Weinstein, who, at age 19, finished third behind Bobby Fischer and William Lombardy in 1960-61 U.S. Championship and who soon thereafter developed severe schizophrenia and was permanently institutionalized on Ward's Island in New York City."

The reference Schenk used for this shocking information was a web site at www.samsloan.com/weinste.htm authored by Sam Sloan, a chess aficionado. Here are excerpts from this site:

I HAVE FOUND RAYMOND WEINSTEIN

by Sam Sloan

Today, Sunday, September 1, 1996, I spent 45 minutes, from 4:15 PM until 5:00 PM, talking to International Chess Master Raymond Weinstein at his home overlooking Manhattan.

I had been searching for Raymond Weinstein off and on for the past 18 years, ever since I had a dream in 1978 that I broke him out of jail and entered him into a chess tournament, which he won.

Raymond A. Weinstein was born on April 25, 1941 in Brooklyn, New York. He won the 1958 US Junior Championship in Homestead, Florida. Weinstein played a total of five times in the US Championship. The greatest achievement of Raymond Weinstein came in the 1960-1961 US Championship. There, Weinstein finished third behind Fischer and Lombardy..............

However, after this great achievement by the still 19-year-old Weinstein, his flame began to flicker..... The last event of Raymond Weinstein was the 1963-1964 US Championship. Weinstein had the unusual result of 5 wins, 6 loses and no draws! Weinstein defeated Robert Byrne, Reshevsky, Donald Byrne, Evans and Steinmeyer....... That was the end of the chess career of Raymond Weinstein. He apparently never played again.

I knew Raymond Weinstein during the early stages of his chess career. I played in the 1958 US Junior in Homestead, Florida, which he won, in the 1959 US Open in Omaha and in the 1960 US Open in Saint Louis, where he also did well..........

The Raymond Weinstein I saw today was not recognizable as the skinny kid I knew 36-38 years ago. He is obese, weighing at least 250 pounds. He looked sluggish and dull. Nobody could have imagined the brilliance and promise which he once had. He did not physically resemble the kid I knew, either. Back then, he wore incredibly thick glasses. He still wears glasses now, but not so thick as before. He occasionally rubbed the side or underneath of his nose. I seem to recall him having that tic when he played chess. Otherwise, if the attendant had not told me that this was Raymond Weinstein, born 4/25/1941, I would not have believed that this was really him.

The entire 45 minutes was spent with me trying to talk to him. He did not say even one word while I was sitting with him....... There was no sign of recognition on his face. He stared blankly at me the entire time. Occasionally, his eyes drooped a bit and seemed almost to close. Yet, he never actually took his eyes off of me.

I recounted all the details of his chess career, details which hardly anybody other than myself would even remember......There was no recognition that he even knew what I was talking about. Yet, I am sure that he did know what I was talking about.

There were also long periods of silence. When I could not think of anything else to say, I just sat there for up to five minutes, hoping that he would say or do something, anything. Nevertheless, he just sat there, staring at me blankly.

When 5:00 PM came, which was the end of visiting hours, he got up and went to the attendant and told her rather heatedly that he wanted to go back to his ward.

After he had left, the attendant told me that I had been his first visitor in many years. She said that when she had told him that somebody had come to see him, he had replied that nobody ever comes to see him. It had taken her some convincing to get him to come down. The attendant was under the impression that Raymond Weinstein has no family at all. She was surprised when I told her that I know one of his relatives. Apparently, he does not receive or send any mail. .... here is the address of Raymond Weinstein:

Raymond A. Weinstein

Kirby Forensic Psychiatric Center

Ward 3W

Ward's Island, New York 10035-6095

Now that I have seen him face to face, I can understand why there has been absolute secrecy as to the whereabouts of Raymond Weinstein for the past more than 30 years......It is apparent to me, based upon what I saw, that Raymond Weinstein will never get out and will be institutionalized for the rest of his life. He seems simply incapable of functioning in the outside world. I find it strange that a human brain of such brilliance could become so twisted.........

This completes the quotation from the Sam Sloan web site.

Sloan's information upset me deeply. I would prefer to disbelieve the information he provides, except that I know in my heart that it must be true.

And there is more according to recent information on the internet. Why was Ray institutionalized? Just a few months after we traveled together in Europe he returned to Holland, assaulted a chess player, and was expelled from that country. Back in the U.S., he sought shelter in a half-way house and there – it's almost unbelievably horrible – killed an 80 year-old man by cutting his throat.

The great question of why humans suffer has perplexed philosophers for ages. The major religions of the world claim to provide least partial answers. The Book of Job offers perhaps the most brilliant exposition. Job's suffering is explained by his friends in various ways, all proven false when God Himself speaks the awful words: "Who darkens my counsel with words without wisdom?" God is saying that you, mere humans, are trying to understand something you cannot. Other religions explain suffering as the byproduct of desire. Still others claim that the evils of this world will be righted in the next. As a book title once put it, why do bad things happen to good people? Alfred Frieze saw his career at the New York Philharmonic terminated by a road accident, and ended his long life betrayed by his only child whom he had loved. Raymond Weinstein's brilliant mind was destroyed by disease, apparently paranoid schizophrenia, in his early 20s. Frieze at least enjoyed a long life and left the legacy of many devoted and grateful pupils. Poor Ray Weinstein, once my good friend, cut down by mental illness over 40 years ago, merely left the world a few fine chess games. He never had a chance. Why do such terrible things happen?

When discussing the above with one person whose opinions I have often found valuable, it was suggested that asking "Why?" is a futile question. If suffering is essentially inexplicable, or merely the product of random events and bad luck, dwelling on "Why?" merely adds to one's own suffering and hence to the pain in the universe. The alternative was offered that it may be more constructive to instead ask, "How?" If we can understand how bad things happen - what is the mechanism of their occurrence - one can then attack these problems in one's own life and work. Mental disturbances, both of criminality and certainly of schizophrenia, have causes. By asking "How?" we can try to understand those causes and hopefully develop cures. That is, after all, what medical research is all about, and I have devoted much of my life to such research.

There appears to be merit in focusing on the "How?" Yet, I still cannot help also asking "Why?" During my years in medicine, I have seen many examples of people who were crippled, blinded, or killed by a single

DNA error in their genes, by one tiny plugged or broken blood vessel in their heart or brain, by a unique cell that replicates wildly into cancer, by a biochemical malfunction in a part of their mind - while the rest of them, the remainder of their bodies and brains, were entirely normal. But that sole defect did them tremendous damage. Why were they chosen to suffer? We work earnestly to better understand genetic, cardiovascular, malignant, and mental diseases, and we shall doubtless make progress in their understanding and their treatment. It may even be that political and other methods will evolve to reduce the massacres, tortures, mass starvations, and brutality to which millions of innocent people are subjected. Yes, it is good indeed to know "How?" and still better to be able to use that knowledge to do something positive about human distress. But there still remains the great problem: why should such things happen at all?

I believe we shall always be left to ponder why suffering is not only vastly unequal in distribution, but seemingly pointless and inexplicable. Yet I also refuse to desist from the unanswerable question. Why is the world so made that Ray Weinstein has been alone for four decades in a cell on Ward's Island with his once fine mind and gentle spirit damaged beyond repair? Unreasonable as it may seem, I persist in asking you "Why? Why??"

Rongeur-Nez de France

It seems impossible to like the French, and also impossible not to like them. This nation manifests some of the best and the worst characteristics of human behavior and modern civilization. Dickens famously labeled the era of the French Revolution the best of times and the worst of times. France today is the best and the worst of countries.

Take the positive side. France is marvelously innovative. America may have given the world the cotton gin, revolver, telegraph, telephone, electric light bulb, phonograph, transistor, and computer, the British may have invented the railroad and the steam engine, but the French have developed the rongeur-nez. This last is a small cylindrical device sold in Parisian drugstores for 15 Euros. It has a nozzle enclosing tiny blades attached to a manually rotated base. One inserts the tip of the device into one's nostril, rotates the base to and fro with the other hand, and - voila - one's nose hairs are cut. For men, who have struggled for centuries against intranasal hirsuitism, this invention is more revolutionary than modern telecommunications. The rongeur-nez also has other important benefits when used in the right setting. Shortly after making my purchase, I sat down on a green bench in the little park behind the apse of Notre Dame cathedral, inserted, and began to rotate. The occupants of adjacent benches rapidly departed, leaving me considerable extra space in which to trim away while enjoying suddenly unobstructed views of the flying buttresses, gargoyles, and rose gardens of the magnificent church. The exodus of my neighbors may be explained by their hypothesizing that I was snorting cocaine through the device or that I may have recently been discharged from a local mental hospital, or perhaps merely reflected fear of what could appear at the business end of the device when removed from my nose. I am confident that using the rongeur-nez on the Parisian subway will get me a seat even in the heure d'affluence. I intend to try that out tomorrow.

Speaking of nasal hairs, one of my adolescent nephews was stopped from getting on a aircraft after 9-11 when a minuscule forceps intended for clearing his nares was seized. My nephew tried unsuccessfully to convince security that this little pincer represented no hijack hazard, saying he believed no pilot would respond to such potential threats as, "Turn this plane around or I'll pull." Maybe he will have better luck if he wants to take a rongeur-nez on board.

So much for French inventions. Let's discuss their work ethic. President Bush is said to have complained that the French economy is in trouble "because there is no word in French for entrepreneur", although some of GWB's political enemies dismissed that comment as compelling evidence against the possibility that "intelligent design" accounts for human evolution. It is not true that the French are lazy. In many shops, bars, and other enterprises in France one encounters men and women with energy, enthusiasm, and professionalism. The thin man who serves morning coffee and croissants in record time at the Bar Castiglione near the Place Vendome is so efficient that I am trying to hire him to replace two physicians at our Institute in Fairfax. The thoughtful service received from one Parisian optical retailer was world class. The manager of a boutique selling fine mechanical watches was so intelligent, articulate (in French and English), well informed, and lovely to look at that she would be a top employee in America or anywhere else. But then, alas, there are all the others: the museum guards, mostly from Africa, who do nothing but talk to each other continually and start to close museums like the Orsay 45 minutes ahead of time so they can quit precisely by the end of each theoretical "work day"; dishonest, rude, and sometimes plain crazy and dangerous taxi drivers; impolite or indifferent waiters whose automatic 15% tip is built into the price of every item on every menu in France; and many others. The universal view is that government workers, and their cousins in the French unions, represent the very bottom of the employment barrel. One bright French lady referred to French government employees as the "world champions of laziness." One has only to experience - as many of us have - waiting in line an hour or more at Airport Charles de Gaulle to get a piece of paper stamped to avoid paying the 19.6% tax on purchases made in France, or have one's travel disrupted by any of the countless strikes ("greves") by the government workers of modern-day France, to cordially agree with this opinion.

The very worst of France is represented in its long history of political corruption, violence, instability, and defeat. The French Revolution replaced an intolerable royalty by the even more intolerable slaughter of thousands by lunatics like Robespierre, Marat, and Danton. Then Napoleon, still viewed as a great hero by many of the French, ended the Revolution and engineered wars in Europe which, harnessing the power of artillery, killed more people than any prior armed struggles. Since that time, the French have been bitterly divided between the Right and the Left in various forms, while losing war after war. You would, of course, not know this from a visit to the National War Museum, nor from various monuments and plaques scattered throughout Paris. From these sources, you will be informed, for example, that French forces were chiefly responsible for the Allied triumphs in both World Wars and that the defeat of Rommel in the deserts of North Africa was accomplished by the French army with minimal assistance from the Americans and the British. Furthermore, there really was no collaborating Vichy government, and the regrettable Jewish deportations to death camps never involved French cooperation. And the later collapse of French colonialism and defeat in Algeria were artifacts due to coincidences which fail to disprove the greatness and glory of France.

The persistence of communist appeal, the adoption by France of socialism and the welfare state on a massive scale, the growing demographic disaster from North African Moslem immigration, resentment of American wealth, arms, and successes, "hommes politiques" famous for opportunism, hypocrisy, and corruption are among the problems which deeply stain the French national fabric. In France can one see today numerous posters saying "Stick with the Socialist Party" and "1905-2005 The First Hundred Years of Socialism". In France in 2005 can one read the following, selected almost at random and translated by me from today's newspaper: "A new allocation. The government announced today the creation of a new allocation to permit parents to stay unemployed at home for one full year after the birth of their third child......The benefits will be additive to those already applying to all families, who already receive 512 Euros each month until their child is age 3 in case they do not work....The new benefit will comprise between 700 and 1,000 Euros per month, according the National Union of the Associations Familiales who inspired the new legislation.......The program will cost about 1.3 billion Euros each year, but will not increase the national government debt because it will be considered instead a deficit of the National Fund for Familial Allocations [which however is also part of the government].....The added benefit, limited to one year for each family, is designed to encourage women to 'mettre au monde' a third child while ensuring that they will not be penalized in their work life." In Paris today one sees posters printed by the government pointing out that illegal immigrants should be encouraged to exercise their rights to free legal care, and that government-supplied condoms are Paris' contribution to keeping love alive in the land of "l'amour." Meanwhile, medical and surgical treatments are being rationed, and many bankrupt hospitals are closing in the Alice in Wonderland of socialized medicine. Enough of French politics......

So then, why do we still visit here? Paris is beautiful, with incredible architecture and artistic masterpieces. The food in many restaurants is terrific. Cafes are great places to be together. Some fine people are here, like the outstanding French musician whose harp Dixie bought last year, or the emeritus professor of gynecology who is one of my close friends. It is necessary, however, to select very carefully, to tune out the idiocies which every day impair the quality of living of decent French citizens and infuriate visitors, to appreciate despite annoyances, to develop some pachydermy. A simple example from today will suffice. In the shade of chestnut trees at late afternoon in the Luxembourg Gardens, Dixie and I sat enjoying the light, the early autumn colors, the tranquility of the fountain and the reflecting pool. An elderly French woman seated herself about one foot away from me and lit up a cigarette. I was trying to alter a setting on my cell phone when I was engulfed in smoke. This grizzled female then informed me that I was disturbing her with my phone adjustments and should do that kind of thing only "chez moi". Of course she was rude, and of course I could have responded by telling her, in suitably sarcastic French, that she should try limiting herself to smoking at home. But rather than do so, we moved on. The vicious old lady puffed away as we strolled together through the sunlight amidst the flowers, and enjoyed the rest of a gorgeous day in Paris. What happened in the Luxembourg is a microcosm of what anyone will sometimes experience in France, and it is well to anticipate it or to stay away.

Come to think of it, I should have pulled out my rongeur-nez when she pulled out her cigarette. I'll keep that in mind for next time. Bet it would have worked......

Save the Sea Turtles

Some time ago while walking on a beach in Florida I noticed a small zone of sand surrounded by sticks and yellow tape warning of a sea turtle nesting area. An adjacent sign stated that the penalty for disturbing a sea turtle nest was $250,000. This struck me, and it may possibly strike you, as a bit steep.

The fines for interfering with sea turtles, amphibious reptiles of slight utility except as mating objects for other sea turtles, vary by location along the Atlantic coast, but are commonly $100,000 or more and can include a prison sentence. Not long ago the Herald Tribune described the case of a 73 year old woman whose beach access had been obstructed by tapes placed by volunteers around a zone they believed might contain a turtle nest hidden in the sand; she defiantly moved her beach chair into the forbidden region on her own property, was arrested, and faces up to 5 years in prison. On Hilton Head Island, it is reported that the maximum fine for disturbing a sea turtle nest can be as high as $390,000 and up to 56 years in prison.

Harming the turtles is considered to include letting light fall upon them. In some beach communities in Florida, all street lights are extinguished during the sea turtle breeding season from May through October, seemingly without regard for elderly people liable to stumble and fall in the dark. This is because it is thought that street lights could interfere with sea turtle mating or return of hatchlings to the sea. Scores of thousands of windows in personal and commercial property near Florida's beaches must be tinted or modified to reduce the possibility that interior lighting might confuse the sea turtles. Florida's power companies modify street lighting patterns and fixtures at massive cost to help the sea turtles. Residents near beaches are told to close their window curtains at night to save the turtles.

An entire department within the government of the State of Florida exists to promulgate, modify, enhance, refine, and otherwise implement sea-turtle-saving behavior by Floridians and visitors to the Sunshine State. The Florida Fish and Wildlife Conservation Commission has published a document running to just under 100 pages about saving the sea turtles; the cover of this publication shows a swirl of tracks on sand supposed to represent the confused wanderings of disorientated baby sea turtles. The Federal Environmental Protection Agency has made sea turtles the poster child for its activities involving endangered species. Thousands of volunteers patrol the beaches of Florida looking for and reporting alleged sea-turtle-harmful behavior. Millions of people have been taught to believe that all this makes sense.

Do an online search about the *costs* of sea turtle protection and you will find almost nothing on the subject. Try it. In contrast, you will note links to hundreds of articles about the essentiality of saving the turtles and cutting down on beach illumination. In addition to many articles from various environmental lobby groups will be found advertisements from companies selling such products as turtle-safe windows, window tinting systems, window coverings, and more. As for estimates of aggregate expenses to make Florida, let alone the world, safe for sea turtles, little information seems to be available. One gets the impression that it is absurd, even obscene, to seek such data.

It would take a truly heroic effort to attempt to arrest the freight train of environmentalist activism over the sea turtles. The current writer would be an idiot to even try. But having something of a scientific background, he found it interesting to look briefly under the hood to see what, if any, scientific basis exists for believing that light in a condo several floors above a Florida beach harms sea turtles. The paucity of data is remarkable.

Assertions that light may harm sea turtle breeding fall into two main categories: (1) female sea turtles prefer to nest on dark beaches and (2) hatchlings can be disoriented by illumination reaching nesting beaches. For reviews and further references one can refer to such advocacy publications as "Understanding, Assessing, and Resolving Light Pollution Problems on Sea Turtle Nesting Beaches" by B. E. Witherington and R. E. Martin, and the "Coastal Roadway Lighting Manual" created with inputs from the same sources. Both of these are readily available as .pdf files online. Witherington and Martin are marine biologists whose careers are profoundly linked to and have obviously benefited from the sea turtle protection movement. They summarize data from an advocacy perspective, but appear to recognize that some apparently plausible science must offered to support the activist movement they and similarly inclined colleagues caused to happen.

Nest counts seem to indicate that reproductively active sea turtle females prefer darker beach areas. In this regard, they are perhaps not very different in mating behavior from Floridian teenagers. What is not proven, however, is that having some beaches which are lighter than they would naturally be affects the total reproductive capacity of the Atlantic sea turtle population. If all that happens is that more turtles go to darker beaches and fewer to lighted ones, there obviously might be little or no net effect on aggregate reproduction. It appears that nobody knows to what extent, if any, having some lighted beaches affects total turtle nesting success.

As for the hatchlings whose ability to find the sea is alleged to be impaired by man-made light, the situation is not only complex but ambiguous. Sea turtle babies hatch out of their eggs mostly in the middle of the night. The darkness of night presumably enhances their ability to escape predation until they manage to crawl back into the sea, which is asserted to be their most immediate goal. Of course, many baby turtles which reach the sea later die there from natural forces including sea-living predators. But it is believed that the first goal of hatchlings is to head into the ocean, and it seems well established that if they wander away from the ocean and cannot find it again they soon die.

There are anecdotal reports that clusters of baby sea turtle bodies have been occasionally been found under street lights in parking lots near the ocean. This and other evidence indicates that hatchlings sometimes move toward bright lights. The problem however is figuring out how light affects baby sea turtles getting into the sea. For example, if they are attracted by light, how do they deal with the brightest light in the night sky, namely the moon? The answer is, really, that nobody knows. The full moon is far brighter than almost any other light source on most beaches. The moon appears to move across a significant part of the night sky from east to west, and the full moon virtually "moves" from horizon to horizon in a single night. Yet during the nights when the moon is brightest, tracks of hatchlings show the highest frequency of moving straight into the sea. How do they do this? Nobody knows. There is speculation, but it is only that, that the hatchlings "see" the illuminated ocean horizon and move toward it while somehow ignoring the even brighter moon itself. On moonless or nearly moonless nights, tracks indicate that the babies do more "disoriented" wandering. But so what? It is presumably harder for the babies to see when it is dark, but it is also presumably harder for predators like sea gulls to find them during the longer time it takes them, on average, to get into the ocean. The babies may also be helped to find the ocean by the sound of waves, or even the vibrations from breaking surf. The few studies which have tried to understand how baby sea turtles see light suggest that the seven species of sea turtles detect wavelengths of light of differently, but all see blue light best; some actually react aversively to yellow light. Studies which temporarily limit the visual fields of baby turtles suggest they more easily orient toward light which is close to the horizon rather than high overhead. The babies are hypothesized to orient toward light by aiming their heads so that equal illumination reaches both eyes.

But - and here is the key point - it seems that nobody knows HOW much light of WHAT type and at what DISTANCE can have a significant adverse effect on seaward movement by babies. The scientists involved actually assert that this cannot (and therefore should not) be determined by measuring intensity of light via metering, since the meters might not act like a turtle's eyes and brain. So rather than admit that they JUST DON'T KNOW the information that is really needed to make rational decisions about beach lighting, the key advocate scientists decided to promulgate very simple but fundamentally non-scientific standard for such lighting. I quote their advice - which is now backed by the force of law involving huge fines and jail sentences - in the following sentences taken from the publications previously mentioned and which state their views:

"Because sea turtles perceive light differently than humans, it is inappropriate to try to determine if a light will cause a problem based on its brightness or broadcast properties." [Note: We shouldn't even try to determine these key parameters]. **An artificial light source is likely to cause problems for sea turtles if the source of light can be seen by an observer standing anywhere on the nesting beach"** [bold emphasis is in the original.] "This basic rule of thumb will allow light managers to easily identify potentially problematic light sources."

The above is the core belief of the save-the-turtles movement, namely that ANY light seen from a beach is bad.

The same sources go on to make the following assertion: "Depending on brightness of the light source and the distance of the reflective surface from the beach, indirect lighting can be just as disruptive to sea turtles as direct lighting." [This statement gives no parameters for when such light "can be" and when it may not be disruptive, because such parameters are not only unknown, but also can't be assessed since "sea turtles perceive light differently from humans" and "it is inappropriate to try to determine if a light will cause a problem.."]

The following is the recommended good method to measure for harmful light: "A good method for determining if light is reaching the beach is to stand on the beach facing the ocean and hold a piece of white, rigid material (e.g., poster board, clip board, etc.) at arm's length away from the light source. This positions the observer between the light source and the material. From a standing position, slowly move the material from side to side. If you cast a shadow on the material, light is reaching the beach." How clever, and how quantitatively scientific! It is also added that "The more extensive the illumination, the greater the potential for problems. Light visible from a crouching position on the beach (simulating a turtle's perspective) is likely to be more disruptive than light only visible from a standing position......although both situations warrant remediation". In other words, *even light that the baby turtles can't see but which a human can see standing anywhere on the beach* is bad for the turtles and "warrants remediation."

That is what is being claimed. That's it. I am not kidding. And this shameless pseudoscience is currently enforced by regulations, fines, and jail sentences.

We are in the process of replacing two storm windows at our condominium in Palm Beach and according to the installer before the windows can be put in a permit is needed, for which purpose a government inspector will actually be paid to go out on the nearby beach at night and determine if he can see any light escaping from our illuminated condo. If he can see any light at all, the windows must use specially tinted glass. This explains why most beach front homes in Florida have opaque brown windows instead of ones with normal clarity. I guess it helps with privacy if you prefer to walk around nude in your lighted unit at night. But whether or not it helps the turtles is different issue.

A whole army of special interests now supports, enforces, and strengthens this folly. These include but are not limited to the manufacturers of the light-protection windows and other products, the scientists who get grants to study sea turtles, the government agencies at the local, state, and federal level whose employees owe their jobs to this kind of thing, the "volunteers" who enjoying serving in the "light police", the condo owners who feel good believing they are doing their part to save nature from a light-polluting mankind, the fixers, lawyers, and not-for-profit groups in the environmental lobby, and publications like the National Geographic.

As for the sea turtles, nobody knows whether they have been helped by all this or not, and if so by how much, making it impossible to determine possible sensible tradeoffs of costs and benefits for sea turtle light-control programs.

And while it seems true, as suggested in a prior missive from this author, that Florida may have the lowest average functional IQ of any state, not everyone who resides there is a fool. Lots of Floridians know that the sea turtle thing is crazy. These folks laugh, put up with it, and pray they won't trip and fall some night on a darkened beach or street. Their candid views are mostly unprintable. When our window installer asked my wife whether or not she and her husband cared about whether our new windows had to be tinted or not, I privately muttered a four letter epithet about the turtles. She returned to the installer with the comment, "We'll take whatever windows are required, but I prefer not to repeat exactly what my husband said about it." The installer, who was a bright guy by the way, just laughed and added, "I've heard it before."

Seven Diamonds for Number Nine

It is almost too easy to poke fun at the recent decline and fall of the former Governor of New York State, and there has been no shortage of humorists doing exactly that. He was one of the nastiest figures in public life, and built his career by destroying the jobs and reputations of other men. But what goes around, comes around. His disgrace could not have been more complete if it had been personally engineered by Hank Greenberg. And as the most revealing indication of his character, during the whirlwind scandal which overtook the Governor not a single man or woman came forth to publicly say anything nice about him.

But that is the past. We offer here a new interpretation of the fundamentals underlying the Governor's collapse. He failed not just because he was excessively hungry for power - that is commonplace among politicians. Not merely because he was unfaithful to his spouse - that is a widespread practice among even ordinary voters. Nor was it just because he is a very mean SOB - there are millions of them inside and outside of public life who remain unscathed despite a lifetime of nasty misbehavior. Our view is that the Governor went down and out because he was something universally disliked - a rich cheapskate.

"Wait a minute," you may say. "A cheapskate? Here is a guy who regularly paid a hooker with a Seven Diamond rating five thousand U.S. dollars for each hour of her time! You call that cheap?" You might even be tempted to further correct me with the observation that a real example of "cheap" is that other politician who paid a mere one-hundred and fifty dollars for nominally similar services, although he likely got not an hour but more like five minutes of that lady's time, and we are not even going to talk about quality. You could even add that cheapskates don't get laid at Washington's elegant Mayflower Hotel, although even I've done that though it doesn't count because it was with my wife.

But I am sticking to my guns. The Governor lost his job because he was a miser. Let's review some facts and do the math.

Assume that Number Nine, as he was sometimes known, visited Washington twice a month to obtain Seven Diamond services. We note in passing that the top grade of "seven" is non-standard in the rating of diamonds, which are normally ranked by size (carats), color, cut, and clarity. The most valuable diamonds are internally flawless, and we can safely assume that the Governor's hooker met that criterion. She was doubtless also well-shaped, or "cut." But her size and color were most likely unremarkable. The National Enquirer or another similar publication will doubtless soon expose to public scrutiny the detailed basis for her top rating.

Now $5,000 per hour twice a month, with say four weeks off for family vacations, is about $5000 x 22 = $110,000 per year. This may sound like a lot of money to the average john, even if we assume the Governor was lucky enough to have all other costs of his trips to Washington paid for as "official business" by New York State. But consider the limited alternatives available to him: (1) keep his fly closed when away from home, mentioned here only for completeness as a theoretical possibility; (2) get a divorce, an outrageously expensive choice and hence not worth serious consideration; or (3) support a mistress meriting the Seven Diamond rating.

Now outstanding mistresses do not come cheap (forgive the unintended pun). Nor can they generally be neglected for two weeks at a time, lest they feel lonely and become faithless, or even transfer their full interests to a more attentive wealthy man. So let us assume an average of not less than weekly visits to the mistress. Elementary analysis suggests that if the Governor had supported a seven diamond mistress it would have cost him far more money than the seven diamond hooker. Consider the following estimated *minimal annual* expenses for a top-quality mistress in a major American city:

Rent: $30,000

Furniture and decoration: Up-front cost likely to be at least $40,000

Automobile: $25,000 (say, a pretty Jaguar convertible amortized over 5 years)

Basic subsistence: $24,000

Booze: $5,000

Medications, contraceptives, K-Y jelly, personal toys, etc.: $3,000

Restaurants and entertainment: $25,000

Furs (assuming one mink coat or equivalent per year): $15,000 or more

Jewelry: Not less than $50,000 per year, more likely "the sky's the limit"

Vacations: $20,000

Pocket change, minor gifts, flowers, investments, and miscellaneous: $60,000

The above are believed to be conservative estimates derived from experienced sources considered to be reliable, and the actual expenses obviously could go much, much higher. But even this minimal total approximates a quarter of a million bucks per year. So by using the hooker, that cheapskate Governor was just about halving, or more than halving, his potential expenses.

Then of course, there was his saving not only of money but of time. The hooker doubtless did not waste time - to her, as to lawyers like the Governor, time is money. Billable time. In a professional relationship, nobody wastes billable time on romantic nonsense like watching TV together, listening to music, reminiscing about the last vacation getaway, ordering from Domino's, smooching, and so forth. There are more important remunerative things to do once the basic exchange is completed.

And finally, a top hooker is professionally conditioned never to confuse sex with love. She wouldn't try to marry the Governor, nor fall in love with him, nor complain about all the time he spends with his wife and kids. She won't ever forget that business is business, and her business depends upon discretion and clarity of purpose. She knows that sex for money is, for many good reasons, the oldest and not necessarily the least honorable profession.

We now pose this query: If it had been revealed that the Governor had merely kept a girl friend instead of having a relationship with a prostitute, would he have been forced to leave office? The question almost answers itself.

He would have apologized and continued to humbly serve the millions of fine citizens of the great State of New York. The Governor would have been almost appealingly revealed as yet another ordinary, vulnerable, flawed human being, a tragic victim of circumstances, a mere mortal whose marriage was, alas, sadly imperfect. There would have been little reason for his imperfections to become really major news, and he might have even gained sympathy from the many men and women whose marriages also leave something to be desired.

But enjoying a hooker at $5,000 an hour - nobody gets cut any slack for doing that! It's way beyond what the average man can hope for in his wildest erotic dreams, so jealousy and ridicule fell upon the Governor. And when that happened, like the snake in the Garden of Eden he didn't have a leg to stand on. In contrast, if he had been less of a penny-pincher and simply used some of his substantial inherited wealth and fat salary from the State of New York to really pay up for a great mistress instead of a Seven Diamond whore he would still - after a few mea culpas - be living in that mansion in Albany, planning more attacks on businessmen and sex rings, and contemplating a future run at the White House.

Huey Long was smart enough to figure out such things on his own, and his meteoric political career was ended only by an assassin's bullet. The former Governor of New York was less smart than Huey, though equally ambitious and dangerous. We should be relieved that a wide open fly and narrowly open wallet have terminated his political career.

Sixty-fifth Birthday Address

Dixie and I would like to thank all of you, our dear friends, for being with us on this special day.

It is conventional, one might almost say "normal", for the aging celebrant to be victimized on his birthday by being roasted, compelled to listen to acquaintances recount examples of his adolescent behavior - for example, that he once lasciviously participated in a panty raid at Wellesley, or had posted above the entrance to his dormitory room that immortal quote from Dante, "Abandon hope all ye who enter here." We wish to alter that tradition this evening by having the celebrant tell a few brief stories on his own.

Let me start by expressing how reassuring it is to have finally arrived in safety at the age when I no longer have to take care of myself. At 65, I have been enfolded in the protective womb of the federal government. Uncle Sam now provides me with free health care, even free eyeglasses, and my bank account automatically receives social security checks to help pay for my wife's jewelry. I am confident that I can look forward to more such goodies as our aging population votes for itself ever greater benefits to be paid for by our children and grandchildren. And you can always count on Uncle to get the incentives right. Not long ago, I received a letter from the Social Security Administration pointing out that I was to lose $1 of benefits for every $2 dollars I had earned while irresponsibly and misguidedly trying to support myself this year. I decided to obtain clarification by calling the SSA. The first message I heard said, in English, "Press one for Spanish." That was when I hung up.

Of course, even big government still can't do it all. Take sex, for example. It still must be accomplished without government assistance. But that eventually stops being a problem. As George Burns explained as he approached 100, sex at his age was "like playing pool with a rope."

One of the few advantages of getting old is that one can tell stories based on many years of experience. In my view, it's moments of humor that most deserve recounting. Nobody who thinks needs to be reminded of the tragedies we have each experienced, and which seemingly tend to increase among ourselves and those we love as age advances.

Not too long ago, my wife went to send something out via "Mailboxes" near our home in Maryland. On line in front of her was a woman with a stroller which she wanted to have packed and shipped. The lady behind the counter - who incidentally was the local Mailbox "Employee of the Month" - said, "We can't ship this." The customer protested, saying that she had sent it before. The agent came around from behind the counter, looked at the stroller, and said, "Oh, we can do it. I thought there was a baby inside." As the agent disappeared to get a box for the stroller, the customer turned to my wife and whispered, "Did she actually say she thought there was a baby in it??"

Hearing that true story made my day. Things happen in real life that are funnier than almost anything one can imagine. Take, for example, the time Dixie and I visited San Francisco. At the airport, we had the ill luck to enter a cab which then careened wildly at high speed toward central San Francisco in the hands of its disheveled, dirty, long-haired maniac of a driver. He was so obviously on drugs that we feared angering him by asking to leave the taxi. Praying the whole way, we arrived at the entrance of the Fairmont Hotel. I emerged from the cab in my tie and jacket, and at the same time the scruffy, drugged-up driver crawled out. The uniformed doorman ignored me, walked up to the taxi driver, and said to him, "Welcome to the Fairmont." Presumably, he thought the driver was a movie star.....

I can't resist telling another story involving my good wife. We were at a celebration where pictures of the partygoers were being taken. Dixie and I posed together in one of the groups. As we walked away after being photographed, Dixie said, "Joe, that was your hand on my ass, wasn't it?" Unfortunately, however, that was not my hand..........This incident made me recall the Peter Sellers movie in which Inspector Clouseau is in a hotel lobby with a dog next to him. The dog suddenly turns and bites another man. "Your dog just bit me," the man yells at Clouseau, who replies in Franglais, "My dog does not bite." The man is now screaming and pointing at the animal, "Don't give me that. This damn dog just bit me." Clouseau continued, "Zat is not my dog."

Allow me to return to some additional true stories of our government in action. Less than a year ago, I received a letter from the Internal Revenue Service explaining that I owed back taxes of hundreds of thousands of dollars on a check I had received from the Social Security Administration in the amount of one million, four thousand thirty-two dollars and 67 cents. I forwarded this letter to my accountant, who with my permission and my name deleted shared it electronically to provide hilarity to hundreds of tax accountants and tax attorneys. Never in its entire history has the Social Security Administration paid any individual a check of this size. Of course, a formal reply to the IRS had to be composed, with the usual lost time and money.....

Another IRS-related story concerns a sperm donor at our sperm bank in Virginia who claimed that he was not an independent contractor. At tax time, the donor was short the thousand dollars or so he owed the IRS for his "work" of donation, and he protested to the IRS that he should have been treated as an employee, with wages withheld, instead of getting a form 1099 as an independent agent. The IRS thus undertook to formally determine whether or not a sperm donor is an employee or an independent contractor. The agency has developed a list of standard queries for resolving this issue in any type of situation. With the help of our attorney, we composed deadpan replies about sperm donation to some of these questions, such as:

"Does the individual provide his own equipment?"

"Does the individual perform a similar service for others?"

"Does the individual engage in this activity at or close to 35 hours per week?"

And my personal favorite, "Does the company provide training?"

I am happy to report that, in the end, the IRS ruled that sperm donors are indeed independent contractors for whom withholding is not required. If any of you are thinking of becoming sperm donors in the near future, please be apprised that you will be responsible for paying your own taxes.......

Even the U.S. Secret Service can be a source of humor. Some years ago I attended a fund-raiser in the Four Seasons Hotel in Washington, DC where U.N. ambassador Jeane Kirkpatrick was the featured speaker. As the cocktail hour wound down, a young man with something in his ear and wearing a suit which barely concealed his bulging muscles came up to me and said to my complete surprise, "Are you ready to escort Ambassador Kirkpatrick to the podium?" I replied that I would be happy to do so, they should just let me know when the right time came. A few minutes later I was told to proceed, but as I approached the Ambassador there was a flurry of activity and I was suddenly advised that a mistake had been made. At the time, of course, I didn't know Jeane Kirkpatrick except by reputation. But some 15 years later, Dixie and I met her through a mutual acquaintance and she actually did become a personal friend of ours. Jeane was a brilliant and courageous woman, and her recent death is one of the tragedies to which I earlier referred.

Well, I have talked long enough, and already sufficiently imposed on your time and goodwill. Furthermore, as Calvin Coolidge once philosophized, "You don't have to explain what you didn't say." We shall have to leave other stories, such as the evolution of our company's "no bra" policy, or my invention of the word "dimbo," for another time and place.

But I would like to close with one possibly amusing story with an embedded moral. In the late winter of 1999, Dixie and I visited the famous Carlsbad Caverns National Park. The caverns are deep underground, and in the elevator leading us back to the surface were a couple of junior National Park Service employees. They were animatedly discussing their recent successes with buying technology stocks. Dixie and I found this rather funny.

But looking beyond the humor, we wisely concluded that when speculation in technology equities had infected even Park Service workers in rural New Mexico it was time to avoid holding such securities.

So I conclude with the hope that as each of us continues our journey through life, we will laugh a lot but also ponder the significance of what we are laughing at. The infinite varieties of human foolishness and frailty easily become sources of humor. But their consequences are real, and far from funny. Thus there remains much serious work for each of us to do after we are done laughing.

Thank you again for being with me today and joining my birthday celebration!

Socialism and Medicine

One reads a lot these days about the death of socialism, and how capitalism is sweeping the globe. Don't be so sure. Take a look at health care.

The government is heavily involved and becoming ever more prominent in America's health industry. The reason that President Clinton was nearly able to nationalize one-seventh of the U.S. economy with his so-called health care reform is that health care is already largely socialized. If you doubt that, try to imagine Clinton attempting to nationalize food or housing. It wouldn't work, although food and shelter are just as necessary as health. The free market for food and housing is comparatively intact. In health care, the incremental change to socialism was much less, and the nearly full nationalization of the health industry in some Western countries like Canada, England, and France showed that it was politically achievable.

The government's involvement in health care is massive. In a real market, B pays A to provide services or products to B. The situation is not changed if B elects to use insurance paid for with his own money to level costs and to protect against the risk of a large expense. But, to borrow William F. Buckley's model, in health care we have the perfect example of C, D, and E getting together to decide what A shall do for B. A is the health care provider, B the patient, C the government, D is B's employer, and E the insurance or managed care company. C always has a huge role. That's what used to be called socialism.

Hold on, you say. We don't have socialized medicine in America. Let's take a look. Medicare is fully socialized already. It forcibly redistributes income. The government sets the fees for nearly all health services to individuals age 65 and older, and it is illegal for the patient to pay anything more to the physician or hospital than the "allowed" socialized rate. In some states, if a physician does not want to accept Medicare patients voluntarily, that's OK but he will lose his state-granted medical license, and practicing medicine without a license is a crime - even though the previously licensed practitioner retains all his skill and experience. Medicaid is socialized charity. Socialized Kidicare is coming. When your employer pays an insurance company for your health care, special laws allow him to do so with your pre-tax dollars instead of the usual post-tax dollars you use to buy food or pay the rent on an apartment; thus, every health care expense deprives Uncle Sam and usually your friendly state government of revenues they would love to have. The same goes for the numerous breaks given to tax-exempt hospitals. The Food and Drug Administration controls the supply of drugs and many other health care products for the entire country, adding billions of dollars in annual expenses for the pharmaceutical and biotechnology industries and delaying the introduction of new, lifesaving drugs in the name of "safety". State and federal governments control the licensing of physicians, hospitals, dentists, pharmacists, and laboratories producing limitations of supply, higher costs, and further government intrusion and control. State and the federal governments control the terms and conditions of many health care contracts and insurance plans. The federal government has a powerful presence in setting funding priorities for medical research. Regulation is of gargantuan proportions throughout the health care industry; examples are endless. None of this remotely resembles a free market. It is the partial defeat, not the triumph, of capitalism.

Everyone has been forced to accommodate to a bad system by adaptations that make it hard to change. There are deeply entrenched interests in the present health industry. These include physicians, hospitals, managed care companies, bureaucrats, medical researchers, pharmaceutical and medical instrument manufacturers, contract research organizations, and so on in an almost endless list. But we should not assume this system can't be changed. There was a time when having a voluntary military was unthinkable. Communism was once considered, even by some of its opponents, an unstoppable wave of the future. School vouchers and tuition tax credits may yet become realities. Free market change consistent with choice, personal liberty, and a safety net for the poor can come in health care as well. The crisis in Medicare funding, and the rapidly growing dissatisfaction with managed care, are some of the many signs that the present system isn't working. Government controlled programs never do. But the prodigious technological advances in health care mask the harmful effects of government, making it difficult to recognize how much further health would improve with a larger role for the free market.

Health care is America's largest heavily socialized industry, education vying with it for this dubious distinction. It doesn't have to stay that way. But don't expect anything but opposition on this from the academic health care field and especially the elite medical schools, whose budgets benefit heavily from government funds and whose faculties so clearly demonstrate the propensity of many intellectuals for leftist thinking. Also in opposition will be some widely read medical journals like the New England Journal of Medicine and the Lancet, which are generously larded with propaganda supporting health care nationalization. These folks know that further governmentalization of health care in America will broaden socialist influence on other sectors of the U.S. economy and around the world, which is exactly what they want. They also recognize that if, on the other hand, American medicine moves in the direction of privatization and the market, it will race far ahead of the levels of innovation and quality in other countries, forcing free market changes there as well.

American health care is thus a critical battleground for leftists. They haven't disappeared, and they won't give up without a fight.

Solving America's Job Crisis

We all know it's almost impossible to find people to hire these days, with the economy being so strong. Getting single mothers off welfare and back into the work force has helped a bit, but many jobs require more education and training than these women usually possess. What can be done?

Recently I heard about a medical organization in Northern Virginia that was having success hiring staff while almost across the road from them hot companies like UUNet, AOL, Cable and Wireless, and Nortel were unable to find new employee candidates who could read or speak English, perform basic addition and subtraction, and understand how to end "Num lock" on their computers.

The company I visited has been in the medical business for more than 15 years, and has over 200 employees. As a condition of allowing me to interview its employees, the organization requested anonymity, and is referred to henceforth as Company A. It is rumored that last year over 100% of its employees turned over. Yet Company A seems to be doing just fine, hiring as needed and apparently making a profit. (As a closely held corporation, it does not disclose its precise turnover rates or profit levels.) So this week I visited them to learn how they do it.

I wanted to meet some of their new hires, and the company was happy to cooperate. The first person I was introduced to was a new clinical assistant. She was polite, soft-spoken, smiling, and told me how happy she was to have such a great job. There was a subtle but distinct anatomical thickening of her midsection. I talked with her supervisor in the nursing department. "How did you know she was pregnant?" she said in amazement. "She wasn't pregnant when we hired her on Monday. But two days later she told us that her pregnancy test had just turned positive." Hmmm......

The next person was a young Chinese-American lady who looked about 6 months pregnant. She had been working at the company for a month or so in something called the "RIA Lab". Company A had hired her knowing she was pregnant. But this woman had special skills, asseverated this was going to be her last child, had the right attitude, and was willing to work for fair wages because nobody else would hire her. I began to suspect a pattern.

I asked around. Most of Company A's staff are female. At first blush this seems natural, as they provide medical services to many women with fertility and genetic problems. But my suspicions were further aroused upon discovering that almost half of their embryology staff are pregnant, and the head of one of their laboratories is leaving after having several babies. My hypothesis was cinched when I learned that almost all the females under the age of 40 at company A - and this is the dominant group in their work force - including both married and single women are pregnant, trying to get pregnant, trying to get pregnant again, or were recently pregnant (and now in the short interval between pregnancies). And some are even getting high technology infertility treatments from Company A itself to help them conceive, a workplace benefit more valuable to these employees than Microsoft stock options used to be to the folks at Redmond!

Bingo! Your correspondent has discovered the secret of Company A's successful recruitment efforts. They hire lots of young women who are or are determined to immediately become pregnant. Company A provides all of them with generous obstetrical health benefits. And if a few of the women experience trouble getting pregnant, Company A will medically help them do so. As yet, no other organizations of which your correspondent is aware have stumbled upon the same hiring strategy, but even when they do almost none will be able to match Company A's unique benefits to infertile employees. And few, if any, corporations will be able to provide fecundity-minded women with that special psychological benefit already achieved at Company A: the daily experience of close integration with a virtually all-pregnant work force.

Current Company A administration does admit that their hiring model has modest disadvantages. These include increased staff turnover, absences from work during and after pregnancy, lighter work loads during pregnancy, the necessity to comply with the Family Leave Act, added health care costs, failures of employees to return to their jobs once children or additional children are born, and additional training costs. But at least they can find employees to pay! Furthermore, the Company benefits from the average lower salary of younger new employees, and pockets the forfeited retirement benefits of unvested personnel who quit during or after pregnancy. But beyond all these pros and cons, Company A is an idealistic organization, a rarity these days amidst the cutthroat competition and narrow margins of modern business. Management feels it is doing "the right thing" by hiring pregnant women since they are an oppressed group in our society, the victims of unfair discrimination in the workplace.

Company A proudly feels it is irrelevant that in a country where contraception and abortion are available on demand pregnancy and childbirth are virtually always voluntary choices. The Company also sees negative value in hiring women who choose not to have children, or who reenter the workplace only after their children are grown up. Hiring such females would, to Company A's great credit, seem to them discrimination against the future mothers of America.

Company A's policies deserve wide emulation and praise. The Company is able to hire in very tough job markets, and simultaneously benefits worthy women who are discriminated against and unfairly avoided by less socially conscious employers. This is win-win indeed for business and for America!

So worthy is Company A's approach that we hope our story will inspire other corporations to follow its lead. And, let's not forget that there is a big opportunity for the federal government to help make this a reality. The Feds could easily require, for example, that pregnant women, like veterans, must be given preferences in hiring. This easily justified reverse discrimination would undo some of the harms of past injustices which, as always, fall with particular severity upon poor, minority women. Such a law would also eliminate the shameful specter of women who, desperately needing jobs, are forced to hide the very fact that they are pregnant. Reducing one more barrier for working women to have children would tend to increase our population, eventually augmenting the size of the U.S. economy, creating more future employees to keep Medicare and Social Security solvent for their parents' benefits, and producing many other advantages for our society.

Also keep in mind that the government could provide tax credits to companies who hire more pregnant women than average, since such companies could possibly have added costs if they do so. It would be easier than ever for our wealthy nation to afford such credits now that the President has projected a permanent budgetary surplus. And even if the surplus were to someday disappear, this program could sustain its funding by tax increases on recalcitrant corporations with lower than average percentages of pregnant women in their work forces.

It's exciting to anticipate things like this as America moves ahead into the 21st century.

The Stillbourn: Being a True Account of One Week on a Viking Prison Ship in the Northern Mediterranean in the Year of our Lord 2008

It started innocently enough at a downtown Washington, DC steak restaurant where we dined with two dear companions. The meal was completed, happiness reinforced by amity, delicious food, intelligent conversation, generous cocktails, and excellent wines, when a man known to our friends sat himself down at our table. This portly gentleman, a professional in the hospitality industry, must remain unnamed here. His type is well-known. Let us call him "The Promoter." He quickly brought the topic around to his hiring of a private cruise ship, arranged for the coming summer for a journey along the French and Italian Rivieras. The anticipated joys of participation in this excursion were described at length, and it was allegedly nearly sold out. After The Promoter departed, our friends disclosed that they had earlier agreed to go on this trip. The four of us had just had great fun together. The idea that Dixie and I might join our friends on this European journey was floated. We considered for a couple of days, and opted in despite our rather negative reactions to The Promoter. Thus we signed on through attachment to our companions, while ignoring the wisdom of Margaret Thatcher: "I generally make up mind about a man in 10 seconds, and I rarely change my mind."

In making an affirmative decision, Dixie and I were also influenced by our prior generally positive experiences on the Queen Elizabeth II going through the Panama Canal, and on a different cruise ship along the southwestern coast of Alaska. But not only were these larger and more luxurious vessels not controlled by a single Promoter, they also had the unique advantage of taking us to places very difficult or impossible to visit other than by ship. This hardly applied to towns on the southern coasts of France and Italy, nearly all of which we had several times traveled to in our own automobile.

To be brief, we made the fateful, substantial, non-refundable deposits, and were locked in. Folly is limitless. Embarrassment prevents me from disclosing the cost of our week visiting former Mediterranean pirate coves. Let it suffice to say that it would have been possible to fly to Paris, reside for seven days at The Ritz or the Plaza Athenee, enjoy lunch and dinner every day at Michelin Two and Three Star restaurants, and see the leading museums, cathedrals, and other magnificent sights of the City of Lights for less than we paid for the trip some of whose highlights will now be described.

Our cruise started in Nice. It is not possible to reach Nice directly from Washington, so we flew on SAS via Copenhagen. The overnight flight to Denmark was satisfactory but tiring as usual, and we partially recuperated in the excellent SAS Business Class lounge in Copenhagen. However, the connecting flight from there to Nice was pathetic. Intentionally overbooked, its departure was delayed while SAS auctioned off an increasing number of free miles to find ten people willing to leave in the evening. The business class seats were identical to those in tourist class, but with the middle seat of each trio left vacant. My narrow chair had not been reupholstered in decades. Lunch featured a remarkable meat worthy of DNA analysis to identify its true origin. It was so tough that NOBODY in the front section of the plane ate more than a single bite. The stewardess claimed the dish was pork, but it was beyond possibility that any part of a pig except cross-sections of its hooves could be so incapable of mastication. Dixie had just read a news article reporting that the high cost of food in France had caused a sharp increase in the human consumption of horse meat, and she believed that SAS had served us horse. My own opinion is that it more likely was farm-raised fox. Some of you may be familiar with the tenderness of fox meat, highlighted by the classic recipe for the stew:

Skin the fox, remove its entrails, and place the carcass in a large kettle.
Add water, cut vegetables, and a rock for added flavor.
Cook at a low boil for three days, adding water as needed.
Discard the fox, retaining the rock.
Season to taste, and serve.

The Nice airport was almost a parody of the French air travel "system". Luggage carts that used to be free were chained together and release of each required 1 Euro coins, which we did not have. The only bank machine available to provide Euros in the baggage area was broken. The change machine for turning paper Euros into coins was also not working. And of course there was no porter. After we stood around for nearly one hour in the non-air-conditioned hall, our luggage, marked "PRIORITY", was finally unloaded. We dragged our belongings to a taxi, and instructed the driver to take us to the Hotel Chateau St. Martin in Vence, a 12 kilometer (approximately seven mile) drive from the airport. The cost of the 15 minute taxi ride, using a meter and via a route I drove a few years ago and know to be correct, was 72 Euros (about $110). I shall henceforth try to stifle my complaints against the robbers who drive New York taxicabs.

The hotel, in which we had stayed before, has delightful gardens. Our room had a large balcony offering a splendid view of the hills east of Vence, the ancient St. Paul-de-Vence below, and the distant Mediterranean. Dinner in the special gourmet dining room was superb. Later, the moon rise was reflected over the sea beyond the lights of Nice, a breathtaking sight. Breakfast next day on our patio was delicious, and the sunlit view gorgeous. The entire fabulous experience was French hospitality at its best, and expensive as it was, cost about half as much as a day on the ship on which we were about to embark. There was only one minor negative at St. Martin: we would encourage the hotel management to do away with the unexpected and nearly invisible "foot rinse" on the approach path to the pool, which yours truly managed to step into with his socks and shoes on while turning to read the small sign warning of its presence.

Interestingly, the grounds of St. Martin once was a regional headquarters of the Knights Templar. Remnants of the old walls can still be seen alongside the hotel, and there is a small museum on the history of the movement. As described, the original nine Knights conceived the idea of providing protection from robbers and murderers to pilgrims who journeyed to the Holy Land after its conquest from the Muslims. The Templars were a pioneering fee-for-service firm, and grew substantially from about the year 1100 into the mid-14th century when it achieved thousands of members. The Holy Land had been lost, but the Knights continued as an armed force within medieval France. In that era major political conflicts involved Kings who desired centralization of power, vs. the nobility and knightly clans who opposed royal infringements on their independence. The Knights Templar during the 14th century were early victims in this centuries-long struggle. Thousands were captured in a single night in a plot arranged by the King with the collaboration of the Pope. The Templar leaders were tried for heresy and bestiality, convicted in show trials on the testimony of false witnesses, and burned at the stake. Thus the movement came to its unhappy end. Modern day Masons claim connections with the Templars, the details of which are secrets of those orders.

To get from the hills above Vence to the port of Nice was a few miles further than to the airport. Outrage at the obscene cost involved in this brief taxi ride was muted by anticipation that, now - at last - the Great Adventure was about to begin.

Our first view of the Seabourne cruise line ship, to be evermore known to us as the Stillbourn, revealed it to be smaller and older than expected. English-speaking crew courteously led us to the check-in line for registration. We were identified by our passports, carefully checked against the list of those who had paid up, and photographed. Plastic room keys and identity cards were issued, and our passports were simultaneously taken from us "for safekeeping" throughout the whole journey. Taking one's passport for this reason is, of course, entirely unnecessary, especially since each passenger compartment has a safe; the purpose is to hold one's passport hostage against full payment to the cruise line and its associated travel agencies for all services before termination of the journey. To enter or leave the ship at any time, either directly at a dock or via tender, required showing one's identity card and being bar-coded in or out by guards. A typical departure and return needed electronic recording of identity at least twice, sometimes up to four times, all done in the name of security. The ship was, in fact, controlled like a prison in which the customers were prisoners, the crew were guards, and a predetermined schedule decreed when the prisoners could temporarily leave on probation with a promise to return prior to the required ship departure time.

A cruise ship is, in fact, a kind of floating jail, not altogether dissimilar to the prison ships of ancient days. The analogy is less forced than you might imagine. We admit that the addition of a mechanical ventilation system, modern plumbing, and better food give the cruise ship advantages over the typical prison ship. But consider the many similarities. When the ship is not in port, you are absolutely unable to leave it, and when in port your time on parole is strictly controlled. Your room is not much larger than the cell of an average prisoner; on the Stillbourn, a couple lives for a week in a windowless enclosure of about 300 square feet, only 150 square feet per person. Every nook and cranny is occupied, one must climb over the bed if the partner sits at the desk, all luggage is squeezed under the bed. Each room has a glass door opening onto what was described in the ship's literature as a "veranda" - actually a platform less than one foot deep and bounded by a railing (photos are available to disbelievers). The crew can electronically lock these doors at any time. Since as participant in a cruise you have no car and the port areas of most cities are usually far from the sites most worth visiting, you are trapped even when released unless you pay your guards to arrange something for you on which you will be escorted by them. The Stillbourn seemed a specifically Viking prison ship because its lounge is named after King Olaf, and bears a large photograph of former owners, Harald and Sonja, King and Queen of Norway. We have not researched the history of Olaf, but choose to imagine him as a thuggish red-haired brute of a thousand years ago, clubbing seals on the shores of Greenland and raping natives in Labrador. But that might be unfair - further research could reveal Olaf was just another royal Scandinavian socialist. As for Harald and Sonja, whatever else they were they were smart, since before the Stillbourn got too old they unloaded it to its current American owners, who now milk it for what they can.

You may think I exaggerate, but I plead innocent. As proof, allow me to describe two examples of our days out on parole, one rather briefly and the other in more detail.

The first was at Cannes. The ship docked a half mile or so from the extreme western end of the promenade along the beach area. Our friends and we walked in the blazing heat (no taxis were at the dock) past many closed shops (it was Sunday). We found a cafe at which to sit down, and paid fifty dollars to gaze at the back side of the convention center while drinking Cokes, water, and coffee. Then, trudging east in the blazing sunlight, we advanced to a small restaurant known to our friends. There we did have a truly fine lunch; fresh Dover sole meuniere and good white wine defy complaint. When we left, the thermometer had risen to nearly 100 degrees. One member of our party, swathed in shawl and oversized hat to protect her from the intense UV radiation, opted out of walking back to the ship, and eventually found a taxi driver who took pity on her and returned her to the Stillbourn. Upon entering her cell she stripped naked and collapsed into heat-exhausted sleep. The rest of us eventually made it back to the ship, climbed the long ramp up to the portal on the side of the vessel, passed through security, and spent the remainder of the day restoring normal body temperature and rehydrating with abundant ice-cold Pellegrino, vodka, and Scotch. Such was our total experience at Cannes.

Next day, the ship was anchored offshore at St. Tropez. The Promoter had arranged an exclusive treat for about forty of us. We were going ashore to have lunch at the supposedly exclusive Club 55. As the Stillbourn could not be accommodated in the tiny harbor, several trips on a tender were required to get all of us into the picturesque old port. We then walked about half a mile to a corner of the harbor where an enormous taxi queue had formed. In about thirty minutes, no taxis had arrived. It was just past noon, and extremely hot. We had brought along to fill empty rooms on the Stillbourn - at the group's expense - some Iraq war veterans who had won a lottery at Walter Reed Army Hospital. One of the vets was a woman on crutches who had developed a malignant sarcoma of the leg and was recovering from radiation therapy and six rounds of chemotherapy, and she bravely stood in line along with us. Then word circulated that there were only five taxis in the whole of St. Tropez, all of which were otherwise engaged. The prisoners began to plan a mutiny. The alternatives being discussed were either to flee separately into the town and seek food and shelter in small groups, or return immediately to the prison ship where it was comparatively cooler and more comfortable than on the taxi line.

But then a resourceful fellow-prisoner discovered along the docks a private ferry which was available for immediate charter, could accommodate all of us, and which offered to transport us to and from a beach near the Club 55. The captain, who looked and acted for all the world like a Barbary pirate, assisted by his girlfriend who was the entire crew, was generously disposed to take us to and from the beach near the Club for a mere FIFTEEN HUNDRED Euros. Thus the mutiny was averted, and we returned to the dock from which we had originally disembarked. The ferry appeared, each couple coughed up 50 Euros, and we left the harbor. Mercifully, just before we departed someone located a single taxi capable of separate transportation of the female vet with cancer and her sister to the Club.

The ferry was a pretty fast boat, and we had all anticipated a short ride, but it lasted nearly an hour as Club 55 is on the other side of a long peninsula that juts east of the harbor far out into the Mediterranean. Meanwhile, the pirate-captain's girlfriend sold most of us bottles of water for 2 Euros a bottle. In this single day, a nest egg nearly sufficient for the captain's retirement was being created. It was after 2 PM when the boat approached the beach. To our amazement, no dock big enough for the ferry existed at that beach. We were told it would be necessary to use a very small boat for the final 200 or so meters of our journey to lunch (a four stage process: Stillborn to tender to ferry to inflatable motorized dinghy). This last bounced away from shore piloted by a barefooted youth wearing swim trunks, sunglasses, and a New York Yankees baseball cap balancing erect in the stern above the outboard motor. The dinghy had lettering inside the bow saying, in French, that occupancy was limited to 5 persons. Nevertheless, in a process which was eventually repeated three times, fourteen of us clambered off the back of the ferry, and fell, jumped, or were pushed into the dingy, then held on for dear life as the thing bounced around in the waves and wind and nearly swamped. I later learned that several of those who bravely engaged in this exercise in nautical transportation were actually UNABLE TO SWIM, and that at least one person sustained a leg injury.

The dinghy approached a small dock and at last we clambered out. To reach the Club, it was necessary to wade through a few hundred feet of sand encumbered with a dense collection of human flesh. Masses of pink bodies, packed shoulder to shoulder in endless rows, men and women, beautiful, average, and ugly, children, adults, and elderly, all "topless", covered the beach. Surprisingly, the experience was no more erotic than observing hundreds of elephant seals beached along the coast of California. Like the seals, the people would sometimes grunt, move an appendage, flip sand, or bellow. Sometimes a cloaca was briefly exposed to view. From time to time, the overheated bodies would migrate into the sea, swim briefly, and return to their place for more sleep.

But at last, our half-starved hoard stumbled to the Club, to discover that it served all food outdoors. Overheated as we were, and overdressed as we were compared to the near-naked local bathers, we took whatever tables we could get on the overcrowded patio and ordered our dishes. The monopoly prices we were each charged by Club 55 were an outrage. We then were rushed through the meal by the Promoter who wanted us to hasten back to the Stillbourn for some early evening activities which he had scheduled, and by the pirate-captain who was eager to end his day and deposit his loot in the French equivalent of his 401k account.

Thus the entire transportation process was reversed, with the task of climbing from the dinghy onto the ferry even more difficult and hazardous that the reverse process which had been necessary to reach the Club before lunch. Then too the return trip was delayed as the Promoter asked the pirate-captain to take us directly back to the Stillbourn. But when he did so, it turned out that the prison ship's tender portal, made for side-to-side boarding, could not "mate" safely with the pirate's rear-only exit. So the ferry then had to go from the Stillbourn back to the dock in St. Tropez where we had been many hours before. There we awaited the tender which at last brought us safely back to our floating jail. And let me tell you - boy, were we glad to see it and be re-incarcerated within!

There would be little point in further highlighting the limitations of our experience such as travel plans unilaterally altered by the tour agent (forcing us into changes in our arrangements to visit Florence and the Uffizi gallery, which we still managed to do by alterative means), the awful music played every night on the open decks and in the lounges, the pointless presence of a few cheerleaders from the Dallas Cowboys one of whom was to be featured in an R-rated movie the Promoter was trying to promote, and much more. Another tale involves our luggage. After we unpacked, the assistant assigned to our room offered to "store" the luggage for us, useful since space is severely limited in one's compartment. We, like other Stillbourn customers, subsequently discovered that the luggage had merely been shoved under our beds - this service enhancement presumably provides a firmer mattress and aids the backs or sexual performance of some passengers. And the Stillbourn crew, when offloading our bags at the end of the cruise, utterly destroyed the extensible handle on my main piece of luggage, damaging the whole suitcase irreparably and requiring its replacement later on in Europe. Just another small example involves the room-service breakfasts, where for the first few days our toast arrived blackened to a charred remnant. I then recalled that James Bond always asked for his mixed drinks to be "shaken, not stirred." So I wrote on the overnight room service breakfast menu that the bread should be "TOASTED, NOT BURNED." And, amazingly, this worked! Each night I wrote the same three words, and every following morning the toast was perfect. Ian Fleming knew how to make 'em give it to ya.

We nevertheless managed to salvage some good from the stillborn Mediterranean experience, although this had nothing to do with the ship. It included a deepened fellowship with our great friends, some fine new acquaintances, a fabulous never-to-be-forgotten lunch in gentle breezes high above the Mediterranean at the Hotel de Paris Grill Room in Monte Carlo, and revisiting the magnificent Botticellis, Memlings, Durers, Raphaels, and more at the Uffizi.

So for us at least, there are some lessons learned which we hope will make us wiser in the future. Where a cruise is a travel alternative, instead of a necessary travel element, we will almost always avoid it. Humans have been land-based creatures since our primeval ancestors slithered away from prehistoric amphibious swamps. What we personally want to see of the world is on solid land, and we intend to leave traveling by sea to fish, dolphins, whales, and the like. If cruising is required, we will plan it with great attention to detail, be exceedingly careful about the ship and agent which is selected, and incorporate a maximum amount of independent time away from the ship, hiring a car as needed for land travel. And, of course, if we cruise with others we will want to be sure we REALLY like being with them. On the Stillbourn, where so many other things were not to our personal taste, at least we got that part absolutely right.

Those Who Have Gone Before

A lot of friends have passed on in the last couple of years. Added to those lost in the three score years I've been alive, it's a big number - or so it seems to me. So when I got the chance to visit and see how they are doing, I went for it right away.

First I stopped in to see Milton. While he was at the Hoover Institution, Milton had befriended me and encouraged my politically incorrect thinking about health care. This world-famous economist was having a great time talking to Adam Smith, David Ricardo, and John Maynard Keynes, as well as his brother-in-law, Aaron Director. He said he loves it Up Here, and although he misses Rose he realizes it won't be long before they're together again. Everything is so easy in Heaven. If you want data, you just ask and it's there - no need to spend years digging it up and crunching statistics like he and Anna Schwartz used to do. And there's no John Kenneth Galbraith or Karl Marx around to spread confusion and contradict everything that is true. Anyway, of course, Here everyone knows such obvious things as "Inflation is always and everywhere a monetary phenomenon." In Heaven, scoliosis, heart disease, declining vigor, and all the earthy ravages to the body and mind are irrelevant. You can just think, talk, and watch - in that detached way typical of Heaven - what's going on down below. Milton is having the time of his life, he earned it in our world, and he's been assured by the Highest Authority that it's going to continue forever.

Then I got to see Jeane. The last few years of her life, after she was no longer Ambassador to the U.N., were difficult - broken bones, suicide of a son, declining everything. Here she's her old self again, vigorous, outspoken, self-confident, and happy as can be. She doesn't have to argue with the SOBs at the U.N. any more - in fact, they are in a different place quite far away. When I ran into her, Jeane was in discussion with Plato, debating some of the concepts of the "Republic." Husband Kirk was there as well, joining in. So too was Ronald Reagan, but since I didn't really know him on Earth I couldn't get to talk with him on this visit. Ronny was smiling however, so he too must be happy, and from what I could hear of his comments his Alzheimer's has certainly gone away.

I went by and talked with Marilyn. She passed on also in the past year, very suddenly from leukemia. She keeps an eye on her family back on Earth, and looks forward to Jim getting up here when the right time comes - although she doesn't want him to hurry. Meanwhile, she's been having a great time with her sisters and her many new friends in Heaven.

Lou also was on my schedule. I hadn't seen him for years. He was a top academic physician, then went to work at Merck, and got caught up in the Vioxx lawsuits. The stress killed him, he just suddenly fell down and passed on. Up Here he's far more relaxed than he ever was on Earth, and he doesn't have to prove his innocence to anyone - the only One who counts knew it all along. Lou's not worried about anything now - not his kids, not his wife, not his job, not money - nothing. He's able to talk with Hippocrates, Pasteur, Lister, Semmelweiss, Fleming, Banting, and all the rest to his heart's content. Heaven really is a terrific deal if you make it in.

Menachem was another physician. He had worked in my research lab and became a good friend. Menachem wanted to come to America, but his wife wouldn't leave Israel so he stayed and put up with all the troubles. A stroke turned him into a recluse before the end. Up Here, it was good to see him laughing again with all his old enthusiasm, and running on the clouds like the athlete he used to be. Shalom, Menachem.

Then I visited with John. He had been a bioethicist on Earth and a man of the cloth. But he lost his faith in the religion of his ancestors, his bioethics center struggled for money, his wife of many years developed dementia, and he grew depressed. Then he killed himself. It's a myth that depressed people who are so disheartened they commit suicide can't get into Heaven, as John's presence proves. He spends his time happily debating things with some of the great philosophers. If he wants to postulate a bioethical principle, the system here allows him to look into the future and see how it would all work out - at least on Earth. Incidentally, there's no need for bioethics policymaking by the inhabitants of Heaven, since all that is decided at another Level.

Jim was up there also. He had been an outstanding obstetrician and built a leading Ob-Gyn department. Jim helped to make my Institute a reality by encouraging me and giving me the chance to meet people who backed it. His terminal struggle with colon cancer was painful. But up Here, all that is forgotten and he's as content as can be. Of course, there isn't much need for obstetrics in heaven, nobody gives birth or gets sick, but Jim is happy to be engaged in other things. He has a million friends, and I'm told that he's one of the heavenly few who actually gets to watch sports TV whenever they want. Jim told me he also checks down on the Institute once in a while, and tries to put in a good word for it Higher Up when he can.

238

I ran into my old scientific mentor, Jay. To him I owe the start of my career in medical research. All Jay's relatives lived to be about 100, so he was pretty surprised when he died at 80. Jay loved to do research on genetics and on aging, and Up Here he spends his time doing thought experiments, getting results far faster that would be possible on Earth. He is still as kind and gentlemanly as ever. Jay, as he had expected, is reunited with his many relatives, including several pioneer settlers in Utah.

Russell also showed up when he heard I was visiting. He was a pastor, had ministries from Wyoming to Africa, kept doing good works like personally delivering drugs to needy people in the Crimea even in advanced old age, and was one of the most idealistic men on Earth. Yet down there, he had to watch two of his four children die before him, and the others sort of mess things up. He's with the two children now, they are having a great time together, and he's waiting for his wife, Dorothy, to arrive one of these days. On Earth, Russell never took a drink, believing that he couldn't break a pledge once made to his father. In Heaven, there are different rules, and the Almighty has granted Russell the privilege of drinking all he wants and never getting a hangover. He loves it.

Of course I was able to see my father, Max, and his paternal contemporaries, Larry and Murray. Can you imagine these three, a lawyer, steelworker, and electronic engineer, exchanging stories about the crazy things that happened to them on Earth, while laughing about it all? The great thing about Heaven is that whatever took place when you were struggling on Earth simply doesn't matter any more. Your earthly life, the good and the bad, the successes and the failures, the sick wife, the ill child, the lost money, the countless other stresses and strains of earthly existence become simply topics for detached and lighthearted conversation. Dad told me that the most important thing he learned in Heaven is that it's all going to get better some day - much, much better provided you live your life so that you get Up Here in the end. That's a lesson I plan not to forget.

There were others too that I got to see: Jimmy who lived and died all alone, in and out of depression, never knowing how to make a friend or keep one; Jon, and Marvin, who drank themselves to early deaths, flawed men who avoided the worst sins and so finally made it Upstairs; Marie, good genetic counselor and friend, who had far too much sickness before she made it into Heaven, as we all knew she certainly would; Mary Beth, another depressive suicide. Time was short, and I could only stay with them for a moment, but that they are all joyful and not suffering any more nobody should doubt.

And so I came back after seeing all of them. Naturally, the Rules won't let me tell you everything I learned visiting Heaven, not only about that place but its alternatives. But I have seen that the good people on Earth have nothing to fear and much to look forward to Later On. That's important. I figure that one day we're all going to reach the end of our earthly road, even you, even me. And I look forward to seeing you Up There when the Time comes.

Marginal Utility: Thoughts on Time, Money, and Human Biology

"As the years pass and the time left shrinks, what economists call the marginal utility of time has risen sharply."

Milton Friedman, in this quote from the preface to "Bright Promises, Dismal Performance" (1983), explains why he declined to personally undertake selecting among his published articles for this anthology of his writings. Friedman wrote these words when he was 71.

Is it true that as the years pass the marginal utility of time increases for the average human being? Simple economic theory would suggest that should be true. Economists define utility as roughly meaning "value", a necessarily subjective term. A basic principle of economic thought is that the scarcer a resource becomes, the greater - on average - will be the utility of an addition (marginal) unit of it. The reverse is also generally true. The more abundant a resource is the smaller its average marginal utility. A meal has much greater marginal utility to a hungry man than to one who has just consumed food. An extra million dollars has much less marginal utility to Warren Buffett than to the ordinary working man, since there is almost nothing Buffett can do with an extra million that he can't do without it.

These concepts explain why most people - the "average" person - will decline to bet a meaningful sum when the odds of winning or losing that amount are equal. Consider the person with life savings of $100,000 who is offered the opportunity to toss a coin with the chance to gain or lose $100,000 depending on the outcome of the toss. While the possibility of doubling one's savings is attractive, the perceived potential value of doing so is more than offset by the perceived potential pain of losing one's entire savings. In fact, many people would decline such a bet even if the positive payoff were substantially greater than $100,000. Naturally, this illustration of the declining marginal utility of money does not apply to all individuals. Casino gamblers bet knowing that the odds of doubling their money are less than even; but most people are not gamblers, especially with serious quantities of money.

Does the marginal utility of time keep increasing with age? Does the economic model hold in this case? Direct observation is, of course, one way to confirm or reject a hypothesis. If a unit of time had more value for the elderly, one would expect to see that reflected in their behavior. For example, within their physical limits, one would anticipate that the very old should frequently rush - yet how rare it is to see the elderly hasten. One would expect old people to try to sleep less - yet they generally seem happy to sleep more, whether or not they really feel a need for the extra sleep. One should anticipate that the very old would plan their days with great care and pack into each one as many worthwhile activities as possible, but this is rarely seen. One might anticipate that the elderly would focus ever more intently on each earthly day remaining, but observation suggests that they spend progressively more time thinking about the next world, and often express weariness with the things of this world. Furthermore, the elderly are more frequently afflicted with pain and illness than the young. Pain may be viewed as increasing the *dis*utility of time; if pain is severe, most people would be happy, if it were possible, to skip ahead in time to the period when the pain is gone. We conclude that the hypothesis of the increasing marginal utility of time with advancing age does not correspond to the actual behavioral patterns of most elderly persons. Direct observation in fact suggests the contrary conclusion: that the elderly, even though they know they have less time remaining to live than the young, actually utilize time as if it were less valuable to them than to younger adults.

Let us now consider the interactions of time and money. Money wisely invested generally compounds over time much more rapidly than inflation, and even money invested with ordinary skill grows on average somewhat more quickly than inflation. Many studies confirm the prediction that the elderly own most of the assets in the U.S. and many other countries. A far higher proportion of young than elderly people are poor. Grandma is much more likely than her adult grandchildren to have substantial savings. It is true, of course, that the "wealth" of the young includes the discounted value of their future earnings from work, while many elderly have little or no wealth anticipated from this source. Nevertheless, the conclusion that wealth increases, on average, as age advances is consistent with experience and extensive data, at least in the United States.

It follows that the marginal utility of money should decline with age. Is this consistent with the observed behavior of the elderly? The miser is mythically depicted as an avaricious old man, but most people are not misers, and most misers are not old. Greed, in this writer's opinion, is more often observed among youths and those in the prime of life than in the very old. The old are much more likely than the young to give away money - to make gifts and charitable bequests - and this probably is not solely because the elderly have more to give away, although on average they do. (It is likely, however, that the elderly poor may assign a high average marginal utility to money, even more than they might have when younger, because they lack the potential for future earnings.) We conclude from our observations that the average marginal utility of money does appear to decline with advancing age for most persons, with the possible exception of the elderly poor. It gets easier and easier to spend as the years pass. But the elderly may get less pleasure from a given expenditure than a younger person, since the likelihood of finding fresh, joyful delight from any expenditure tends to be diminished by the expanding history of experiences with similar expenditures, and possible decreases in health and sensory perception. Rare indeed is the octogenarian who enjoys an ice cream cone as much as a child does.

In reflecting on factors influencing the marginal utility of time and money, the overriding importance of biological aging is inescapable. As the riddle of the sphinx tells us, "Man is the animal that walks on four legs when young, two legs when mature, and three legs when old" - the third leg being a crutch. Language is absorbed far better by the brain of a child than an adult. The pre-teen and teen years are often the time for flowering of talent in activities like music or chess. Innovations in physical sciences and mathematics are most frequent in the early professional years. High work output is characteristic particularly of persons in their 20s, 30s, and 40s. Sound business decisions are generally made by persons of experience but with little diminution of intellectual vigor, so it is hardly coincidental that most corporations are headed by persons in their 40s or 50s. Investing may be an exception, as Charles Munger and Warren Buffett claim, if skill continues to improve into the late years (and I do hope they are right about this!). Many people retain excellent intellectual and physical vigor in their 70s, although subtle diminutions generally are evident. In the 80s, decline is usually obvious, and almost nobody in their 90s is unaffected by significant physical feebleness, visual or hearing loss, decline of intellectual skill, illness, and so forth.

Aging is inevitable. Given what we know about the effects of aging, what conclusions might one draw from the above analyses regarding the marginal utilities of money and time? As time advances beyond the middle years, additional accumulation of money is usually less and expenditure correspondingly more utile. But time itself, while in theory more and more precious as age proceeds, comes to have a diminishing, not increasing marginal utility. And the increasing ease with which money may be spent for personal utility with advancing age may be more than offset by the declining pleasure (value) which an expenditure can effect. If rational living is an attempt to maximize - within moral and legal limits - total utility over a lifetime, it follows that to defer utile expenditures into advanced old age (while also risking never getting the time to make them) is irrational.

A tentative conclusion is that it is generally rational to spend more heavily as the years advance, while recognizing that the real net utility derived from most units of expenditure will inevitably decline if life is sufficiently long. Thus, the time to spend money most readily is generally when old enough to afford it, and young enough to enjoy it. For most persons this means their 50s, 60s, and 70s.

The Bible reminds us that only a fool saves all his money so that after he dies another fool may squander it. Accumulating money with the intention of spending it liberally on oneself but only in far advanced old age seems almost equally shortsighted.

The Visitation

Being a medical scientist at the National Institute of Health hardly predisposes toward acts of faith. Genetic science in particular proves that the early part of Genesis cannot be an accurate version of the origins of life. But, after all, this could be a mere blemish in a Bible which was necessarily transcribed by men. And men make many errors.

No. It is innocent suffering, like that seen here in the world's largest clinical research center, which the doubtful believer or agnostic finds hardest to explain. As it must lie within the power of a good, all-powerful, and loving God to alleviate such pain, why does he not do so? Here are children born with a change in one of millions of units of their DNA code. And for this they are granted a life of agony. Some have lungs that barely work, and die after years of slow suffocation. Others are wracked with convulsions. Still others are blind, or deaf, or both. And there are those with failing hearts, slowly destroyed kidneys, liver failure, progressive paralysis, or bizarre mental disturbances. Some of these terrible maladies take decades to kill their victims. And often the sufferers are not mentally retarded. They know what is happening to them, they pray, they hope, they dream, they weep - and they die young, at 13 or 16 or 20. Such terrible ages at which to die!

No satisfactory explanation of why innocent suffering occurs while an omnipotent God exists has yet been provided. Man is hard wired for suffering. Why? Man is sinful, but surely newborn babies need not pay for Man's sins. And why were only some chosen to suffer? Why these and not others? What is God doing while all this is going on? One may explain the Holocaust as a poisonous fruit of man's evil nature. But this explanation fails for genetic diseases. Why? Why? And where is God, if He is anywhere?

Medical researchers often work far into the night. Some experiments take many hours of uninterruptable effort. Data must be analyzed, new disease models considered, innovative studies planned. The scientific literature is ever expanding, and there is never enough time to read all one should. And sometimes the doctor/scientist must spend the night at the bedside of a sick or dying patient.

The huge cafeteria in the NIH Clinical Center stays open until midnight. Brightly flourescent-lit like the rest of the hospital, it is almost empty after the day ends. Here after dark are parents on all-night vigils, physicians, hospital workers, and scientists who that evening will not experience the joys of a relaxing drink, a quiet dinner with family or friends, casual reading, or untroubled repose.

I have just finished my work, and am very tired. Five years of effort have not yet led to a breakthrough on the genetic disease I am trying to eradicate. It is very late. At home, my wife and children are already asleep. The cafeteria attracts me. I pay for my coffee, and looking around see only one other person in the empty room. Blonde and pretty, she sits at a long gray plastic-top table near the window. She is not looking at the darkness beyond, nor at me. She is waiting. Alone. So am I. I hesitate, then decide. I walk toward her.

"May I sit here with you?"

I had expected her to pause, to appraise my white coat, my doctor nametag, my general appearance. She just looks at my face with calm blue eyes.

"Yes." Without hesitation.

Why am I doing this? I am a married man, and not yet so unhappy that I would be looking for another woman. Not yet.

"What keeps you here so late tonight?"

"I'm a normal volunteer on Ward 3."

"That's very nice. Are you a college student the rest of the year?'

She nods. Her face is open, kind.

"Why did you decide to spend the summer as a medical volunteer? Does your family live in Bethesda?"

"No. I volunteered because Jesus told me to."

Whoa!

"Jesus told you to? Are you at a religious school where volunteering was encouraged as a summer activity?"

Gently she looked back at me.

"No, that's not it. Jesus told me to do it."

"You must have found something in the Bible that led you to feel Jesus wanted you to be here. It really is good to help medical research in this way. It makes a great difference."

She is silent.

"Are you saying that Jesus actually spoke to you? You truly heard his voice?"

"I saw him."

I shake my head. "No. What really happened?"

He came to me one night. He spoke to me. This is what He told me to do."

I look closely at her. My shock cannot be hidden. Here is an apparently normal college kid, prettier than most, probably more innocent than most. My doctor mind seeks for evidence that she is delusional, psychotic, schizophrenic, actually a patient from one of the mental units. No, she seems as sane as I am.

"That's amazing. You mean, you really met Jesus. You didn't imagine it?"

It's like she has heard this before. She is calm, not arguing, not persuading.

"Oh, I didn't imagine it. He was there with me. I saw Him and he spoke to me."

This woman radiates complete confidence that what she is saying is true.

"I've never met anyone who said they have personally met Jesus. How can you know it was he?"

She smiled gently.

"It was Jesus. It couldn't have been anyone else."

"I think I would have to see him myself before I could be sure such a thing really occurred."

"It happened to me. Maybe He will come to you also."

Wow! That's too much.

"I doubt it. I am not a Christian."

"What do you believe in?"

"I'm not sure. I don't think I believe in any religion really. But I'm not sure I don't believe either. I want to believe, but I can't."

"I don't believe. I know."

"I take care of sick kids, kids with genetic diseases. It's hard to believe in anything when you watch what is happening to them."

She smiles, saying nothing.

I don't know what else to add, thank her for talking with me, and go home. The next morning I tell my wife and children what happened. They laugh, joke, dismiss the whole thing. I feel foolish to have told them about it.

The next day, after finishing my experiments I decide to talk again with the young woman. I go to the unit where she volunteered. The nurse is puzzled. There are no volunteers on the unit at this time. I describe the student. Perhaps she is a patient? No, she explains, there is nobody here like that, nobody like that all summer.

I walk through the rooms, check the lounge. Not here. Maybe she is in the South unit instead of the North. No, not that either. Nor in the ward above, nor the floor below. She is not there. Seemingly never has been there.

I kept looking, but never found her.

Who was she? What was she? Why did she appear, and disappear? Why was I drawn to her? Is she a person, an angel? Who or what? And had she really met Jesus? What is the meaning of our meeting?

I have not been quite the same person since this event. To believe or not to believe, that is the question. To me, evil and suffering remain unexplained. But since that visitation I want to believe, to trust in God with a faith unweakened by doubt. Perhaps that will happen.

Then maybe I will see her again.

Eulogy for Miriam G. Schulman

Star of David Funeral Home and Cemetery
North Lauderdale, Florida
January 29, 2013

My mother died on January 25th, just about 2 months short of her 103rd birthday. Her life was almost unimaginably long and fortunately ended suddenly and peacefully. I last visited her about three weeks ago, and at that time she was the oldest person I had ever met in my entire life.

Miriam Grossman was born on March 29, 1910 in the lower East Side of Manhattan. She was the third child of Russian-Jewish immigrants, and her father, Benjamin, had escaped from the Czarist army by hiding in a laundry truck and then making his way on foot to Danzig and then America. If he had been caught, he would have been beaten to death by a troop of soldiers. He was a tough man, and yet so sensitive that when his wife, my maternal grandmother Yetta whom I never met, died of cancer at a young age he attempted to cut his own throat and was stopped by the fortunate intervention of my mother - a story I heard from her own lips.

While much information is available about the circumstances under which immigrants lived in lower Manhattan prior to World War I, all my mother would tell me was that the family tried to leave it as fast as they could. Benjamin was an excellent tailor, and one of his relatives, Nettie Rosenstein, was talented enough to become a famous fashion designer, creating the inaugural ball dress worn by Mamie Eisenhower after Ike's election as President in 1952. The Grossman family moved to

Pelham, New York, then still a fairly small community, and my grandfather opened a tailor shop there; it failed, and my mother attributed this to anti-Semitism. They then finally settled in Brooklyn where my grandfather and grandmother purchased a two story home large enough to accommodate themselves and their growing children: my mother, her older sister, Anna, and her older brother, Julius, known in the family as Jack. All the children lived at home with their parents until they married.

The world into which my mother was born in 1910, lacking most of the modern conveniences of today, seems almost primitive - the telephone and electricity were just being introduced, and actually the United States was not fully electrified until about 1940; promoting rural electrification in the remote parts of Texas was one basis of the early political career of Lyndon Baines Johnson. Life was tough, and only the tough survived. Miriam was a survivor.

World War I bypassed Miriam's family, and they thrived in Brooklyn in the booming 1920s. Anna moved out when she married Reuben Schulman, of the so-called "Newburgh Schulmans". She was extremely bright, independent in her thinking, and knowledgeable about business. She was one of America's first female Certified Public Accountants (CPA), but devoted her career to managing the books and working hard in R. Schulman's Department Store, on the main street of Newburgh, New York; this store was a source of some wonderful toys later on for Benita and myself. Jack, stricken with polio as a child and destined to limp ever after, was a handsome guy who looked rather like Clark Gable of "Gone with the Wind" fame; he was a ladies' man and physician general practitioner in Brooklyn for many years and eventually married my aunt Maidie. My mother briefly dated my father's brother, David Schulman, the father of Ronnie Schwimmer, but she didn't like him because he was too assertive for her taste; yet through him she met, quickly fell in love with, and married his more low-key younger brother, Max Schulman, who became my father.

The Great Depression was a hard time for Miriam and Max, but they still had the courage to marry in the middle of it. Miriam had graduated from Hunter College, a free women's school in Manhattan, and wanted to be an elementary school teacher. She placed 5th, according to what she told me, on a statewide exam to assess potential new teachers, but things were so bad in the Depression that she had to wait half a decade to finally get a full-time teaching job.

Max's family were financially better off than my mother's, but Max slept on a cot in his parent's living room until he and my mother married. He was a graduate of Columbia University, had a masters degree in accounting from NYU, and a law degree from the Brooklyn Law School - this last obtained at night while he worked days at various jobs. He tried to start a solo law practice but it somehow never succeeded. It was, of course, World War II and the burgeoning money supply which ended the Depression, and thus allowed my father to be hired in 1940 as a patent attorney and accountant by AT&T. I believe he was one of the first Jewish employees who ever worked at AT&T's headquarters in downtown Manhattan; before the War AT&T's executive ranks had been well-known to be dominated by sometimes anti-Semitic Catholics.

As war threatened, both Miriam and Max did their best to avoid it. Their timing was almost perfect. Being married and having a child lowered one's rank for being drafted into the war. Thus, I was born exactly 13 days after

Pearl Harbor. None of my first degree relatives saw active duty during World War II, although one of my mother's second cousins was in the front lines in the D-Day invasion.

My earliest childhood recollection of my mother was when I was not yet four years old, and she came into my bedroom and with tears in her eyes told me that "The War had ended." Knowing nothing of what this meant to her, I said something like, "So what?" I have repressed the specifics of her angry response, but her scowl and dismissive exit from the room remain engraved in my memory.

As my sister and I grew up and went to elementary school, Dad continued to work at AT&T and enjoyed interfacing with the famous scientists at the company's Bell Laboratories in Murray Hill, New Jersey. My mother worked at a Brooklyn elementary school mostly as a second-grade teacher.

Then tragedy struck Miriam and her family. Always a flamboyant, outgoing, and even "show-offy" woman, she began to show signs of mania - of major psychosis. She hardly ever slept, wandered the apartment day and night quoting the Bible and scaring the heck out of me and Benita; she wore short orange skirts, and finally had to be institutionalized in Kings County Hospital after she gave a $100 tip - about a week's salary for my father - to the postman. She was in and out of Kings County's inpatient mental facilities for about 2 years. My father and relatives on both sides of our family shared the extra burdens of caring for Benita and myself. Her illness marked the only time I ever saw my father cry. As an inpatient Miriam received, unsuccessfully, several courses of electroshock therapy. Through the help of my uncle

Jack, she was being cared for by the head of Downstate Medical Center's Department of Psychiatry. And then a miracle happened. Thorazine, the first major anti-psychotic medication, came on the market and my mother became one of the first patients in America to receive it. For her it was truly a wonder drug, and cured her almost completely. In the decades to follow, Jack and then I became responsible for managing my mother's psychoactive medications, and even in her final years, indeed up until her death, she received Prozac and sometimes Thorazine-like drugs. But the good news is that she came back to her family, to her children, in the 1950s, and was basically normal for most of the rest of her long life.

However, Miriam's illness made it difficult for her to work as a teacher and early pioneer in teaching dyslexic children, and she did only part-time work thereafter. Thus frustrated, she transferred I believe her own ambitions to advancing her two children. Miriam was a paradox: She was deeply interested in art and music, particularly opera, but never attempted to draw, only a very few times tried oil painting, and never learned to sing or play a musical instrument. She never learned to drive a car, never learned to swim. I do not know why she never did these things, and once when I asked her she simply said, "I didn't want to." But she wanted her children to do all of these, and much more.

Miriam was a fierce defender of her children from such things as bullying and nasty schoolteachers. She gave Benita and me a lot of love, but it was not expressed as the unconditional love of modern ideal parenting dogma. You had to perform to receive Miriam's love and approval, and that meant above all performing well in school. Needless to add, both Benita and I did very well at that.

My mother was exceptionally intelligent and energetic and always tried to do her best for her family. But she alas lacked sophistication in some important ways, so her energies were not only sometimes ineffective but occasionally even harmful. I was pushed through school as rapidly as possible, in part to get me to be self-supporting at an earlier age. Some of the associated errors of judgment were striking. I was interviewed at Harvard Medical School and, if accepted, would have entered at just age 19. The two wonderful men who interviewed me at HMS said they wanted me to go there, but I would be the youngest person ever admitted for many years back, and they made me an amazing offer: Harvard would provide a scholarship for me to go abroad to Cambridge or Oxford for one year to help me gain maturity before starting at HMS. I excitedly reported this offer to my parents, but led by my mother it was rejected. That wasn't part of her plan. If I couldn't be admitted to Harvard Medical School after only three years of college, well I could just go to Downstate or some other place that would take me then and there. What difference did it make what medical school I went to? Fortunately, when I explained the situation to the people at Harvard, they understood the problem and - thank God - chose to admit me anyway.

Intelligence and wisdom are not the same things, and my mother and father both had more of the former than the latter. For example, my mother's highest ambitions for her children when Benita and I were young was that I would become a Park Avenue doctor and Benita a school teacher. Fortunately, we both developed in ways that provided us with more sustaining opportunities. In another example, my parents scrimped and saved every penny - literally - to accumulate what they thought would be enough for them in old age. But they never learned how to invest wisely, and inflation destroyed most of the little they had worked so hard to earn and keep. And therefore, of course, in her old age my mother was supported by her children.

Then too my mother had a way of not seeking advice when it was needed. Her failure to communicate with me and my wife, Carol, who was also a very good physician, in a timely way played a significant role in the premature death of my father. So too did her insistence on relying on the physicians at University Hospital when we advised transferring Dad to the Massachusetts General Hospital where I had trained. In the end, my father died through a medical oversight at age 78. Miriam never wanted to marry again after my father died. She was the same age as Max, and lived without a man, to the best of my knowledge, for the last 25 years of her life. I asked her about remarrying, as there were men who seemed interested in her - at 78 she was still vivacious, energetic, and reasonably attractive. She just said she didn't want to do it, it was a lot of trouble, and she preferred to be on her own.

In Miriam's late years, she never lost her sense of humor. Once she was offered a chance to try on one of Dixie's dresses which we thought might fit her. Miriam's comment to Dixie was, "Perhaps we are the same size, but in different places!" And then there is her famous comment when Dixie once told her that "Joe is more than a doctor." Miriam's reply was an incredulous, "More than a DOCTOR?!", as if such were impossible. Memorable too was my father's funeral in this very funeral home, which was orchestrated by my mother without other inputs being sought. Dad appeared in his coffin wearing a light green jacket, a shirt of undefined color, and a yellow tie with large purple polka dots; when some time later I asked her why Dad had been buried looking this way, Mom actually said, "Well, what would have been the point of burying him in a good suit?" Today Miriam will be placed alongside Max in a Burberry dress, a scarf from Brooks Brothers, shoes from Tory Burch, and undergarments from Victoria's Secret. We figure that if she is going to meet her husband again after an absence of almost 25 years, she should at least try to look her best.

In late life, my mother was handicapped by progressive macular degeneration, and eventually lost the ability to read. She had cataracts too, and benefitted for a few years from a lens replacement in her better eye by James Gills, America's most experienced cataract surgeon. She tried to use a computer, but grew tired of the effort involved in reading even the enlarged print on the screen. Recorded books did not help since she would fall asleep while listening to them. Her memory began to weaken. Later still, she fell and broke a hip, remarkably fully recovering after surgery at age 95. She had a transient ischemic attack, a small stroke, recovered, and very near the end of her life had another stroke that made it impossible for her to walk. She was increasingly feeble and bedridden after age 100. Yet she had the energy and determination to enjoy her 100th birthday party, which some of our family celebrated with her at the Colony Hotel in Palm Beach on March 29, 2010. Finally, a few days ago, her heart suddenly gave out and she left us. Now she is with Max - assuming, I suppose, that that is really where she wants to be. If not, my guess is she will find a way to do whatever else she wants to do.

Miriam was a courageous person, and ended life as a still courageous very old lady. Her personality remained agreeable until death, and even in her last years when beset by very advanced age and illness neither Dixie nor I ever heard her complain. I am grateful that she finally died peacefully and still without complaining.

As I saw my mother fading away in her late years, the miracle of her life continued to amaze me. How could this very old, withered, feeble woman once have been a child, then grown to beautiful adulthood, married a handsome man, made love, made babies, and helped to raise adults like Benita and me? It seems almost impossible, but it is true. Thank you, Mom, for doing your best, thank you for all the good you did in your long life. May you rest in peace.

Aunt Maidie, Uncle Jack, and Brooklyn 50 Years Ago

Selma ("Maidie") Grossworth Grossman Eisenberg (aka Aunt Maidie) died a few days ago at 100 years of age. I thought it might be of some small interest to record at this time my memories and impressions of that bygone era in Brooklyn and period of my youth in which Aunt Maidie and her husband, Jack Grossman (aka Uncle Jack), played significant roles.

The period under consideration runs mostly between 1950 and 1970. The memories involved are highly personal, and no claim is made to objectivity or even, after the passage of so many years, perfect accuracy.

Uncle Jack was my mother's older brother, the middle child in the family behind his sister, Anna. He was born in Brooklyn about 1907; I do not recall his actual birth date. Jack had polio as a child, and while I believe he never was put in a respirator (the dreaded "iron lung") he was very ill and was scarred both physically and psychologically by this affliction. He grew up with a badly deformed left leg and foot, was never able to run, and walked with a pronounced gait abnormality. He was embarrassed about his handicap, wore a special shoe with a built-up sole and heel on his left foot, and would never allow me to examine his abnormal leg and foot. It is virtually certain that Jack's polio affected his mental outlook and future life path, as my mother explicitly stated and believed.

Jack was highly intelligent and eventually succeeded in entering Flower - Fifth Avenue Medical College in Manhattan, one of the few professional schools that did not seem to have an element of anti-Semitism in its admission policies in the 1930s. I do not recall where Jack went to college. He related to me tales of riding ambulances in New York as a physician-in-training where part of his job was to help declare dead and collect the bodies of people who had been ruined in the Great Depression and ended their lives leaping from tall buildings. Like my mother, Jack lived in the home of his parents for some years as an adult, and I believe did so until he married.

Despite his deformity, Jack was a virile, handsome man who looked much like actor Clark Gable; he knew it and parted his dark hair in the middle to strengthen that likeness. He was reportedly quite a ladies' man when in his unmarried prime. I do not know how he first met Maidie Grossworth, but I do know that he had a lot of girlfriends and he and Maidie dated for some years while Jack ran around with other women. I believe, although obviously I do not know, that Jack's proclivity for the ladies ended when he at last wed Maidie, who had waited a long time for the marriage to happen. I do not recall when they married, but they were in that blessed state during all the years of my recollectable interactions with them.

Maidie grew up in an apartment in Brooklyn, and I assume was born in Brooklyn as well. I never met her mother. She took me a few times to meet her father, "Willie" Grossworth, who lived in a small, dark flat not far from where Maidie and Jack settled after their marriage. Willie was thin, short, bald, soft-spoken, with a gaunt face and prominent eyes, and seemed to me then to be very old, even more aged than my grandparents. I can recall only two subjects about which Willie informed me. He had come to the United States from Austro-Hungary where, he noted proudly, he had once actually glimpsed, in person, the Emperor Franz Josef. I had no idea at the time why Willie thought this was important. Later I became familiar enough with the history of Austro-Hungary to understand that Franz Josef was viewed by "his people" as a deity ruling one of the most powerful nations in Europe, and indeed in the world. The old Austro-Hungarian Empire was a vast enterprise, the second largest nation in Europe after Russia, but was changed irrevocably by World War I and dismembered thereafter into various complete and partial states of Eastern Europe. Shrunken and bitter Austria soon became a trough of Nazism and was, of course, the birth nation of Adolf Hitler.

Willie, who was a tailor, also told me one other thing. "Be your own boss." He thought that I should become an ophthalmologist like one of his friends. Willie believed that having a Manhattan-based solo medical practice approached, if it did not actually attain, the very summit of human existence.

My earliest memories of Jack and Maidie involved the automobile trips they took with me, Benita, and my mother. These regularly occurred on Tuesdays, Jack's weekly day off from his general medical practice. Jack was almost the only blood relative in my extended family, other than my father's brother, David (also a doctor), who could actually drive a car. Maidie never drove. Jack, usually with Maidie, would pick us up in his grey Desoto sedan with its sloping roof, and off we would go, usually to either Prospect Park or Sheepshead Bay. Neither of these was more than a few miles away. For those not familiar with the anatomy of Brooklyn, Prospect Park was to Brooklyn what Central Park was to Manhattan, and it was due north of where we lived in Flatbush. Sheepshead Bay was straight south of us; at that time it was a lovely inlet, the home of a fishing fleet that brought back catches from the

Atlantic and sold fresh fish directly to customers, like my mother and Maidie, who visited their docks. (I have memories of my mother cleaning and gutting some of these fish in our kitchen, but mostly our fish dinners relied upon Mrs. Paul's Fish Sticks, allegedly containing frozen mashed cod, potatoes, and loads of salt.) Sheepshead Bay, and believe it or not there is a Wikipedia entry on this place, was close to the very affluent neighborhoods of Manhattan Beach, where really rich Jews like the Streitz matzo company people lived, and the more downscale but still picturesque Brighton Beach area. The Bay also had some terrific seafood restaurants, particularly Lundy's, and sometimes we would have lunch there. Today the Bay is still picturesque, but everything on shore is greatly changed. Lundy's was closed for many years after a union action; the owners simply shut it down rather than cave in to union demands. Today in shrunken form it is operated by Greeks. The Russian mafia is said to control Brighton Beach. The fishing boats are virtually gone, and tour boats have taken their place. The Bay region seems seedier to me than it did then, but as a kid I was doubtless rather insensitive to "seediness" so I really cannot really say if this is true. What I am sure of is that all of us, including Maidie and my mother, certainly liked going to Sheepshead Bay.

My relationship to both Maidie and Jack underwent a transformation after my mother's mental illness struck in 1951-2, when I was 10-11 years old. Jack's role in that terrible time was important, vital in some ways and yet far from benign in others. As my mother's brother, he assumed primary initial responsibility for advising my parents as my mother's mania developed and eventually spun out of control. Significantly, he helped get my mother hospitalized at Kings County Hospital and into the care of the chief of its psychiatry department, and this enabled her to become one of the first people in the U.S. to be given chlorpromazine (Thorazine), the drug which miraculously normalized her after electroshock therapy had failed.

Yet kind, concerned, deeply engaged, and well-meaning as he was, Jack and as far as I can recall Maidie too, made the tragic error of blaming my poor father for my mother's troubles. They were heavily influenced by the Freudian and psychotherapeutic orthodoxies of that era, and the dogma that environment was overwhelmingly decisive in determining how happy or psychologically normal anyone would be. Thus delinquent, violent, or otherwise aberrant children were blamed on bad parents, and mentally unstable people were presumed to result from the failures of their inadequate spouses to sufficiently provide for their tranquility and general happiness. No greater injustice could have been done to my father at a time when my mother was stark raving mad than to blame him for her condition. Yet this was done, and I was then unaware of it. This kind of blaming went on among the adults out of sight and earshot of the children, and some of it was done in Yiddish. It was wrong, and the acme of cruelty. The only time I saw my father cry was when his wife was in a mental hospital and he was further burdened by the belief that the disaster was somehow all his fault. I actually now think that if it had not been for the support of his older brother, David, and his sister, Celia, and his love for his two children, my father Max might have despaired to the point of suicide.

But little did I know most of this, and I knew nothing of the way Jack and Maidie blamed everything on my father. What I did know was that my home had become a very unhappy place. I wanted to get out of it, to get away to some peaceful spot. I had learned with my father's help to ride a two-wheeler bike, suffering in the learning process only one bad fall which removed about two inches of the skin from my right knee and momentarily caused the lesion to look like the cross-section of a large carrot before it welled up with blood. I began now at age 12 or so and continued for some years thereafter to ride that bike time and time again to the quite, childless, comparative serenity of Jack's and Maidie's home on Ocean Parkway. Thus began years of an unusually close relationship with both of them. I remember speaking to my father some time later, but before I had reached the age of maturity, about how wonderful Jack and Maidie both seemed to me. Dad never told me about the pain they had caused him, but I do remember him gently responding for reasons I did not then understand: "There are some problems there, Joe, which you don't know about." How true it was!

More about the anatomy of Brooklyn before we take our tale a little further. Jack and Maidie lived in a small apartment on the first floor of a six story building near the corner of Beverly Road and Ocean Parkway. While Beverly Road was a cross-street of minor importance, Ocean Parkway was the residential Champs-Elysees of Brooklyn. It was, and still is, one of the most beautiful streets in New York. Indeed, it was not a street and not a parkway but a wide boulevard. In cross-section from east to west it had a two lane road, one lane of which was used for parking cars (none of the apartment buildings had parking facilities); then a broad bridle path on which real horses with real riders came out from Prospect Park, the northern terminus of the boulevard; then about six lanes in the center for bidirectional north-south traffic; then a concrete bike lane wide enough to accommodate 4-5 bikers abreast; then a paved walkway for pedestrians which was generously provided with iron railings and wooden benches; then another two lane road for driving and parking. There were multiple rows of elm and maple trees shading the cycling and pedestrian areas and the bridle path; in the late years of my childhood a blight killed the elms, but the maples thrive to this day. It was a lovely, lovely place. Ocean Parkway was many miles long and one could bike on it throughout its entire length. Near its southern end was a large building, Lincoln High School, at which my father's sister Celia taught, a substantial VA hospital, and - best of all though beyond where the road officially ended - the edge of that wonderland for kids like me, Coney Island, with its fantastic amusement parks, parachute jump, roller coasters, merry-go-rounds, Nathan's hot dogs, and much more.

Almost unbelievable today is the tiny size of what Jack and Maidie called home, and which also doubled as their workplace. One entered their apartment through a dimly lit art-deco lobby, then went up a few stairs on the left to their door where a sign read "Julius H. Grossman, M.D." Inside was a room about three times longer than it was wide, and able to accommodate about six small chairs; this was the doctor's waiting room, and doubled as the living room and dining room of the apartment at other times - a portable table was set up there for dining purposes and put away before the next day. To the right was a tiny bedroom with a double bed, and through a separate entrance also to the right was a miniscule kitchen. Both the bedroom and kitchen had windows that opened out onto some kind of viewless walled space. At the end of the waiting room was Jack's office, with a substantial wood desk straight ahead, and a metallic examining table and a few small medicine cabinets off to the right. The room was equipped in the most basic medical manner - a reflex hammer, a stethoscope, a mercury-column blood pressure device with an inflatable cuff, some thermometers, and a diathermy machine (which generated warmth intended to relax painful muscles). Off at the left end of the office was a small bathroom. And that was it! The whole space in this rent-controlled office/home was likely smaller than 700 square feet, maybe 20 feet wide by 30 deep in aggregate. And Jack the physician and Maidie his wife, office assistant, and "nurse", lived in this tiny apartment continuously from the late 1930s until Jack died in 1968. In about 1960, an adjacent one room flat with a view out to the Parkway became available, they were able to rent it and break through the wall, adding a living room and bathroom and perhaps another 250 square feet to their habitation/office "complex" for a grand total of not more than 1000 square feet.

It is almost impossible to believe that this was their universe, but so it was. They hardly ever left this space together, except for those little trips on Tuesdays. Jack made house calls on his own and, rarely, saw a patient in some hospital but not with Maidie. They almost never took any vacations. Jack said flying was too dangerous, so he and Maidie never used an airplane during their years together. They never left the United States, indeed I don't know if they ever went farther from Brooklyn than the Catskills and Newburgh, where Jack's sister Anna lived. They had no children because they wanted none, so they told me. So I became something like a son to them, and Benita something like a daughter. For reasons I have never been able to understand, they lived a life far more constrained than my parents or my other close relatives. Some members of the family attributed this more to Jack than Maidie, perhaps in part to Jack's polio and its associated traumas. It may have been that Jack was the victim of mild depression. But who can really say?

And yet when I was young their little home seemed to me to be almost a paradise and an island of peace compared to my own household. I was always welcomed there, given a small meal by Maidie, and all three of us would talk. I learned a little about medicine from Jack. I was accepted and appreciated by Maidie. And sometimes I would hear an interesting story about some of the patients, and other happenings. One of the most interesting involved a visit from two tough-looking guys in fancy suits who said to my uncle something like the following. "Doc, unfortunately we work in a dangerous business, no need to go into details, but sometimes somebody gets hurt, maybe by a bullet or a knife, and we need a doctor to fix that up quietly and without goin' to a hospital or anything, and we was hoping you would be that doc. We'll pay you a lot more than you must be taking in from this little place. We want you to say yes." My uncle just turned them down and pointed out that they should have little trouble finding, right here in Brooklyn, other doctors who would be happy to help them. Despite their implied threat, the mafia goons went away and left him alone.

As I passed into adolescence, through high school, then through Brooklyn College, and up until the time I went away to medical school I continued to have a close relationship with Jack and Maidie. I visited them often, perhaps weekly on average. My memories of these visits are nice ones. Yet when it came time to think about medical school, my other uncle, David, my father's brother, was the positive force within the family encouraging me to apply to top schools like Harvard. Jack felt reaching up like that would be a waste of time, I wouldn't be admitted, and even so what difference would it make? My parents seemed to agree with Jack. I don't recall what Maidie thought about this vital issue. Fortunately for me, Dave was right and I will always be grateful for his optimism and confidence in me. I had a powerful, almost desperate, desire to escape from Brooklyn, to enter the larger world I felt was there beyond it. Entrance into Harvard Medical School provided me with that liberating opportunity.

I left Brooklyn for Boston at age 19. Naturally my connection with Maidie and Jack diminished thereafter. My interests in science and medicine were very strong, my brain was active on many things, and my gonads were pretty active too. Gradually, all my ties with family in Brooklyn diminished. Long distance calls in the days of AT&T's monopoly were expensive, letters were cheap, and I stayed in touch with Maidie and Jack mostly by mail, and of course occasional visits when I came back to visit my parents and others in Brooklyn. I married half-way through medical school, and by then things in New York seemed far away.

Along the Wide Missouri

"Oh Shenandoah, I long to see you,
And hear your rolling river. Oh Shenandoah,
I long to see you,
Away, we're bound away,
Across the wide Missouri."

The Shenandoah in the famous lyrics of this old
song is likely the river in Virginia, in another interpretation
an Indian maiden, or perhaps both. But there's no doubt that
crossing the "wide Missouri" meant going west for the
pioneers, and so it is too with us. What follows is a short
summary of our automobile trip along the Missouri River
in early August, 2013.

The Lewis and Clark 1804-1806 expedition of
course involved exploring the Missouri after the Louisiana
Purchase was completed in 1803, and was done at the
request of President Jefferson. It had multiple purposes
including seeking a waterway to the Pacific Ocean,
naturalistic studies, political foot printing, and more. That
journey long antedated the mountain man era which started
from St. Louis in 1822-26 with the beaver-trapping efforts
of William Ashley and his associates. The pioneer
migrations to California and Oregon in the 1840s mostly
originated at St. Louis or Independence. The Missouri
River region is transformed by modern civilization and the
river controlled by enormous dams and the lakes behind
them, so it is impossible to retrace the route of Lewis and
Clark exactly. Nevertheless, one can follow the river fairly
closely in many segments, and visit its shores at abundant
access points.

There are six major dams on the river, and the gigantic lakes behind some of them like the Garrison, Oahe, and Fort Randall dams in the Dakotas and the Fort Peck dam in north-central Montana each extend about 100 miles or more.

We went to see the beauty of the river and the landscapes of the adjacent regions, and we were not disappointed, although in many areas the Missouri no longer looks like the wilderness river of the early 1800s. We of course were led to think quite a bit about the complex issues related to the Missouri dams. We also had the historical opportunity to witness part of the extraordinary Bakken oil operations along ND highway 85 from Belford through Watford City to Williston - a tremendous development analogous to the 19th century discovery of gold along the American River and silver in the Nevada territory. If you have not read Mark Twain's "Roughing It" recalling his experiences as a reporter in silver-era Nevada you are should read it, and will recognize previous incarnations of Williston, ND. But more about that later.

A little background on the Missouri. It is America's longest river, over 2,300 miles from its origin on the eastern slope of the Rockies along the Montana/Idaho border to its junction with the Mississippi just north of St. Louis. Like all rivers its flow rate varies widely with the seasons and is subject to periodic overloads in years with heavy rainfall or excessive snow buildup in the mountains. At the time of this writing (during a normal summer) the flow of the Missouri at its mouth is about 90,000 cubic feet per second (cfs). For comparison, the Columbia River flow is about 3 times greater, and the gigantic Mississippi has a flow about three times greater still than the Columbia. There is no shortage of water in our nation, although water is very unequally distributed over the land mass. The Colorado is the major river water source in the southwestern United States but its flow is far less than the Missouri - right now the Colorado flow is slightly less than 20,000 cfs. Naturally, water may be removed from many rivers for irrigation and to rebuild depleted reservoirs, so no single flow number adequately summarizes the importance of a long U.S. river. During flood periods after heavy snows and rains, as in 2011, the Missouri flow can reach over 150,000 cfs as water is necessarily released from dam reservoirs under such circumstances, but despite the many dams significant downstream flooding still occurs in some years. In short, the Missouri is a very large and important river, and sometimes dangerous still.

We chose to follow the river going upstream, and also elected not to do so in the state of Missouri where it traverses such densely populated regions as St. Louis and Kansas City. Paralleling the river upstream from "Can Citi" to Omaha is a short journey we made in May. So we started this summer's trip at Omaha. By the way, in addition to learning the correct Missourian pronunciation of Kansas City (above) from a friendly native, I have also been informed from the same source that "Missouri" is correctly pronounced "Misserah". I continue to use Missouri in my written text, and will work on my dialect when time permits.

Driving north from Omaha along the southwest bank of the river we were surprised by the hilly nature of the landscape, densely wooded in many locations. One proceeds on a plateau with various views of the river, and the landscape gradually becomes flatter and more typical farm country. We spent our first trip night at Sioux City, SD on the border defined by the river between Nebraska and South Dakota. "Dinner" was experienced at a Mexican restaurant in South Sioux City (in NE), and the tolerable cuisine was accompanied by a trio of mariachi singers and guitarists who made up for lack of vocal loveliness through very appreciable volume.

Next day we followed the river west and then north to Pierre, SD. For a state capitol, it is not much of a town. Along the way we saw the river at numerous points and visited the Fort Randall dam. The scale of the dam's earthen embankment and concrete spillways was impressive, and the huge lake formed by the dam extends northwest for 60-70 miles and is several miles wide. At Pierre we fed at "Jake's", a bar and grill famous with locals and at the opposite end of town from most of the motels. Wings, ribs, and beer - take it or leave it. We took it and had a good time. Outside "Jake's" in the twilight, a man from Wisconsin was showing off an amazing three-wheeled hotrod - an immense, overpowered tricycle that he claimed could do 80 miles per hour in first gear. He may have been involved in the large motorcycle rally which occurs annually in early August at Sturgis, SD. Dozens of local men and boys snapped pictures of his monster machine, and so did I. Hey, there is not a lot to do before dinner in Pierre in August, or probably in any other month either.

The following day we drove north from Pierre east of the river, then crossed it at Mobridge, and then departing from the river drove along the South Dakota/North Dakota border for many miles, planning to see the Missouri again at Williston, ND. The farmland in the central and northern part of South Dakota is highly productive, green and lovely in August, gently rolling and - as one proceeds west and into regions of lower rainfall - increasingly sparse of trees. There are quite a few aquifers, some with sizeable bird populations. The immensity of the farms growing corn, soybeans, wheat, and sunflowers in South Dakota is amazing, agriculture dwarfing that of the eastern shore of Maryland or the countryside of Virginia. According to a recent article in the Wall Street Journal, corn is America's number one agricultural product, and the area devoted to growing it exceeds the entire area of the state of New Mexico (!) - and after visiting the Dakotas I can believe that statement. Soybeans, by the way, are number two - city boy here would have guessed number two to be wheat. Agricultural markets evolve. America's most important agricultural product in 1850 wasn't cotton or tobacco, it was hay. Esthetically, the South Dakota farmland vistas are far less monotonous than the flat fertile landscapes of Maryland or Illinois.

Reaching almost the western edge of the Dakotas, we turned north on ND 85. The lovely farms under blue sky balanced by a moderate assortment of rounded clouds continued until we reached Belfield near Interstate 94. That was where we saw the first oil pumps. And from there north over the 80 or so miles to Williston - wow, things were very different.

Before we talk about the oil thing, a few more thoughts about dams in general, and the Missouri dams in particular. The subject of dams generates hot debate in many circles, and there are advocates and opponents often unwilling to credit views alterative to their own. A good book on the subject, but partisan in opposition to many dams, is Marc Reisner's "Cadillac Desert", written in the 1980s under the strong influence of the so-called "environmental movement." To such as the Sierra Club, any dam is an atrocity, the product of a conspiracy between corrupt politicians, special farm and construction interests, big businesses involved in agriculture, the Army Corps of Engineers, the Bureau of Reclamation, and other evildoers. Some dams have also flooded Indian lands, for which many feel the compensation paid to the tribes has generally been inadequate. The lakes and related water accumulations behind dams may be harmful or advantageous for birds, a mixed bag for the community of bird watchers. On the other hand, there are many people who find dams worthwhile endeavors, and actually like the results. The Corps of Engineers is facetiously said to have as its mission statement "We can't stand the sound of running water, so we dam it up." Dams are built for four major ostensible reasons: supplying water for replenishment of groundwater or directly for agricultural irrigation, and some for human consumption; flood control; hydroelectric power; and recreation. And they do all these things, in varying degrees. The debates center mostly around the prices which must be paid for big dams - destruction of natural habitat, high building costs, loss of life of construction workers, partial but sometimes inadequate ability to control flooding, and obvious "pork" for nearby towns and counties whose citizens usually receive heavily subsidized water and electricity.

Some people, like Reisner, argue that the early success of Boulder (Hoover) Dam led to a period of dam building from the 1930s to the 1960s which included such major projects as the Tennessee Valley Authority and Grand Coulee. After the most useful dams were built, it is claimed that vested interests led to creating many more which were less useful, and some truly useless. But it's pretty hard to weigh all these factors fairly, it seems to me. For example, Grand Coulee on the Columbia is far larger than Hoover dam. Built starting in 1933 as another of Franklin Roosevelt's public works projects intended to employ men during the Great Depression, the dam had limited irrigation or flood control value. Its massive hydroelectric capacity was considered wasteful overbuilding by many. Yet that electrical power soon found a use, more generators were added, and today Grand Coulee is the largest potential electric power producing facility in the United States with a peak output of nearly 7 gigawatts (its average output is less and exceeded by the Palo Verde nuclear facility in Arizona). Even Reisner notes that it was the massive power from Grand Coulee which enabled the extensive production of aluminum (made via electrolysis) to build the planes to win World War II, and he states that Coulee's power also facilitated manufacturing the plutonium at Hanford which brought the war to an end. Today, the power from Grand Coulee is a major source of electricity for the growing population of the Northwest. And it is clean energy too.

Personally, I am neither for nor against dams in general. It seems to me that for each proposed project the specifics need careful and critical evaluation.

As for the claim - undoubtedly correct - that dams represent a federal subsidy to local people for water, electricity, boating, and more, one rejoinder could be that that is how our national government works for just about everything. Someone in Kansas pays to improve the beltway around Washington, D.C. The pacifist's taxes support the Department of Defense. The Sierra Club member has tax payments partially used to flood a wild valley, and the bookworm in Manhattan pays for someone to use a houseboat on Lake Powell. The rich Texan pays for welfare in Baltimore. As Kurt Vonnegut often wrote, "And so it goes."

This discussion of dams and their importance - or exaggerated importance depending upon your point of view - for energy generation relates to the goings on in western North Dakota and eastern Montana involving the exploitation of the massive Bakken shale oil reserves liberated by breakthroughs in "fracking".

Dixie and I drove through the region to the east of Theodore Roosevelt National Park a few years ago, when the Bakken thing was just beginning. What we noticed then was an occasional field with an active oil pump, unexpected difficulty in finding a motel room, "cowboys" talking about oil and property in every cafe, and more trucks on highway 85 and on I-94 west of Dickinson than we had ever dreamed would be there. But that was nothing compared to what is going on today here on a prairie where in the geological past there existed a large sea and the abundant plants and animals whose organic remains have been luckily transformed into vast deposits of oil and natural gas. The traffic is a complete snarl in such towns as Watford City and Williston. Hotel and motel rooms are almost unavailable (we got the last room reservation at the large MainStay hotel in Williston, and it could be had only for one night). There are innumerable trailer parks, houses of all sizes and configurations - mostly tiny - being built for workers, road construction adds to the problems, new shopping centers, all restaurants - however poor - packed with field workers, painters, and all other kinds of manual laborers. Every imaginable tool, truck, and oil parts and services business is here. Schlumberger has an immense facility with more trucks on its property than I have ever seen together anywhere. The composite scene is mind-boggling. The Bakken is without doubt the modern equivalent of the California gold rush of 1848. It is really, really big. I am no longer surprised by the claims that it and other similar geologic formations like the Marcellus under the Appalachian Basin will mean oil and gas independence for the United States, and transform us into a nation with oil and gas excess for selling to others. It is going to be hugely beneficial for our country, and I believe for the world too, but at least for the next few years don't plan your next vacation or drive in the country anywhere near Williston, ND. Especially not on a day like the one just after our visit when - I kid you not - the U.S. Secretary of the Interior and a host of her flunkies from Washington descended upon Williston to view the Bakken activities first hand and, allegedly, "help". We escaped from Williston at the crack of dawn a few hours before this flock of worthies touched down in North Dakota.

By the way, ladies, the gender ratio in Williston is about 10 or 20 men to every even marginally viable woman. If you like blue-collar men, head to North Dakota without delay and you can take your pick. I asked the innkeeper at our motel, an overworked and seemingly bright guy, how many whorehouses were in Williston. He smilingly said he "didn't know of any", but then claimed that he had never bothered to inquire and admitted that his knowledge might be incomplete. Reflect on the mobile saloons, gambling dens, and prostitutes who moved with the western end of the transcontinental railroad as its construction proceeded from Omaha to Utah; today you can find the equivalent, doubtless in establishments more discreet and air conditioned too, in boom towns like Williston.

And here's something else on energy. The gas stations in South Dakota sell 87 octane regular gas at a HIGHER price than 89 octane super grade. That because the 89 octane has 10% ethanol. That ethanol comes from corn, a major crop in the Dakotas. The demand for ethanol for fuel raises the price farmers get for corn, thus elevating the cost of corn worldwide since our country is a major corn exporter. In the world's poorest countries some of the poorest people are now unable to afford corn who would otherwise be nourished by it, due to the powerful ethanol lobby and the farm interests it serves. Naturally, the oil industry opposes the ethanolists with lobbying on behalf its own special interests. That's the way the game is played when big government and its regulators decide who gets the next dam, whose additives get into gasoline or are kept out of it, how much farmers pay for subsidized electricity or water, and much, much more.

It's amazing what thoughts come to mind when you have a few days to wander in the heartland of America.

Next day we were off to see the Fort Peck dam in eastern Montana. This monster is 4 miles long, 250 feet high, and the lake behind it is 130 miles long and has more shoreline than the state of California. We expected it wouldn't be a dull day, and it wasn't. The Fort Peck dam is in a very remote location far from any interstate highway or significant city, a few miles south of tiny Glasgow, Montana. If one was inclined to think a bit about dams on the Missouri and elsewhere before visiting this enormous structure, one will think even more about this afterward. Visits to the dam powerhouse and its interpretative center are under the supervision of the Army Corps of Engineers. The Corps built most of the big dams in the U.S., and was once a political powerhouse. Today it just isn't the same. Its representatives to the public at the center were two pretty young women, one of whom was chewing gum while introducing the facility to 10 or so visitors. Another Corps hostess was an older lady with oxygen flowing into her nostrils through nasal catheters. The Corps' literature now asserts recreation (on the lakes behind dams) is the first priority in its list of the benefits of dams - the others of lesser importance being hydroelectric power, irrigation, flood control, and navigation in that order. In the good old days, that list would have nearly been reversed. At the interpretative center, before our guided tour of the powerhouses, we were the only two people to watch a really excellent movie on the history of the dam construction. I wish that movie were for sale - its black and white footage from the 1930s is vivid and rare, the narration intelligent, and we learned a great deal from it.

Fort Peck dam was started in 1934 as another one of the early public works projects of the Franklin Roosevelt administration. Its purposes were initially described as improving flood control and navigation on the Missouri, and creating jobs. It is hard to see how navigation could be much of a purpose, especially since the dam blocked any river access upstream of itself, and steamboats had formerly gone all the way to Fort Benton over 100 miles further west (see below). The conditions for trying to build this monster structure were unprecedentedly difficult. During the winter of 1934 temperatures in this region fell to -60 degrees Fahrenheit, yet work continued. About 10,000 workers who came from everywhere in the depths of the Depression received 50 cents an hour for doing dangerous, dirty work directed by the Corps engineers on site and in such remote locations as Omaha. Whole "cities" of huts and shanties were hastily built to house these men. Workers doing the most hazardous tasks like cutting through over a mile of shale to create the 4 huge passageways for the entire Missouri flow to be directed through turbines spinning huge generators got paid up to $1.50 per hour - which was real money in 1934. The dam took about 5 years to build. It was the largest filled earthenwork project in the world, and its design involved much experimentation. The "earth" to fill the dam, originally planned to be in cross-section like an inverted V with a 1:1 slope on each side, came from the mud of the Missouri delivered through large pumps and pipes moving gigantic quantities of slurry long distances to the dam site. The downstream architecture was changed during construction to 1:3 to further strengthen the dam. Despite the incredible efforts, things did not go well at many points. In 1938 came a major disaster when a giant mass of slurry inside the dam escaped, causing a partial collapse of one wall of the dam while many workers were nearby. They fled for their lives, but 8 died, 6 of whom are still inside the dam. The hazards implicit in this giant project are recognizable from the deaths involved in its construction: they total 59. No information was provided about the number of serious injuries, deaths not counted (such as some of those from pneumonia, tuberculosis, dysentery, etc.), and the total of plain old human misery. But you can vividly see evidence of that suffering, especially on the faces of the workers, in the Corps' movie.

The finished dam is 4 miles long with a two-lane highway on top of it about 250 feet above the base of the downstream slope. The huge lake behind the dam extends west for about 100 miles, and it is actually not even the biggest lake made by dams on the Missouri - those behind the Garrison and Oahe dams are larger still. Only two of the four tunnels built with such incredible difficulty have been used - ever. These two are linked to power houses with turbines and generators making a total of less than 200 megawatts with maximum power online, only about a fifth of what a typical conventional modern power plant (gas, coal) produces today. One of the two generators is only infrequently used due to lack of cost-effective demand.

Three miles east of the dam are the gigantic spillway and gates opened only when necessary to prevent overfilling of the lake. The spillway is one mile long and was being repaired during our visit. In 2011, these gates were opened after a very rainy season and record snows in the Rockies caused all the Missouri dams to be forced to unload some of their excess water. Water at 160,000 cubic feet per second, several times the normal flow of the

Missouri, surged downstream and caused considerable flooding. How bad the flooding would have been absent the dams nobody can say. But even the incredible chain of large dams on the Missouri has not completely eliminated floods from the river. The Fort Peck dam is now, obviously, at least to some extent an enormous white elephant.

Like I said, it makes one think. And not just about dams. How many of the great projects of today will, in 80 years or so, seem of long-term importance? How many will later come to be viewed as gigantic blunders? Who can say?

Upon leaving the Fort Peck region, we followed the Milk River, a tributary of the Missouri, west to Havre and then drove southwest toward Great Falls. For the last half of the "leg" from Havre to Great Falls we again were following the Missouri, and visited Fort Benton and an amazingly lovely overlook of the river just south of that historic town. As noted before, Fort Benton was the highest point on the Missouri which could be reached by steamboats; until the railroads ended its importance it was a gateway for people and produce to settlements in the Pacific Northwest and even western Canada. It is now a sleepy town in a river valley with a few tourist shops, a gas station, and a past.

We spent the night at Great Falls, MT. Here the famous falls of the Missouri have been ruined, perhaps irretrievably, by a dam and power house built right at the falls - absolutely ugly. We saw the same kind of desecration a few years ago at the Shoshone Falls on the Snake River, falls which were considered second only to Niagara in size and magnificence but which have been aesthetically wrecked by a dam and hydroelectric station of Idaho Power.

Great Falls has a museum with many examples of the paintings, drawings, and sculpture of cowboy artist Charles M. Russell. The museum is not without interest, even though the writer does not consider Russell a great artist. At the time of our visit the Charles Russell Museum had a special exhibition on the history of the bison in North America. Everyone knows that native bison once numbered in the millions, and that during the 1870s and 1880s they were nearly exterminated by sharpshooters acting formally or informally on behalf of the U.S. government. As General Phil Sheridan famously said in 1866, "Kill the buffalo, and you control the Indians". (He is also inaccurately claimed to have said, "The only good Indian is a dead Indian"; the correct quote is "The only good Indians I have seen were dead.") It is claimed that the surviving number of wild bison was reduced to only about 30-35 animals! These were then protected and bred with the help of private parties, both white and Indian, and now there are many thousands of bison descended from these few. Bison burgers, from ranched bison herds, are sold in many western restaurants. Bison meat is tasty and has a lower fat content than beef, and if you haven't ever eaten a bison burger, take your favorite cowgirl out west and try some - they are excellent, and you will both also enjoy seeing some of the loveliest landscapes on earth.

We are almost at an end. From Great Falls we followed the Missouri via Interstate 15 southwest through magnificent canyons, a route first discovered by the railroads, to Helena, and then southeast to what we consider the river's origin at Three Forks, where the rivers Jefferson, Madison, and Gallatin - all arising in the Rockies not far to the west - come together to form the Missouri. A small state park is located at this lovely spot in a remarkably green valley, only moderately urbanized. A few hundred yards downstream from the start of the river is a gravel factory which constitutes the whole village of Trident. And not many miles below that factory is the first of the smaller dams on the Missouri.

These are harbingers of what lies further downstream all the way to the Missouri's junction with the Mississippi, as the river flowing over 2,000 miles drops less than 2 feet per mile from about 4,500 feet of altitude at Three Forks to 1,400 at Omaha and a bit less at St. Louis.

We retain many pleasant memories from this journey of over 1,500 automobile miles, but probably the most vivid are the incredible spaciousness of the unending prairie, the pale blue of distant mountains, the varied beauty of the Missouri in its serpentine natural channel sometimes bordered by limestone cliffs, and of the amazingly extensive, rolling prairie of the Dakotas with its green fields of corn, warm tan of limitless wheat, bright yellow sunflowers, metallic conical-peaked silos glistening silvery in the sunlight, and the blue, blue sky with small cumulus and high cirrus clouds wind-driven above. If you haven't roamed the Dakotas in early August, seen the still-wild Missouri River, or rolled across the prairies as the Bearpaw Mountains and Rockies distantly appear you are missing something. Try to visit if you can.

Mexican Rockets Slam into Texas

Hello, children, and welcome to your basic world history 7th grade class. I am your new teacher, Miss L. Santayana. Today we will study from the history curriculum prepared for all U.S. students by the Federal Department of Education. As you know, since 2030 the material from this department is the only history which can be legally taught in schools in the United States except for other content or textbooks which have been approved in advance by the FDE.

Our topic today will be the war a few years ago along the southern border of our country between the people of the Mexican Strip and the United States. You can see some of the newspaper headlines from that time online such as "Mexican Rockets Slam into Texas, SAMAH Rejects General Disassembly Call for Cease Fire". This unfortunate conflict resulted from deep misunderstandings by our country about the origins of the wretched conditions of Mexicans living in the Strip. Let me guide you through the highlights of what took place in 2044, how things came about, and what happened afterward. You can find more information in chapter 14 in your history textbook "We Are All Equal" which was written by scholars employed by the FDE. They really know what they are doing, and they should since the FDE is now the largest employer of university-level historians in America.

The "Texas-Mexican Strip Disagreement", as the 2044 fighting is now generally known, had its roots deep in history. FDE has confirmed, and you all already were told that history is always written by the winners of any conflict, so you should remember that despite our best efforts to be fair, history teachers like myself may be biased by our sources of information, or may be transmitting to our students our own unconscious biases against people from other cultures. Regardless of anything you may think based on what you learn in my history class, I hope you will at least come away with the core lesson that the FDE wants all American students to learn: ALL CULTURES ARE EQUALLY GOOD.

The ancient history of Mexico is confusing, and there is little point unless you are a genius in trying to learn the differences between the Olmec, Mayan, Zapotec, Nahuan, Toltec, and Aztec cultures. What you should remember is that according to modern historians these were mostly agrarian (that means "farming") peoples who peacefully inhabited the region now known as Mexico, at least back to more than 20 centuries before the Common Era. Some of you may have heard that these were just tribes or primitive empires which regularly practiced slavery, tortured captives, and carried out human sacrifices – but recent research by the FDE proves the unfairness and falsehood of such rumors.

As you have already been taught in previous classes, on the other side of the world from the peaceful Mexican lands during the 15th century arose one of the greatest tragedies in human history – the beginnings of colonialism. While there was some spreading of European ways at an earlier period, by such as Vikings from the formerly warlike Scandinavian countries (apparently they really had warriors in those days) or traders like Marco Polo, the exploitation of New World people essentially began in the 1400s as the Portuguese and Spaniards used ocean-going ships and iron weapons including firearms and to seek gold, valuable spices, and slaves throughout the world.

In the early 1500s, a particularly brutal Spanish warrior named H. Cortez and about 500 of his fellows invaded Mexico in search of gold and silver which the Aztecs, then the leaders of the Mexican government, had accumulated in places like Mexico City, their capital. After using trickery, modern firearms against the peaceful Aztecs, and the spreading of smallpox which killed millions of innocent victims Cortez managed to kill the Aztec kings and conquer Mexico. It is probably true that exposure of the Aztecs to smallpox was initially accidental, but once their vulnerability (that means "innocent weakness") to it became known FDE research now proves that it was mostly disseminated (that means "spread") to them on purpose. As you already learned in your 4th grade history classes, later on the same form of extermination – killing with smallpox – was intentionally done by European settlers who wanted to steal land from our own peaceful Native Americans (still sometimes incorrectly called "Indians").

As you may recall from your required class last year on contraception, gender choice, AIDS victims, and sexually-transmitted diseases that one such disease is syphilis. For many years it was believed that the native peoples of America had sex with their European conquerors and were responsible for introducing syphilis into Europe as a kind of deadly exchange for the natives receiving smallpox from the Europeans. Syphilis in its original form did in fact kill millions of Europeans in this era. However FDE researchers have recently concluded (that means "voted") that it is highly unlikely that such a terrible disease would have been naturally endemic (that means "there") among the peaceful natives of Mexico. FDE also finds it hard to believe that any of these natives would have agreed to have sex with their brutal Spanish conquerors, except for the many who were coerced (that means "forced").

So Spain took over the land of Mexico and imposed (that also means "forced") the Spanish language upon its inhabitants. The Aztecs and other native people became slaves working gold and silver mines for the enrichment of the Spanish king. Other Spaniards sought gold elsewhere in the New World and one of them, the sailor J. Cabrillo, became the first to claim ownership for Spain of the coast of California.

But gradually relations between the good native peoples of Mexico and the Spaniards improved. Many of the Spaniards came to the New World as fortune hunters and bachelors. Unlike the settlers of our own country, who hated Native Americans so much that they would not marry them, the Spaniards readily developed families with native women. In this way, the Spanish proved that they were more broadminded (that means "fair") than the bigoted settlers of America. Over time, this miscegenation (that means "marrying out") resulted in a new race which used to be called "mestizos" and which we now call Hispanics.

For about 300 terrible years – three long centuries – the peoples of Mexico suffered under Spanish colonialism. But then in 1821, these heroic people revolted from Spain much like our own country did from England, and Mexico shook off the shackles (that means "took off the handcuffs") of Spanish rule. After that, things got much better for the Mexican people. Some of you may have heard phony rumors to the contrary – rumors that the Mexican revolution was followed by economic instability (that means "poverty"), civil war, suspending of the Constitution, and dictatorship. The FDE now has discovered that such reports are either false or greatly exaggerated.   Research by the FDE has further shown that more than 95% of all revolutions result in happier populations, and the Mexican revolution was another example of this.

Not long after winning its independence, Mexico faced a threat from the north. A group of white men came down from the United States into the northern part of Mexico, pushing out the native peoples and sometimes cheaply buying their land. These so-called Texans, whose name comes from the Spanish "Tejas", were led by the Austin family, one of whom – S. Austin – used to be considered an American hero. The Texans created many troubles for the Mexican government, and some of them even brought in slaves although the Mexicans had officially abolished slavery in 1829. Although it was obvious that Mexico had every legal right to Texas, the intruders from the north started a civil war and tried to take Texas away from Mexico. The Mexican president, A. Santa Anna, bravely led the Mexican army in an attempt to stop Texas from being stolen from Mexico. He personally commanded the troops at the battle of the Alamo, in which the Mexicans – wrought to an understandable state of frustration by the insurrection (that means "trying to take over") – killed all the Texans, even bayonetting the wounded and slaughtering the few who surrendered, except fortunately for one Black man. Among those killed at the Alamo was J. Bowie, the inventor of a large knife which the Texans had used to slash many Mexicans to death. It may not seem nice to us today, indeed it upsets even me a little, that at the Alamo the Mexican troops massacred (that means "killed") all the Texans who survived their attack, but after all it was the Texans who started the civil war and the Mexicans had every right to try to protect their land and their loved ones.

Texans, however, cared nothing about the rights of the Mexicans. Even while the Alamo battle was occurring, Texas declared itself an independent nation. Eventually Santa Anna's troops were defeated by S. Houston and his followers at the battle of San Jacinto. Santa Anna was captured, but because he was such a great man Houston released him and he returned to Mexico.

Later, Texas decided to become a state inside the United States. The Mexicans did not intend to allow their northern territory to be stolen from them by our country and tried to stop this. A war broke out between the United States and Mexico called the Mexican-American War of 1846. The United States, its territorial greed stimulated by one of America's worst Presidents, J. Polk, and with troops commanded by General Z. Taylor (whose military successes later made him President) managed to win the war. Our nation grabbed Mexican land all the way to the Rio Grande River and also seized the northwestern part of Mexico which included a good part of what we call California. Is it any surprise that Mexicans to this day despise the United States, and want to correct the historic wrongs which our nation forced upon them?

The loss of Texas to the U.S. also had terrible consequences for American Blacks. Texas became a slave state. Mexico had banned slavery, but after Mexico lost Texas about 30% of all Texans became slaves. Texas fought with all the other slave states in the Civil War. Probably not all Texans favored slavery, and it has even been claimed that Texas' first President and Governor, S. Houston, did not want Texas to fight for slavery, but many other Texans did. Of course, slavery was ended officially in Texas by U.S. President A. Lincoln, but for many years thereafter Blacks in Texas never got fair treatment. The FDE historians are now doing an analysis of how much better off Blacks in the Tejas region would have been had that territory remained part of Mexico.

Some of you may also want to know that the fighting connected with the stealing of Texas from Mexico by the United States helped to make the American Civil War bloodier than it might otherwise have been. It was in Mexico that R. Lee, formerly a hero in our South but now discredited as a misguided fool, first fought and learned how to kill. The same goes for many others who became military leaders for the South in our Civil War, including the President of the Confederate States (that means "the South in the Civil War") named J. Davis. Many now consider it an error that neither Lee nor Davis were executed as traitors at the end of the Civil War – most FDE historians believe they deserved death and that only politics saved them.

After our own Civil War ended, Mexico continued its own slow but peaceful evolution. It did experience a few rough spots along the way including an invasion from France, several dictatorships, the murder of President F. Madero, military government, political repression (that means "less democracy"), and economic inequality and poor development. Meanwhile, the United States, under the corrupt administration of former general U. Grant, who had also learned to kill in Mexico, and several subsequent administrations was forced into rapid development by a group of rich industrialists known as the "robber barons". Americans started to reach for prosperity by exploiting the mineral resources of our country – big steel, big oil, big coal, and big railroads were our real leaders. More and more people came to the United States from Europe, and as they spread west forced Native Americans off their own land and into reservations. In contrast to peaceful Mexico, where citizens were never allowed to carry guns,

Americans were allowed to be armed and in many western settlements minor disputes were settled with gunfire. Is it any surprise, children, that with so many guns we have so many murders today in our big cities?

In the 20th century, fortunately behind us long before any of you were borne, America grew richer and richer. This was largely because of the two World Wars which devastated Europe and Asia. The United States exploited the resulting weakness of other countries for the benefit of American business. The dollar became money instead of real gold. American oil companies acquired monopolies in the Middle East. Americans developed experience with nuclear power by dropping the atomic bomb – not once but twice – on Japan with the alleged purpose of ending the Second World War; it did end the war, but at a great cost to humanity. A few Americans got lucky and capitalized early on computer technology, with men like W. Gates and L. Ellison becoming obscenely rich billionaires. By the first part of our own 21st century the United States was affluent, powerful, bent upon world supremacy in everything. Meanwhile, Mexicans peacefully continued to raise their families and hoped to someday – somehow – fix the historical wrongs that our country had forced upon them. But they were poor and weak, while we were rich and strong. We had nuclear weapons, they did not. We even had a veto in the United Nations, they did not. How could they ever manage to obtain justice from us?

Meanwhile, not all Mexicans wanted to stay poor in Mexico. They wanted to come to America to work. Americans had stolen their land, murdered their soldiers, exploited their mineral resources, forced upon them bad economic deals, and kept them in poverty. Surely, they felt, the least the United States could do was to open its borders to Mexican workers – to all of them who wanted to work here. We were rich and could easily have done it. And we could also have afforded to help Mexicans who came here and fell victim to circumstances where they could not work, where they were pregnant, where they got sick. We did of course let some Mexicans in to work at our lowest paying, back-breaking jobs like picking grapes in the torturing heat of central California, laying bricks, cutting lawns, re-roofing buildings. But many could not enter legally. They could not come in to work on lands that were, by moral right, really theirs – Texas, California, Arizona, New Mexico. So with no alternative they tried to get in illegally, and many of them succeeded. Those who got in, even illegally, found jobs, got free schooling for their children, got free health care, were even free to protest as illegals right in front of the White House without being arrested. They were starting to get what they deserved from our country. And millions of others Mexicans saw what was happening and wanted the same thing for themselves.

But, children, did we open wide our doors to these people whom we had mistreated, whose land we had stolen, whose poverty we had exploited, some of whom died in our southwestern deserts while seeking work in the United States? No, we did not. Instead we built fences between the United States and Mexico. We patrolled our borders and even sent some people back to Mexico. The pressure built up. More and more Mexicans pressed close to the border with the United States. The Mexican government, hoping we would help them soon, built shanties and provided tents to Mexicans near the border. The United Nations provided food and humanitarian relief to the people shamefully trapped in poverty along the southern border of the richest country in the world. In short, children, this is how the Mexican Strip began.

Soon the Mexican government wanted little to do with the masses on the Strip. It was expensive to support the growing numbers of poor people denied admission by American. Unemployment and crime became rampant (that means "common"). The UN gave still more aid. The shanty towns grew. The Strip population, despite deaths from disease, crowding, and poor nutrition continued to increase.

The Strip became a recruiting ground for mobsters handling illegal drugs and controlled by billionaires. It also became a place where violent ideas, provoked by desperation, could take hold. Weapons appeared in certain hands, some supplied by the drug lords, some from nations which hated the United States, some from the oil-rich Middle East. The United States had many enemies, and often for good reason did they hate us. The Strip underwent a political evolution (that means "change") toward autonomy from Mexico. Revolutionists arose, threatening, assassinating, inciting. Their money came from outside. They soon created a rogue "state" within a state, ignored by Mexico, ruled by terrorists, mobsters, and killers. The leadership said they would regain the lands stolen from them many years ago by the Texans and Americans. Soon weapons intended for use against the United States appeared in the Strip. Spy satellite overflights and human intelligence bribed out of the Strip revealed rockets in the Strip which could only be intended for use against the United States. Tunnels were dug in secret below the fences guarding the American border, even under the Rio Grande, and terrorists infiltrated through them into such locations as El Paso.

What did America do in response? Did we take these poor, suffering people into our hearts, open our doors wide as a nation, treat them as equals, love them as brothers, and give them the full "right of return" to their ancestral homelands? No, children, we did not. Instead we strengthened our fences and built the incredibly expensive Titanium Dome, an anti-missile defense system that could defeat all, or certainly most, of the types of missiles which the Mexican Strip had received from FARC, from Iran, from Russia, from revolutionists who united against the power, the wealth, and the arrogant success of America. American science might be the envy of the world, America might be a nuclear power, America might be affluent, Americans might mostly live in peace with each other, and America might be known everywhere as a "democracy" – but all that made the desperate population and their violent leaders hate us more. And with nothing to show for what they had promised to accomplish - to take back lands from the United States, to force America to recognize the "right of return" – the leaders of the Strip set their course toward violence against us. It was the only way they could stay in power. And they counted on the rest of the world to help them achieve their goals.

The leaders of the Strip had formed a powerful political party which became the only one allowed to represent its population in the court of world opinion. This party, which been elected by its desperate inhabitants, was known as SAMAH, an acronym for "So All Mexicans Are Happy". The name also forms a palindrome (too complicated to explain this word, kids, but it sort of means "opposite") when coupled with SAMAH's sister organization in the Middle East known as HAMAS. Indeed SAMAH knew history, and was acting with full awareness of HAMAS's missile attacks and underground infiltration from the Gaza Strip against the U.S. puppet state, Israel, many years ago in 2014.

There were many parallels between the situation faced in 2014 by HAMAS in the Gaza Strip and that confronting SAMAH 30 years later in the Mexican Strip. As the FDE summarizes it, in each case the leadership controlled a poor population that could not easily escape. In each case a rich and hated northern neighbor protected its own interests from that of a population whose land it had seized in warfare. HAMAS launched over 1,000 missiles at Israel, kidnapped Israeli soldiers and citizens, and killed anyone in the Strip who dared oppose such actions. What then happened? Israel's missile shield, called Iron Dome and much like our own Titanium Dome first promoted by President R. Reagan, blocked most of the missiles. Then Israel struck back hard. It invaded the Strip, bombed it, destroyed the tunnels, attacked the missile launchers, and blew up ammunition dumps some of which had been created in schools. It did not need to use its nuclear weapons. Thousands of Gaza residents were killed. The United Nations called for a cease fire. HAMAS refused to give up. The destruction by Israel continued. Finally, there was little left to destroy in Gaza, and HAMAS had used up its rockets, ammunition, and even its food. HAMAS then agreed to a cease fire. But only on condition that the world would help them since they were, after all, innocent victims. They had done nothing wrong except try what they could to reverse some of the injustices of history, in their case wartime defeats against Israel, the hated usurper (that means "thief") of their lands. Now Israel had destroyed their homes, their hospitals, their schools, had shut its doors even tighter on unlimited migration from the Strip. HAMAS and its people deserved help, they were suffering. They were not to blame, Israel was.

And the world helped the Gaza Strip. Money was poured in by the U.N. and other relief agencies, much of that money indirectly from the United States. Israel itself provided some aid. Today, Gaza has better buildings, better hospitals, and better schools than it did before Israel destroyed the old ones. There is still not peace, of course. And why should there be? After all, someday the process can be repeated even if the historic grievance – the injustice as our FDE now calls it – cannot be corrected.

And that, of course, is just what SAMAH did with the Mexican Strip against the United States in 2045. The Mexican missiles were launched while America was asleep, and despite Titanium Dome scores of Texans and a few people in Tucson and San Diego died in their homes. President Chelsey Hernandez, who had even married an illegal Mexican immigrant during the campaign before her election, was severely criticized. So what choice did she have? American armed forces struck back and in a few days thousands of Mexican Strip residents were killed, maimed, wounded, burned alive, blinded. Juarez became a pile of rubble. For a while brave Mexicans continued sending their rockets against the U.S. while the world called for a cease fire. But at last the one-sided battle was ended and the U.S. had "won". What happened next? The Strip is still there. It has been totally rebuilt. Its buildings today are far superior to the shanties that used to be there. The United Nations, which serious criticized our country for its over-reaction to the desperation of the Mexican Strip, provides large amounts of support to better the lives of the poor victims in the Strip. SAMAH, like HAMAS, has helped its people, though many of them were necessarily sacrificed for such progress. Indeed, the world provides many examples of this kind of vigorous, courageous leadership. The successors to SAMAH and HAMAS continue the fight with different names.

About 80 years ago, an Englishman named Peter Sellers made a movie called "The Mouse That Roared". This old movie is still available free for viewing on the FDE website at www.FDE.gov   In the movie, a mythical nation called the Grand Duchy of Fenwick, desperate for money and represented by the mouse, famously observes that the solution to their problem is "to declare war on the United States and lose". HAMAS and SAMAH both applied this concept in real life along with, of course, some screaming, bleeding, fear, pain, and dying. But perhaps, children, as some FDE historians now suggest, that may be the necessary price of progress.

Next week, following the rules given by the FDE, we will practice debating the following question: "Should SAMAH have sent its missiles into Texas?" Equal time will be provided to each debater. I will assign a side of the debate to each of you for preparation, and will choose the actual participants just before class time. In the opinion of FDE, this is not an easy question to answer.

Class is ended. Have a nice day.

Twins and More

This is a personal analysis of genetic issues involving children and the impact, if any, of normal varieties of parental influence and peer and other non-parental environmental issues on what kind of adults emerge later on. My thoughts have been influenced by recently reading, and in one case rereading, the references noted at the end. But they are also the product of a longstanding professional interest in genetics, reproduction, and developmental biology. That said, please be aware that the opinions expressed here may not match some widely held orthodoxies.

Judith Rich Harris is an author with widely read opinions on this subject. Her book "The Nurture Assumption", recently reissued, is very well written and pungent, although it doesn't have the many graphs and data tables I seek in books by primary researchers in genetics, psychology, etc. I read it first about 1999, and recently again. Contradicting the conventional dogma that parents have large influences on what their children become, Harris summarizes various studies and offers the conclusion that parents (except for their genes) matter virtually not at all, genetics is the key factor in the adult that emerges, and that peer group influences are important and explain the remainder of the variability of outcomes. Harris vigorously sums up her perspective in a rejoinder to British poet Phillip Larkin, who had quite a messy personal life. Please forgive use of the four letter word below, but I am quoting exactly from both the poet and Ms. Harris and assume my readers are adults who have seen this word before. Larkin famously wrote, referring to his dead parents and to everyone's parents too, in a passage that has

provided millions of messed up adults with someone to
blame:

> "They fuck you up your Mom and Dad,
> They don't mean to but they do.
> They fill you with the faults they had,
> And add some extra, just for you."

Since the deceased parents could not reply, Harris
offered the following rejoinder on their behalf:

> "How sharper than a serpent's tooth
> To hear your child make such a fuss.
> It isn't fair – it's not the truth,
> He's fucked up, yes, but not by us."

Harris gets to her principle conclusions in two main
ways. One is by looking at the generally similar but still
not identical adult outcomes of identical twins, whether
reared apart or reared together. The other is by using the
considerable evidence that adoptive parents have negligible
long-term influences (beyond early childhood) on their
children. My view is that she is only partly right and I will
try to explain why I think so. To anticipate, I believe she
fails to take genetics, prenatal events, and randomness into
sufficient account as the predominant factors explaining
differences between identical twins and, by implication, as
key influences on all childhood outcomes.

We start with a little background on the evolution of
insights about human development and child rearing. In
the not too distant past, limited attention was paid in the
western world to the details of how children grew up.
Children were generally taught to read, write, and do
simple sums, usually inculcated with a morality based
directly or indirectly upon the Bible or at least some of the

Ten Commandments, and when old enough were put to work. Wealthier children in nations like Britain often had even less interaction with their parents than the children of the poor; richer kids were wet-nursed, raised by a nanny, and the boys went off to boarding schools while the girls learned to sew, play a musical instrument, dress becomingly, and behave with decorum. The 18th and 19th centuries were not child-centered worlds.

Sigmund Freud and his contemporaries, and some of their many followers in the new fields of psychiatry and psychology, usually receive credit – if that is the right word – for a subsequent near total transformation of ideas about human development. Freudian interpretations of reality are hard to define because of their variability and, as Nobel laureate Peter Medawar famously asserted, their non-provability, but they basically claim that early childhood phenomena like resolution of the Oedipus complex, excretion and toilet training, repression of early childhood memories, inhibitions, and similar elements critically influence the nature and balance of the three deep psychic elements – the ego, the id, and the superego. Much of what is going on in the mind is hard to uncover because it is hidden in something called the unconscious. Therefore if an adult's head didn't work right, Freudians were likely to probe for something that didn't happen right in childhood, probably early childhood. Tools like psychoanalysis and the interpretation of dreams were used to facilitate self-understanding thus allowing childhood traumas to reach consciousness and be dispelled. Freudianism has been analogized to a kind of religion with special indoctrination (psychoanalysts must themselves undergo psychoanalysis), numerous disciples, and many variants of belief. The wide diffusion of Freudianism was also greatly facilitated by its assertion, though Freud himself was a medical doctor, that psychoanalysis and psychotherapy could be practiced successfully by therapists lacking any experience in health care.

Among the many consequences of the Freudian revolution was the burden it placed upon parents, who obviously were the principle actors in the infant's early experiences. Consider the "psychic pain" of being born. As one psychiatrist friend parodied it, "For 9 months you are in a quiet, warm place, being fed and protected, and then one day all that ends. Suddenly it's light. You are wet and cold. And then someone holds you upside down, smacks your bottom, and makes you cry." The first of many traumas! For mental health baby's future traumas, like being told he can't make love to mother or defecate wherever he wants, need careful management by parents. If these and other developmental issues are not handled in the "right way", the result will be a messed up adult. One prominent Freudian disciple, Bruno Bettelheim, became well known for telling parents of autistic children that they had caused their child's autism through their own abnormal personalities and errors; some of the accused parents felt so guilty they committed suicide.

Buried deep within the Freudian vision is the implication that we are what our environment makes us. It claims we are each born with a blank mental and emotional slate, and our parents do the most important permanent writing on it. While it certainly was not Freud's intent, the interpretation that man's nature is highly malleable provided a deeply misguided justification for Communism and its view that social engineering can transform mankind, creating a new kind of man. Lysenko, a Lamarckian pseudo-scientist who influenced Stalin, even asserted that improved characteristics acquired through such engineering would be inherited by offspring.

As psychotherapeutic ideas spread from Vienna throughout the western world, scientific insights about human development were being developed initially by others who had nothing to do with psychology. The work on pea plants of genetics pioneer Gregor Mendel was rediscovered in the early 20th century, and Mendelian principles started to be applied to human diseases. The last century has witnessed a vast expansion of genetic information; the technologies and scientific work that provided it have enormously altering knowledge about human biology. Specialists in "behavioral geneticists" and scientists from other disciplines have applied genetic techniques ranging from gene sequencing to studies of multigenerational trait persistence to provide important and provable, testable, independently-confirmable data on how we develop and the main determinants of the characteristics of the adults we become. Their many insights are far too numerous to summarize here, or probably anywhere. But two key take home messages can be highlighted:

1. The kind of adults that children become correlates negligibly with characteristics of their adoptive parents, and significantly with those of the biological parents who did not bring them up.

2. Identical twins which are "genetically identical" even when reared apart are remarkably similar in a wide variety of characteristics including intelligence, personality, talents, and many other major attributes.

These critical findings, which have been repeatedly confirmed, support the counterintuitive view that parenting matters little and heritability matters hugely in determining what kind of adults people become.

These conclusions are recently supported by data from an unexpected source, a professor of economic history. As described in his book "The Son Also Rises", Gregory Clark from the University of California – Davis used the creative tool of following what happens over many generations to the descendants of people with very rare surnames. For example, start with a prominent scientist, politician, or otherwise socially distinguished man with a very rare last name and follow individuals with this rare surname for several generations using records available in countries like England, Sweden, Japan, and some others. In all countries studied so far, social prominence persists far longer in the same-surname and presumably genetically related descendants than the time course predicted by chance. Not only do traits for prominence and achievement manifest inheritance from the initial prominent man, but there is also a tendency for highly accomplished people to marry spouses who are talented or come from families with prominent members – a phenomenon called assortative mating. Clark's important point is that the persistence of multigenerational social prominence can be explained by genetic factors and his data are inconsistent with transmission through environmental factors ("nurture") like wealth, parenting styles, or other factors. Interestingly, the delayed multi-generational regression toward the mean (approach toward the expected population average over time) is also seen but in a reverse direction when people at the bottom of the social heap have their rare surnames followed for many generations. Their descendants tend to gradually rise from the bottom regressing upward toward average social positions, but at a rate far slower than expected if genetics did not matter – and matter a lot. Thus the book's title, "The Son Also Rises", but the sons rise very slowly most of the time.

OK, so genetics matters. But let's return to Ms. Harris. She correctly states that identical twins are very similar, but their adult characteristics are not all the same. She also finds in adoption studies compelling evidence – as have many others – that despite Dr. Freud's opinions about parental influences on toilet training and Oedipal challenges and more modern theories of the importance of parenting behavior on adult outcomes, parents hardly matter at all in their non-genetic impact on their children. Thus she concludes – and much of her book is about this – that the non-trivial adult differences between identical twins must be due to peer group influences. In sum, peers matter and parents don't. Thus in Harris' interpretation, parents are off the hook on outcomes except for their influence – if any – on trying to select the child's peers. Parental abilities to influence peer factors naturally diminish over time, and are quite limited once children go to school, play with other neighborhood kids, or are to significant degrees away from parental control. Harris thus concludes that about all you can do is be nice to your kids and maybe, just maybe, they'll be nice to you when they grow up, but as for how they will live their lives in other ways – forget it. Their genes and their peers will make them what they become.

Although there is a hard-core group of genetic deniers who maintain that with better early parenting, extra pre-school enrichment of education, more money, etc. any child can become anything it or its parents want it to be, most of us have figured out that every child does not have the innate capacity to be a star athlete, top musician, or a math genius. But there are persistent disagreements about how much "nurture" matters and what kind matters most. Some say peers are most important, others say parenting, others say both are highly significant. Might they somehow all be wrong?

"Identical twins" should more accurately be called twins with the same initial code in their DNA. The DNA of an embryo encodes a program – an immensely complex many, many step biological program – for making a baby. Though both twins descend from one cell with its particular genetic code, twins don't end up exactly identical because of many random biological events which occur before birth. And the aggregate impact of these random events are likely to be considerable. Let's follow what happens from the start.

Identical twins are usually envisioned as arising from a common one-cell origin, the zygote (one cell embryo) produced by the fertilization of one egg by one sperm. The human zygote is so small that a microscope is needed to see it. By a truly miraculous process, this zygote will over about 9 months turn into a newborn baby – or, in the case of identical twins – two babies. There is some debate about exactly how identical twinning starts in very early embryonic life. The zygote divides into a two cell embryo, then into four, and the cell number increases from there. (The average adult has about 37 trillion cells, and a newborn certainly has at least one trillion. It takes a lot of cell divisions to get there – see below.) There is speculation about when and how one embryo sometimes becomes two. Nobel laureate Robert Edwards favored the view that it happens at about 7-9 days of embryonic life when the embryo "hatches" from the gelatinous shell (zona pellucida) that surrounds it and is ready to implant and burrow into the inner lining of the future mother's uterus. By the time of hatching the embryo already has many cells, and during hatching the enlarging embryo forces its way out through an opening in the zona. This has actually been observed in some laboratories performing IVF (in vitro fertilization) research. If part of the embryo that has already emerged breaks free from the part still inside, two cell masses are created. The one inside can also hatch out and implant like its twin.

But even at this point, everything is not the same for the twins. Before hatching, the embryo has done more than increase its cell number. It has also developed at least two multicellular elements – an inner cell mass and a surrounding layer of cells. If the embryo is female, each cell in the inner cell mass will have already randomly inactivated (permanently turned off function of) one of the two X chromosomes in each cell, and it won't be the same X chromosome in each cell. So when the embryo "twins", the resulting two cell masses won't be exactly identical any more. Almost surely, one will have more cells from the inner cell mass than the other. Almost surely one will have more of the surrounding layer of cells than the other. And if the embryos are female they also almost surely won't have exactly the same proportions of cells containing in active form the X-chromosome from the mother vs. the X from the father. So even before the two embryos implant, "identical twins" are not completely identical.

Now imagine what follows. Each cell in each embryo is running a program encoded in its DNA. The program to be carried out is so complex that most of its steps are not yet understood by modern science. On average, each cell in the embryo will divide, including completely synthesizing and doubling its DNA, about 40 times yielding a total at birth of about 1-2 trillion cells. Some of the cells of the just implanted embryo will turn into brain cells with extensions in some cases stretching from the brain to the lower spinal cord, others will become heart muscle cells which will contract several million times before the twins are born, others will become part of the over 270 different bones each baby will have at birth. All these cell divisions, all the differentiation of cells into different types, all the organization of these cells into normal organs, and much, much more – including "unknown unknowns" we don't even suspect today – go on before the birth of any normal baby. The biological programs encoded in the embryo DNA code require a vast number of steps for execution. Many molecules have to interact to add even a single base, one of millions, to replicate the DNA in even a single cell or to add one amino acid to create new proteins for any additional cell. Given the trillion or so functionally specialized cells needed to make a baby, it is impossible that as each of the two twins develops every single step in every single cell will be carried out at exactly the same precise moment in time – biology just don't work like a cesium clock. The random timing differences may each be fairly small, but in aggregate they will not be. Furthermore, biological processes have error rates. For example, DNA replication errors are well known and in the course of making a trillion or so cells, random errors are certain to be introduced and they won't be identical. Some segments of DNA get inactivated by a complex process called imprinting during development, and that can't happen either at the exact same moment in the cells of both twins. So on these considerations alone identical twins should not be expected be identical when born.

But there is more. The twins can't both land in the exact same spot in the maternal uterus. One may find a luckier, better nourished spot with better blood flow than the other. And the identical twins may develop intrauterine conflicts; some twin pairs have connections between their largely separate vascular systems resulting in one twin being overloaded with blood and the other seriously deprived, and occasions where this happens to a smaller, subclinical degree are likely not rare. As they get larger, twins also compete for space in the uterus and one may be more mobile or compressed than the other with unpredictable consequences for neuromuscular and skeletal development. At birth, one twin will have a slightly or perhaps considerably different weight than the other. Fingerprints are different due to frictional effects in the uterus. One twin may have a higher Apgar score, a rough correlate of neonatal health. After delivery of its sibling, the second-born twin may experience a partial separation of the placenta from the uterine wall, and hence interruption of its oxygen supply, before it can breathe on its own. And there can be many other differences too.

So, to summarize. Identical twins are not completely identical at birth, and can't ever be exactly identical. Though similar, they necessarily have different phenotypes. The phenotype is what you are. The genotype is what your DNA program code is. Not the same thing at all. And the differences can be attributed to a vast number of random events.

If we could study large numbers of identical twins who were truly identical in all ways –with identical genotypes and phenotypes at birth - and if these could be separated at birth and reared apart and some raised in different countries, some by different sets of parents, some sent to different schools, some exposed to environments enriched in saints and others in sinners, some having a good mentor and the others not, some granted admission to Harvard College and others not, and so on it might be possible to rationally end debates about how influential parents, schooling, peer groups, mentors, and other environmental factors are in child development, at least on average. The debates continue not because everyone has a closed mind, but because there is insufficient information to correctly inform the many intelligent open-minded people who want to know the truth.

What are my personal views, or more correctly my partially informed biases? I believe that genetics is hugely important. If you want to maximize the chances of having a smart kid, genetic odds work in your favor if you are smart yourself and find a smart spouse with as many smart blood relatives and ancestors as possible (to reduce the chance your potential spouse's superior intelligence is in part a random event). Same for athletic ability, beauty, musical talents. On the environment, the "nurture" part of things, my bias is that it matters much less than the genes except if it is truly a horrible factor like living in a slum city in India. As long as kids are brought up in American homes providing environments within a broad normal range, their innate characteristics will largely determine their future. Of course, if you are lucky enough to have a gifted child facilitate developing those gifts, and if you have a child with handicaps do what you can to provide extra assistance and training. Don't overprotect your kids, part of their job is to become independent people. And while parents can have only limited control over peer issues, almost none in late childhood and early adult life, and social life involves many unpredictable events it is common sense to discourage interactions with inappropriate peers.

In summary, parents should primarily encourage their kids in a loving, comfortable, and affordable manner that feels right to them, and entrust the rest to fate or to God. Most children will do just fine and become adults their parents will like, and who will like their parents. But some kids will fail repetitively, a few will change into adults you'd rather not know, and rare ones may turn into something really, really bad. Bad outcomes can be tragic, but as with the kids who turn out well they mostly don't happen because of what parents did or didn't do. I feel Ms. Harris' rejoinder to Phillip Larkin got it right. But we should also remember that messed up and wrong though he was, Larkin still managed to become the poet laureate of Great Britain.

Selected References (all readily available books):

Clark, Gregory: "The Son Also Rises"

Harris, Judith Rich: "The Nurture Assumption: Why Children Turn Out the Way They Do"

Segal, Nancy: "Born Together, Reared Apart: The Landmark Minnesota Twin Study"

Skenazy, Lenore: "Free Range Kids, How to Raise Safe, Self-Reliant Children"

Wade, Nicolas: "A Troublesome Inheritance: Genes, Race, and Human History"

Matriarchy on the March?

On March 28, 2015 the Wall Street Journal (not the New York Times) published a review headlined "Matriarchy on the March" about Melvin Konner's new book "Women After All". The reviewer was David Barash, "an evolutionary biologist and professor of psychology at the University of Washington" whose "most recent book is 'Buddhist Biology'". Above the headline is a quote from Joseph Conrad "Being a woman is a terribly difficult task, since it consists principally in dealing with men." Below the headline is a large full color picture of a fierce-looking, yelling woman in military uniform in front of a bunch of male soldiers; the photo is labelled "DISTAFF SERGEANT Army recruits at Fort Rucker, Ala., 1990". Near the center of the page in large letters is the take-home message: "Humans who carry a Y-chromosome are more likely to break the law, more likely to die in accidents, more likely to commit acts of violence. Who needs them?"

When I saw this in the early morning, I first wondered if I were still dreaming. Then I read on while sipping and trying not to regurgitate my initial cup of tea. In the first paragraph I found "Here is a stunning fact: There is a single chunk of DNA, known as SRY, that dooms its carriers to shorter life spans…and an increased risk of being violent.....More than 90% of people who run afoul of the law and are currently incarcerated carry this gene – although, to be fair, nearly one-half of non-felons are similarly afflicted. It's a tough road for those unfortunates who are forced, through no fault of their own, to deal with such defective genetics: There is no cure." Barash is referring, with some inaccuracy, to the Y-chromosome of all human males.

The reviewer then claims that Dr. Konner, a professor of anthropology whose prior book was asserted to be a "magisterial tome" about childhood, "makes a powerful case for a provocative thesis: that women are, in nearly every way that really matters, superior to men" and that "this superiority is finally becoming evident in our societies." In support of this assertion, Konner is quoted as claiming that "In addition to women's superior judgment, their trustworthiness, reliability, fairness, working and playing well with others, relative freedom from distracting sexual impulses, and lower levels of prejudice, bigotry, and violence make them biologically superior.....And, of course, most fundamentally they are capable of producing new life from their own bodies, a [biological burden] to which men literally add only the tiniest biological contribution – and one that in the not-too-distant future could probably be done without."

After this paean for the superiority of women, Barash notes that "the crux of Dr. Konner's narrative [relates to] those increasingly unnecessary and troublesome individuals suffering from X-chromosome deficiency disorder". By this Konner means "men", who have only one X-chromosome in each of their cells, while women have two X-chromosomes per cell. We return to this genetic "deficiency disorder" below.

The review closes with a prediction from Professor Konner who, despite his own personal affliction with SRY, "regards the future with hope [because] as women gain in influence, the world will become more democratic, more socially compassionate, more equal, less discriminatory, less sexually casual, and less pornographic". Professor Barash admits that "it remains to be seen if the upcoming generation of women [including "politicians, and "yes, soldiers, sailors, and pilots"] will generate a professional cohort that is more competent, compassionate, thoughtful and socially responsible." But he closes by stating, "I'm betting yes."

All this is perhaps little different, except in tedium and length, than the message "Move Over Men" on the bumper sticker of a car driven by an apparent woman which passed me on the right at about 100 miles an hour on an eastern highway some months ago. The message is simple: Women are going to take over the world, it's time for men to get out of the way, and if they don't the women will make them do it anyway. And when that happens, we will all be better off.

Shall I agree with two backscratching professors and one speeding female? Do you? I'm betting no.

Almost everything in the book review, and the principle assertions attributed to the book, are ridiculous. Indeed they are beyond ridiculous, and are downright wrong and dangerous.

Nobody would dispute that males have a higher frequency of criminal behavior and higher frequency of violent behavior than females. But so what? Even according to the two professors, about one-half of non-felons are similarly affected by what they call defective genetics for which there is no cure. Translating that into plain English means that almost all of the nearly half of the world who happen to be male are non-felons. That makes close to 4 billion male non-felons. Let's say about 1% of males might reasonably be considered criminals, and a smaller percentage, say 0.1 to 0.2%, of females might be so classified. That still means that about 99% of males are not criminals, and a tiny bit more, say 99.9%, of females are not criminals. Expressed in that way, the obvious conclusion is that the SRY gene and the Y-chromosome which carries it are in almost all instances accompanied by normal behavior, and are associated with criminal propensities in only about 0.5% of the human race. Would a sensible person call this "defective genetics" for which there is "no cure"?

Then there is the issue of "X-chromosome deficiency disorder". The good professors both seem unaware that while females normally have two X-chromosomes in each of their cells, only one of those X-chromosomes is genetically active. The other X-chromosome is randomly inactivated very early in embryonic life. Males also have one active X-chromosome per cell, and in no way have an X-chromosome deficiency. Furthermore, males have an active X-chromosome plus an active Y-chromosome in each of their cells. Thus men might claim to have more functioning human DNA per cell than women, even to thus be "more human". Indeed, reasoning like Barash and Konner, one might assert that women are suffering from a partial DNA deficiency condition for which there is no cure.

Of course, this kind of speculation is ridiculous. Men and women have genetic differences. Everyone knows that anyway. Furthermore, these genetic differences expose the developing brain of the male to male hormones produced by the testis from early in intrauterine life. But what do these differences mean, and why should they be considered bad?

The Barash-Konner's of the world would have us believe that the genetic attributes of men are less undesirable, those of women more desirable. But how can that possibly make sense? If for species survival maleness was undesirable in evolutionary terms, why would maleness persist over many millions of years of mammalian evolution? There are other forms of reproduction in plants, animals, and insects which differ substantially from the male/female pattern found in human beings. Few sensible people would deny that there must be important reasons – very important reasons – that both men and women exist. The human type of sexual differentiation simply must be the one which favors survival of the human species. And if so, it will take more than a couple of anthropologists' loony opinions to bring about a world in which men "in the not-too-distant future could probably be done without."

Let us assume that women have many positive attributes. Should we deny the same assumption for men? Let us assume that women differ in having a wide variety of individual strengths, talents, and weaknesses. Should be deny the same assumption to men? Let us assume that women are sometimes good and sometimes bad. One does not have go back to the Eve of the Bible to discover bad women, nor back to the Cain of the Bible to find bad male behavior. Everyone knows that some men and women are geniuses, and others have intellects at the other end of the bell curve. We all know that there is an enormous overlap in the talents and accomplishments of men and women. Gender does not define human limitations. Gender does not predict who will be better in mathematics, or who will develop into a better nurse, or become a more loving, dedicated spouse.

The world needs both men and women, and they are going to be with us as long as mankind survives on this planet. Do we need the "nurturance" of the nursing mother? Of course we do. Do we need men who are strong enough, tough enough, and determined enough to populate a police force or an army if our survival is threatened by evil? Of course we do. So far, most of the world's inventors have been males and most of the world's saints have been women. Over time, the proportions of gender representation in these categories may change, and that is fine if it does or if it doesn't.

The greatest problems of mankind significantly include that the average IQ is only 100, the average level of human goodness is lower than desirable, that there is a scarcity of the best among us, and that evil people exist. There will always be fewer wonderful people in the world than we need, and we should value those we have and provide every opportunity to allow more to develop. We should recognize the terrible toll on human lives and human aspirations taken by poverty, by disease, by corruption, by lack of education and do what we can to relieve those conditions. If our goal in the most important sense is to make the world a better place we handicap ourselves enormously by demonizing half of that world and claiming that a genetic curse affects the world's men. It is utter folly to make such claims. The distorted visions of academicians like Barash and Konner deserve our contempt, and they certainly have mine. To their ideas, I say no. To hopes for a better world for both women and men, I say yes. What about you?

Family Newsletter

Well, it's that time of year again. Here's where I get to tell you about all the great things that happened to our family during the past 365 days in, as the German polymath Leibniz first put it, this "beste aller moglichen Welten". As you may recall in "Candide", Voltaire expressed minor disagreement with the great mathematician's theocratic attempt to explain away the many troubles in the universe. But let's face it: Voltaire was a cynic without modesty or morals, and had no compunctions about contradicting one of the world's greatest geniuses, the man who arguably beat Isaac Newton to the invention of calculus. And who am I to argue with Leibniz?

Mother died a little while ago, but there is a better way to put it. One of our grandchildren cried when told that his cat died while he was at camp. He said, "Couldn't you say it nicer?" So we told him that his cat had gone up on the roof and we couldn't get it down, and he liked that better. I haven't told him yet about Grandma, but when I do I will just explain that Grandma is up on the roof. And I'll also tell him that now Grandma is happier being safely up in heaven with Grandpa and all the friends she outlived. We all wish Grandma had suffered a little less from her pancreas, but during the three years she was sick we all joyfully rallied round and visited a lot and showed her how much we cared, and she always would smile so we knew she didn't mind being a little uncomfortable and not having her surgery work out exactly as she hoped. Well, you win some and you lose some, and the world goes on its merry way whether you win or lose. I mean, everyone one has to lose sometime. So why look at the dark side? All in all, Mom's suffering was an inspiring experience and all of us who attended her funeral will always remember how happy we were since she was no longer in pain. All's well that ends well I always say.

I also had a good year, made a little money in the market, played all the golf I wanted, watched us all get older and mellower, watched the grandkids grow – all the usual things that add so much to one's joy and fulfillment. It's also true that I needed a hip replacement, a stent, and my anemia isn't any better, but dealing with each of these has made me a better, stronger, and wiser individual. And it also gave me a chance to get to know my doctors better, although actually I only saw each of my doctors once, but that gave me plenty of time to reach out to all the other health care providers who were so wonderful helping me with my insurance. I am not walking so good after the hip replacement, and I did have a touch of infection that was treated with IV antibiotics for about 6 weeks, but all this is fine now and the surgeon feels the limp will improve if I will just keep up my physical therapy. By the way, the PT lady is a very beautiful 22 year old blonde, not married, who told me she likes older, rich men; this made me feel so good that I told my wife about it and my wife said she was very happy to hear it.

My wife also had a year filled with personal growth, fulfillment, and the successful search for meaning. She got involved with a charity that supports kids with IQs under 100 who need remedial reading assistance so they can go to the University of Missouri through its special affirmative action program. We both think that is just a terrific thing for her to be doing, and she is now reaching out with her friends to get Yale to start doing the same thing. And as Harvard now has a woman as its president, we hope to inspire a similar program limited to females of color. We feel the U of M program is very successful - last year fully 40% stayed on at the school to become sophomores, and only three of the dropouts went to jail. My little woman is also enjoying herself playing golf, lunching with friends, and shopping. She is proud that she has mastered the complex art of online shopping, and this year alone accumulated over 700,000 American Express points. I don't know if I should even bother to mention that a few of her friends passed on this year, and several lunches had to be cancelled, but you should have seen how the women rallied together and rescheduled without any trouble. Such challenges strengthen one's abilities to adapt to changing circumstances, and is one more way that She moves in our lives to help make us better people.

Now, about the children. Sammy is doing well in his career as a community organizer in Chicago. He and Fred went to Provincetown for the summer, and they are thinking of buying a condo in Key West once Fred finds a job again. They have three dogs, all French poodles dyed different colors (the pink one is my personal favorite), and they always carefully scoop and bag when they take them out for walks. Shawna has become a partner in a marketing firm in Weehawken, and she loves her job selling solar panels to people in the slums where clean energy is of particular importance. Margaret is having a wonderful time as a social worker on the upper East Side, but she said she actually earns more from her new second job where she works nights with some other girls out of an apartment on East 73rd Street; I'll share with you more information about this second job as I learn more myself, but Margie says it allows her to meet a lot of energetic, rich men and pays extremely well. We're delighted with the wonderful lives that all of our children are making for themselves.

As for the grandchildren – well, nothing could be more important or more perfect. As you know, we have 6 of them and we are SO proud of what each of them is doing. As you know, Margie had three of them, one from each of her husbands, and they are all doing such great things. Alisa is the oldest of course, she is now almost 26 – can you believe it! She loves to travel, and took time off from Bennington to go to – you won't believe this – Pakistan of all places. She is learning Arabic, which is a difficult language, even harder than Hebrew, and has recently decided to change her name to Saleema. And while she was in Karachi (that's in Pakistan) she met the man of her dreams – Mohammed Jihadi. They are planning to return to the U.S. soon, unless that lunatic Donald Trump becomes President. The wife and I are so proud and happy – it looks like she will be the first of our grandchildren to marry!

The next oldest is Timothy, and he's doing a great job in his sophomore year at Roxbury State. Last year he was at MIT, and you'll never guess how clever he was to get admitted there – he actually told them his grandfather was a Native American. But even with all their wonderful teachers he still had a little trouble with math, and so the very nice counselors they have at MIT – you have no idea now sweet they all are – helped him to transfer, with full credit, to become an English major at Roxbury State. And he's doing great there, and we are so proud.

Margie's youngest, Mata, is in her last year at the New School of Bronxville which was started a few years ago by parents who were wise enough to understand the hidebound futility of the old fashioned, narrow focusing of high school education on reading, writing, arithmetic, and White History. At NSB, Mata can flourish studying anything she wants, as much as she wants (or doesn't want), the teachers are consistently affirming, and the counselors say that she can go to almost any college in the country despite her grades because she is so outstanding at football. Isn't it wonderful that women's football has become such a big thing on campuses all across the country? I hope she goes to a college in a warm place so the wife and I don't have to freeze our asses off watching her play like we've done at the NSB home games. I like football, though to be honest I prefer to watch women's beach volleyball; but dear sweet little Mata doesn't have the right figure for it.

Oh, let me tell you about the others. We can't forget them, can we? Sammy and Fred have "adopted" two babies who are now both 4 years old. Actually, they didn't just adopt them the old-fashioned way. They are so clever that they found some wonderful clinic that fixed them up with an egg donor and then somehow mixed her eggs with both their stuff at the same time, and put the babies into a surrogate and they adopted their own children from her. It's something they love to tell everyone about, and you may recall that Fred was so happy with the lawyer they found to help them with this that he even talked about going to get a law degree. But he changed his mind, and now is having the most wonderful time every day playing with these adorable little kids. While Sammy is out community-organizing, Fred takes the little ones to the park along with the dogs and does all the other fulfilling things the parents of little kids get to do every day.

Shawna has only one of our grandchildren, but last is not least in our family. Little Harry is some kind of genius, which we think is all the more remarkable since it's not clear which of Shawna's admirers was his biological father. Here is Shawna, working and raising Harry all by herself, and even with that kind of handicap Harry is just so smart. He is only 3 years old, but he can spell "CAT" and he can speak in short sentences. The wife and I are convinced that he is destined for future greatness. But even after he becomes extremely successful, we hope he won't look down on any of our other grandchildren. I mean, each of them is so perfect, so special, so unique – it makes no sense to think one is "better" than any other. We have a diverse family, and we believe each member is perfect in her own way.

Well, this letter is probably already too long. There isn't time to tell you about all the other things – both good and perhaps less good – that enriched our lives this year. Yes, some of our friends lost spouses or died themselves, but the wife and I got to Paris. A few folks we know are quite sick now, but Saleema visited Karachi. Some people of our acquaintance have lost their jobs, but I made a pile in the market. Don't let any of this bother you. Never forget that these different outcomes are all part of the harmonious diversity in the universe, all part of the plan that Leibniz so perfectly described.

A last comment. We just heard from Paris that the poor nations of the world will receive hundreds of billions of dollars from the richer nations to forestall climate change. This is wonderful. The money will not be wasted in these poor places on vaccines, antibiotics, wells supplying clean water, fighting corruption, building better schools, and other such things; it will instead rightfully all go to saving our planet from its worst possible disaster – a predicted temperature rise of one degree or so over the next century. I am really excited about this, and am doing what I can to make the world greener and keep mankind, and all the other animals and even the plants, happier and healthier and I hope all of you will join me in this effort. My New Year resolution is to do the following: I will cut my showering to once a week, and reuse my towels until they absolutely must be changed. I will lick my plates as clean as possible and use the dishwasher less. The wife will use no detergent in our laundering, and no dry cleaning will be done on our clothes since this pollutes the air with dangerous organic chemicals. We will no longer heat our pool or our hot tub. We will change our green lawns into a water-saving desert mix of cactuses and sand. We will discontinue using gas heat and refuse to accept electric service from the power companies whose fossil fuel plants are so dangerous to the world. We will install costly solar panels on our roof, and encourage more windmills for generation of clean power and ask to have them placed in our own neighborhood. Lastly, we will do everything we can to intimidate, ridicule, and embarrass both in public and in private anyone who is a climate change denier. We are broadminded and will reluctantly tolerate uninformed people who want to see more prisons, who think the police are of public benefit, who are opposed to race preferences, who favor private health care systems, even those who want people to be able to buy and carry guns everywhere like they do in the Israel of Mr. Netanyahu, but we will NOT tolerate climate change deniers. This Earth, right now, is the best of all possible worlds, and nothing can be more important than for all of us to do our utmost to keep it that way.

We hope each and every one of you has as perfect a New Year as we know we and our whole family will have! And we will update you on all the good news in next year's family newsletter.

BELIEVE IT OR NOT

Here is an assortment of real life happenings selected after decades of witnessing folly. The judges were a man and woman with few hang-ups about absurdity, political correctness, and four letter words. Many of these real life events are funnier than good jokes. A few jokes are included too, try to guess which they are. Laugh and enjoy!

"I'd like a glass of Burgundy."

"OK."

After first man leaves, another says to waiter "Son, there was no Burgundy on the menu".

"True. But what I gave him was burgundy colored."

"Let's get out of this bar. I know a place where you can get three drinks free and get laid in the parking lot."

"Wow, how'd you find out about that?"

"My wife told me."

After receiving burned toast for breakfast on a cruise ship, man writes on the next day's breakfast menu "Toasted, not burned."

Worked like a charm. The bread arrived toasted, not burned.

Man arrives at a fancy hotel, spends a week in the honeymoon suite with his young bride, and when checking out asks for – and reluctantly is given – the 10% AARP discount.

Man hands a blind man a piece of matzah. Blind man feels it and says, "Who wrote this crap?"

Gynecologist says to his dentist, "You know, in my field one can never ask patients to open wide."

Dentist replies, "And I can never tell my patients to let their teeth fall apart."

Pig tears down a farmer's fence. He says, "That's one."

Same pig kicks over the trough. Farmer says, "That's two."

Pig knocks over farmer's pail. Farmer says, "That's three" and shoots the pig.

Farmer's wife hears the shot, comes out of the house, and sees what happened.

She shouts, "Why the hell did you shoot the pig?" Farmer says, "That's one."

Man at roadside shop asks saleslady, "How long does it take to get from here to Ft. Collins?"

"Depends how fast you drive."

Menu cover giving location of a Chinese restaurant within walking distance of a Washington, DC tourist attraction: "Two blacks from the National Zoo."

Woman sees the special offer and buys a cupcake at a 2 for 1 sale. She receives three cupcakes. The kid behind the counter explains that she bought one and then he gave her the other two because of the sale.

American lady in France wants a certain cheese for dessert. Wanting "Eppoises" she orders "Epuissee" (exhausted).

Woman says to gardener, "I asked you to spray for scale."

"Yes, but I only had the spray for blight."

Doctor doing camp physicals says to a 10 year old, "Bend over and spread your cheeks."

Boy bends over, places index finger of each hand in his mouth, and pulls them apart.

Doctor tells an 80 year old man that having sex with his young bride could be dangerous.

"Well, if she dies, she dies."

A golfer makes an unusually long drive, and it hits another golfer. The first golfer races to the second in his cart, jumps out, apologizes, and asks, "Did I hit you on the fly?"

"No, on the leg."

First golfer goes back to tell his friends this story. They collapse and roll around on the tee.

Woman tired of coddling of criminals sees headline: "Ohio Governor Clears Death Row".

She is disappointed upon reading the article to learn that 167 people had their sentences commuted instead of being executed.

Hillel said, "If I am not for myself, who is for me? If I am only for myself, what am I? And if not now, when?"

Wife quoted this as, "If not now, when? And if not me, who?"

Just one line: "We're here, ain't I?"

In Paris, an American tells her husband, "I need to buy some mousse for my hair."

Husband says, "Do you know the French word for mousse?"

"I'd like six wings."

"Buffalo or crab?"

"Just chicken please."

Man buying a train ticket is distracted by the breasts of the lady behind the counter, asks for a ticket to Titsburgh instead of Pittsburgh, and embarrassed at his error starts to apologize.

The guy behind him says, "Look fella, don't feel so bad. We all make Freudian slips. Why, just this morning I meant to ask my wife to pass the sugar and instead I said, 'You bitch, you've fucked up my whole life."

A couple's passports are examined by a security agent before leaving Switzerland.

"You don't have the same last name. Are you married?

"No."

"Do you live together?"

"Yes."

"Do you like it?"

In a rural community in North Dakota, a traveler asks at local garage about where he could get breakfast.

He tells his wife, "The guy mumbled that the best place is The Coat of Arms and it's just down the road."

They can't find it until the wife says, "I think I see it. Dakota Farms."

"What does 'eleemosynary' mean?"

"It's Latin for 'pro bono'".

Man asks college-student waiter, "This menu says the steak is served with potatoes Pont Neuf. What is that?"

"I don't know but I'll ask the chef."

A few minutes later, the kid returns and says, "The Pont Neuf is a bridge in Paris."

"I know that son, but what are potatoes Pont Neuf?"

"I have no idea."

Woman buys a new pair of shoes. At home she pulls the box from the bag, and a few minutes later throws the box down her apartment building's trash chute. Unfortunately, she forgot to first remove the shoes.

Sign near the pro shop at a golf resort.

"No clubs, no shoes, no balls – no problem."

Overhead at a restaurant:

"That new Viagra ad is incredibly clever. 'If your erection last more than 4 hours, call your doctor'"

"If my erection lasted more than 4 hours, I wouldn't call my doctor, I'd call the newspapers."

Man in business attire arrives at his hotel in San Francisco after a hair-raising ride from the airport in a taxi driven by an unshaven, drugged-up cabbie wearing a filthy T-shirt and soiled chinos. As they both climb out of the cab, the doorman approaches, ignores the passenger, and says to the driver, "Welcome to the Fairmont."

Couple arrives at Zion National Park during a heavy rainstorm.

At the entrance booth the driver asks the Park Service lady, "What's the chance of rain tomorrow?"

"60%. Today it's 70%."

At a fancy restaurant a man asks the waitress, "Is it really true at all your steaks are Prime?"

"Absolutely. All our meat and seafood are prime."

In the Old City of Jerusalem a driver is struggling to find a parking space. Signs say "No Parking" everywhere, but cars are parked beneath all of them except one.

So the man asks a policeman, "Can I park there?"

The cop says, "No, don't you see the No Parking sign?"

"But what about all these other guys?"

"They didn't ask."

Judge asks, "I see here you've been married for 61 years. And now you want a divorce. Why?"

"We wanted to wait until the children were dead."

Orthopedic surgeon to pretty woman, "You're not old enough to have arthritis." Looks again at her chart. "Yeah, I guess you're old enough. Do you experience morning stiffness?"

"Usually."

"How stiff is it?"

"Mostly 8 to 10".

"How long does the stiffness last?"

"Maybe 30 minutes."

"What do you do to relieve it?"

Woman leaves, hoping to find a doctor who understands double entendre.

Adam is lonely in the Garden, and asks God to fashion a perfect companion for him.

"I CAN DO IT, BUT IT WILL TAKE AN ARM AND A LEG."

"What can you give me for a rib?"

Sign by the road:
Mexican Water Restaurant
Don't Drug and Drive
Crawl-ins Welcome

Little girl is standing at the edge of the Grand Canyon.

Her mother is trying to take a picture and says, "Back up."

"BACK UP?!"

Brazilians don't like their former colonial masters, the Portuguese. Here's a story they told a visiting professor:

"World math contest is held in Portugal before a big crowd. The best Portuguese mathematician is about to be selected, but there is a last question he must answer correctly.

"What is 3 plus 4?" "8"

Crowd yells "Another chance, another chance."

"Let's try 4 plus 2?" "7"

Crowd yells "Another chance, another chance."

"Last try. What is 2 plus 1?" (Thinks hard) "3"

Crowd yells "Another chance, another chance."

At a gas station in rural Colorado, the urinal is so high on the wall that the normal sized man using it has to pee upward.

He comes out and cleverly jokes to lady who owns the station, "You must have had a really tall plumber!"

"Really? Nobody's ever said that to me before."

Man asks the young woman behind a motel desk for the price of a room.

"Sixty-five dollars."

"I'm in AARP. So how much would that be after the discount?"

"I already applied the discount when I saw you walking in."

"Honey, I just heard a funny one. What's the difference between a pussy and a cunt? A pussy is something very nice. A cunt is what owns a pussy. Ha, ha, ha....."

"That's the same as the difference between a dick and a prick."

George Burns was asked by a friend, "George, what does your doctor say about you smoking all those cigars?"

"I don't know, my doctor is dead."

An elderly man is giving out samples of the jam and crackers he is trying to sell in a supermarket in Utah. He's wearing surgical gloves for sanitation.

He then goes toward the toilet. A man and woman are watching him, and the woman says, "I'll bet you he comes out still wearing those gloves." The husband just laughs and says, "You're kidding!"

The man comes out a minute later wearing the gloves, and returns to giving out samples.

The plastic garbage pail was missing. Later it was discovered that a cleaning woman had placed it in the trash compactor.

Sign in a clinic parking area: "Family Planning. Enter in rear."

Country club Merry Christmas bulletin: "The clubhouse and restaurant will close at 2 pm on December 24th so our employees can go to their home and mate."

Woman gets into car and hears a strange voice. "Powering off."

Later, a crushed Bluetooth speaker is found on the driver's seat. Those were its last words.

These events led to serious consideration of reporting a new disease, ADAIS: Acoustic Disorientation and Anal Insensitivity Syndrome.

An American in Paris, who speaks just a little French, notices the sign "Cireur" near a public toilet. He remembers this a few days later as he develops early symptoms of diarrhea while wandering around the city. "Ou est le cireur?" he asks a passerby, and is greeted with a blank stare. His symptoms get worse, and he asks the same question again, now pretty desperate to find the place. "C'est urgent, pressante, ou est le cireur?!" The second Frenchman ignores him as a lunatic. Almost doubled up with cramps, he finally finds the Cireur ------ only to discover this word means "Shoe Shine" (from "cirer", "to wax"). The nearby urinoir unfortunately lacked booths for people with diarrhea.

Sign in a public restroom: "Toilet Broken. Please Use Floor Below."

During an interview, a professional basketball player agreed the performance of his team was poor.
"Yep, the ship be sinking."
"How low can it go?"
"The sky's the limit."

Only 8 of the above brilliancies are jokes, the rest are real. If you bought this as a new book at full price and send me a letter with a prepaid stamped envelope bearing your return address I will tell you which ones they are. My personal favorite is perhaps the last, since its final lines are applicable to so many things that seem to happen in the world - "How low can it go? The sky's the limit."

The Unprotected

There is no need to wonder what happens in an unarmed community without effective police. The world is full of many examples, and so is America.

Stalin, that evil genius, understood it well. Read, if you can stand doing so, Solzhenitsyn's "Gulag", Vassily Grossman's "Forever Flowing", Shalamov's "Kolyma Tales", or "Kolyma - The Arctic Death Camps" by Robert Conquest. It's simple really. Take some normal people, say a group of political prisoners or other alleged enemies of the state, and pen them up with real criminals. Tell the guards to look the other way. The criminals take over. They intimidate, shake down, torture, and kill the normal people. They also kill some of themselves. But the criminals control the prison. Fear, violence, and death become the daily way of life for everyone. Of course, forced labor, intense cold, and semi-starvation added to the miseries in the Gulag, and were additional factors making life there a living hell. But all you really needed was to throw together criminals and ordinary people and walk away. Stalin - a gangster, murderer, and bank robber long before he took over the USSR - proved this with millions of victims.

Author Philip Roth gives some examples from our own country. Read "American Pastoral". One of Roth's characters describes what happened in Newark, New Jersey about 30 years ago in a neighborhood formerly populated by immigrants and small businesses: "The major industry now is car theft...... [and] the worst kind of hatred in the world. A car is coming the wrong way on a one way street and they ram me. Four kids drooping out the windows. Two of them get out laughing, joking, and point a gun at my head. I hand over the keys and one of them takes my car. They ram cop cars in broad daylight. Every heard of doughnuting? They steal the car, top speed, slam on the brakes, yank the emergency brake, twist the steering wheel, and the car starts spinning. Wheeling the car in circles at tremendous speeds. Killing pedestrians means nothing to them. Killing motorists means nothing to them. Killing themselves means nothing to them. They killed a woman right in front of our place, same week they stole my car. Doing a doughnut. I witnessed this. It made my blood run cold. The car groaning. Ungodly screeching. Just driving her own car out of 2nd Street, and the woman, young black woman, gets it. Mother of three kids. Two days later it's one of my own employees. A black guy. But they don't care, black, white, doesn't matter to them. They'll kill anyone."

If you think this didn't happen in American cities 30 years ago maybe you weren't alive then, or at least sentiently alive. Maybe you also don't remember how major parts of several inner cities including Washington, DC were torched by some of these nice folks. Maybe you don't know that in my own company the boyfriend of one of our black secretaries was killed in a drive-by shooting, and a black contract worker - a painter and one of the nicest guy in the world - was choked to death when, over the weekend, he tried to break up a fight in a DC slum between two of his crazed neighbors. Maybe you never talked to the fireman in Tampa who told me that when his fire truck was racing to put out a blaze crowds would gather to block the truck from reaching the burning building - and this happened many times. Maybe you don't know, or maybe you forgot, that in our inner cities about 90% of murders of black people are committed by other blacks - not by the police, but by vicious black criminals. And the bad guys do a pretty good job killing each other too. My wife found an article in a major newspaper which disclosed that in Baltimore, one of the murder capitals of America, the average number of prior arrests of the murder victims in that city was 13.

Yes, things were that bad not so long ago and many believed they could only get worse. Then some brilliant people started to work out ways to make them better. The size of police forces was increased. NY Police Chief William Bratton, Mayor Rudolf Giuliani, and others showed in practice that the Broken Windows theory works - arrest the turnstile jumpers, the bums who harass normal people on the street, prevent crime, put police back in the neighborhoods where they are needed, empower then to stop and search people behaving suspiciously, monitor the success of police in preventing crimes as well as catching criminals, bear in mind that the bad guys committing "minor" crimes are often the same committing the worst ones, and that criminal acts are often repeated by the same perpetrators. And it worked. The violent crime rate in New York City during the 1990s was driven down to less than 50% of what it had been. The homicide rate fell by 73% between 1990 and 1999. Arrests went up, and crime went down. Many of the bad guys were taken off the streets, out of the parks, out of the lives of normal people and into the prisons where they belong. This success was copied with similar results in many other cities. The biggest beneficiaries of this progress were the people who lived in the worst neighborhoods where most crimes are committed - poor people, black people, Hispanic people, working class people.

This remarkable progress is in danger of being lost due to recent political pressures to weaken America's law enforcement in the name of avoiding "police brutality", unreasonable searches, etc. (the Ferguson effect). The murder rate in Chicago, in New York, and in many other cities has risen sharply in the past year. The data are there for anyone to examine. The police are retreating, at least for the time being, and the bad guys are winning, at least also for the time being.

Many responsible reporters and others are describing these events and their consequences, perhaps none better than Heather McDonald of the Manhattan Institute's City Journal. If you haven't read what McDonald has to say, check out some of her writings. And thankfully she is not alone.

Yes, black lives do matter. And the way to save them, and non-black lives too, is to have an effective police presence to protect the law-abiding from violent criminals. If you live in Scarsdale, in Bethesda, in McLean, in Palo Alto, or dock your sailboat in Sausalito none of this is likely to make a personal difference to you. You, and I too, are what commentator Peggy Noonan recent called "The Protected". But not all are so well protected. The people who will be hurt, hurt a lot and killed a lot too, if the police withdraw even partially from the battle against vicious criminals will mostly be the poor, the weak, women, and people of color. These must not be allowed to become America's criminally unprotected.

Oklahoma Cops and Other Tales

My wife and I have traveled extensively, mostly by car, in the varied vastness of these United States and have now visited every state including Alaska and Hawaii. America defies generalizations, and the incredible contrasts between, say, Washington and Florida, or Maine and Arizona defy summarization. We offer here just a tiny assortment of mostly humorous and seemingly informative moments from our travels.

Our sampler begins with Oklahoma. We have driven across this large state, which is 464 miles east to west (and west to east too) several times. It's a long uncrowded drive mostly on I-40, enjoyable in good weather. Naturally, one is inclined to want to cover many miles when driving here and the faster one goes the more miles one covers. Which reminds me of the time I asked a lady in Colorado how long it would take to get from her jam store to Fort Collins. Her reply was, "Depends how fast you go."

Anyway, we were driving about 80 mph across Oklahoma and a police car maliciously hidden behind a shrub in the median pulled out after us. The blue lights flashed and I pulled over. Oklahoma is different than most states in that the cop invites you into his car while he checks your license and registration. In this case there was one policeman doing the talking, and another sitting silently in the back seat. At some point the officer asked me what type of work I did. I said I was a physician with a special interest in genetics. His eyes lit up and he said, "Boy am I glad to meet you. I have a child with a rare genetic disease." He then proceeded to ask me many, many questions about the illness his kid had, and I gave him a lot of information since I actually was an expert on this particular disorder. We spent over 20 minutes on these personal questions and answers. I figured that the outcome of this would be a warning, rather than a citation - and maybe even a thank you. Instead after all this he wrote out a ticket and I later paid his town about $150. But that is not the end. A couple of years later, I was stopped in almost the same place by another policeman. I knew the drill, and he seems like a rather nice guy. So I said to him, "I hope you won't mind if I tell you a little story. A few years ago, I was stopped near here by another policeman who found out I was a medical geneticist and who spent about a half an hour asking - and me answering - all kinds of questions about his child with a genetic illness. He then gave me a ticket anyway. I hope you will be nicer to me than he was." This cop had a sense of humor. He smiled and said, "I will be. I won't ask you any questions about genetics." He then wrote out a ticket dinging me $188 for going 1-10 miles over the speed limit.

Let's now go on our magic carpet to New Haven, CT, the home of Yale University, an acme of wisdom and scholarship. Its students are all brilliant, its faculty peerless (or so they say). Across the street from the Yale campus is a collection of restaurants, and at dinnertime we entered a rather attractive French one located in a former mansion. It was mid-summer, and the waiter was obviously a kid from Yale doing a summer job. After studying the menu, I was thinking of ordering the steak, but it was accompanied by something called "potatoes Pont Neuf". So I asked the waiter, "What are potatoes Pont Neuf?" He said that he didn't know, but he would find out. He came back from the kitchen and said, "The Pont Neuf is a bridge in Paris." Trying to keep a straight face, I replied something like, "I know that, son! What I am trying to find out is "What are "potatoes Pont Neuf?" To which the kid's brilliant response was, "I have no idea."

In case you're curious, I ordered the dish and the item in question was a stack of pommes frites (better known in New Haven as French fries) arranged in a little tower that was supposed to represent a pillar of the bridge.

I can't help relating another travel story that happened on a cross-country flight some years ago, and it involves - you guessed it - the state that Huckleberry Finn so admired. In business class, occupying the aisle seat next to me was a man who appeared to be in his 70s. He said nothing to me, and consumed a bourbon before the plane took off. He had a second one not long thereafter, and began on his third. He then leaned forward, pulled out from his briefcase a book entitled "The History of Arkansas", and began to read. The man looked familiar to me, and then I knew. So I said to him, "Excuse me, sir, but are you by any chance the former Senator from the great state of Arkansas?" He put down the book, looked at me, and J. W. Fulbright began to talk. Well liquored up by this time, he spoke freely about himself. He was retired from the Senate, and earning money as a representative of the Arab oil interests. At some point, Ronald Reagan was mentioned, and then his comments turned nasty. He made no effort to disguise his hatred for Reagan. And he memorably said to me in a thick Southern drawl, "That's what happens when you let a cowboy (which he pronounced like cow baw), an ignorant cowboy, become President of the United States!" After a while, he drifted off into sleep leaving me with the strong impression that he was one of meanest SOBs I'd met in my life.

Parenthetically, it may be of some minor interest that the very last of the 50 states we chose to visit was

Arkansas, which we had always avoided for much the same reasons as Huck, and because I wasn't sure I could figure out the meaning of "is". But in the end, the wonderful Crystal Bridges Museum of American Art in Bentonville, AK became so strong an attraction that we caved in. This truly amazing museum - masterpiece after masterpiece - proves that even today it is possible to create a world-class museum through a combination of limitless wealth (Alice Walton) and excellent taste (former National Gallery of Art Chairman John Wilmerding, and Walton too).

Now on to Florida. And this story is moving rather than funny. In fact it involved my mother's funeral near Fort Lauderdale. My mother was Jewish and born in 1910 in the immigrant ghetto on the lower East Side of Manhattan. She died at the age of 102, and had been cared for in her own home for many years by a principal caregiver and four assistant caretakers. All were black women from Jamaica, and very likely illegal immigrants. The funeral service for my mother was held in a Jewish chapel, and was attended by several family members. Remarkably, all the women who had been paid to help to look after my mother also showed up, plus another 7-8 of their friends. The service was initiated by a rabbi, who in a pre-conference meeting confided that he had become a rabbi because he couldn't get into medical school. After the rabbi finished, I had the honor to invite each member of the family to follow me to the podium to say a few words about my mother. They each did so, and tears began to flow from the listeners. But after the family members completed their eulogies, unexpectedly the first of the black women arose to speak with remarkable eloquence about my mother for perhaps 15 minutes. She was followed by each of the others, including some who had only been secondary assistants to the other caregivers. Each of them found something kind and admiring to say about Miriam. For the finale, also unanticipated by me or other family members, a Jamaican woman walked before us and began to sing Gospel songs in a most wonderful voice. She was a Sunday singer at her church, and she had a blessed musical gift. Her performance lasted several minutes and the audience members abandoned themselves to crying. So my Jewish mother was sung to her grave by a Jamaican woman inspired by the Gospels! It was a profoundly moving and unforgettable experience.

Let's go from Florida to Alaska. I was invited to join a fishing expedition near Lake Clark, about 100 miles west of Anchorage, by the head of a Christian organization known as "World Vision". Our donations to this charity had provide medical education for a promising young man in Columbia, and created wells with clean water for several villages in sub-Saharan Africa.

I flew to Anchorage a day before the rest of the group, had thought about renting a car to see a bit of Alaska on my own, and so went into a store in the airport to buy a road map. The shop girl said, "There is not much point in buying a map, Alaska has only three roads." Assuming she was joking, I bought one anyway and upon reaching my hotel room discovered that she had not been exaggerating. Anchorage is pretty small, and there is only one main road that leaves the town. It was a long way to Denali and the weather was bad (as it usually is, even in August), so I holed up in the hotel until the others arrived. Next morning, we boarded two chartered airplanes for our flight to the camp near Lake Clark. The arrival runway on was unpaved and barely wide enough for the aircraft to land between (and over) talk evergreen trees. The next day several of us boarded a one-engine De Havilland pontoon "Beaver" to take us to a river where the salmon were running. The aircraft's one engine ran so roughly that I actually feared to let it take off with us on board. The joy stick had part of its controls affixed with silvery duct tape. Miraculously, we became airborne and landed safely. In disembarking I stepped off a pontoon into a soft muddy bottom and badly twisted my left knee. I spent the rest of the week in considerable pain while my colleagues ignored me and happily went fishing.

And I was not the only casualty. A day later the same De Havilland took off carrying 9 people to fish another river; I remained safely in my bunk with my bad knee, trying to grin and bear it. The fishermen returned a couple of hours later and told me that as the aircraft left Lake Clark and headed toward the mountains its sputtering engine died. The good Christians on board burst into prayer as the plane began its untimely descent toward the trackless marshy vastness. One of the men told me he had never heard such praying in his life. The pilot turned the plane while gliding it down, and it just barely got back over the lake and plunked safely on the water. Nor was this near mass fatality the end of our Alaskan air adventures. A longer flight using two twin-engine aircraft was planned for us to go to another river to catch more salmon. I was sufficiently recovered by now to try a little fishing myself. Our plane got through without difficulty, but on the other aircraft a side door near the back of the plane popped open in flight! The aircraft suddenly tipped sideways almost 90 degrees. Fortunately, the man sitting next to the door had his seat belt on or he would surely have been swept out. Two other men managed to crawl toward the open door, and with great difficulty hauled it closed using a chain to which its open end was attached.

Even that is not the end of the Alaskan aircraft saga. Both twin engine planes were needed to take us back to Anchorage, along with some dead salmon that a church-going amateur taxidermist in the group offered to preserve for us. I refused to board the aircraft with the defective door, even though someone claimed it had been fixed. As I sat in the other airplane, I watched the aircraft with the door that had "been fixed" preparing to take off ahead of us. I actually saw a man approach the plane with a rubber mallet and, while the engines were turning, hammer the door repeatedly to, presumably, make it less likely to open again in flight. But the plane I was on had its own issue, not discovered until after it took off. The pilot of this plane for the prior several days had been from the lower 48, he told me he wanted to try flying a little in Alaska just for one summer, and he also said that the pilots who flew year-round in Alaska were "crazy" - and of course he was right. This pilot had been replaced by a madman jockey to take us back to Anchorage. In flight this lunatic informed us that to save time we were taking a "shorter" route back than the circuitous flight around the mountains which we had initially used to arrive at Lake Clark - we were now going to fly over the mountains. What he failed to say was that the mountains were near the maximum altitude of which the loaded plane was capable, the aircraft had no radar, and we had a cloud ceiling of about 6,000 feet. As the aircraft ascended blindly into the clouds and toward the mountains I felt that my life had a significant probability of ending prematurely. As we approached the apex, the cloud cover opened up momentarily and I watched with horror as we barely skimmed over the rocks and shrubs on the mountaintop. I silently cursed the pilot who had stupidly exposed all of us to this needless risk.

A friend who is an expert on air traffic control has confirmed that Alaska is the scene of innumerable air fatalities due to many factors including poor runways, inadequate navigation and radar systems, crazy pilots, drugs, alcohol - and above all, the weather. But there are indeed almost no roads in Alaska, the size and wildness of the place have to be seen to be believed, and so if you want to get around the interior of Alaska you pretty much have to fly. My advice is to skip doing any of it, and buy your salmon in a grocery store.

Oh, what about my pink salmon trophy? Well, I heard nothing about this dead fish for a year or so, and got no replies from inquiries to the taxidermist in Mississippi. Then without warning, it arrived at my home in Washington in a crate - C.O.D.! Without advance notice I barely had the cash available to make the necessary payment. The guy did a nice job on my fish, although it isn't the same size as the fish I gave him - but who can tell "his salmon" from someone else's? The stuffed and rather fierce creature now arches over a doorway in my home in Maryland, and is a souvenir that I can look at whenever my knee aches or I am tempted to go salmon fishing. As for flying again in Alaska I can't even imagine a reason to again do something that dumb.

So now to Pennsylvania, home state of my dear wife. She had some distressing osteoarthritis in her fingers and thumbs and so went to see a noted orthopedist at the Hospital of the University of Pennsylvania. University hospitals have surgical trainees, who are already medical school graduates, interview patients who are to be treated by the more senior physicians; and these trainees also assist the senior surgeons during operative procedures. So at Penn the following exchange took place between the surgeon-in-training and my wife. As you read this and note the man's inability to perceive double meanings, please bear in mind - out of respect for the rest of the medical profession - that orthopedic surgeons are usually jocks from the bottom third of their medical school classes.

"You seem too young to have arthritis." [Then looks at her chart] "Oh, you're old enough!"

Wife is silent. Doctor-trainee looks at x-rays and sees she indeed has arthritis.

"Do you experience morning stiffness?" Note that he didn't ask what was being stiff.

"Yes, regularly."

"Please rate the degree of stiffness on a scale of 1 to 10."

"It varies."

"How long does the stiffness last?"

"About 30 minutes."

"Is there anything you do that relieves the stiffness?"

"That also varies." She is trying to keep a straight face.

Then the senior doctor enters and this hilariously unwitting exchange ended. The senior then injects one of Dixie's thumbs with a steroid, and asks her how uncomfortable it was.

"OK. Not too bad."

The trainee then added, "Well, the next one's going to hurt a lot more."

To which my wife replied, "You didn't have to say that!"

After which the senior surgeon turned to him and said, "She's right!!"

And so it went at a famous university hospital.

We now make our last magic carpet journey, for the moment, to Ocean City, Maryland in the summer of 2016. This substantial oceanfront community and tourist center is on one of the many barrier islands along the Atlantic coastline. Ocean City has an amusement park, a boardwalk several miles long, a fishing pier extending far out into the sea, numerous hotels and restaurants, an amazing display of gigantic kites from one concessionaire, and remarkably wide, well-maintained, clean sandy beaches. There are thousands of visitors on every summer day. The population of boardwalk strollers and beachgoers is highly varied, or to use the modern jargon "diverse". Many are teenagers, the girls wearing tiny bikinis and sometimes joining the guys in beach volleyball. At least one-third of the visitors are black, and it is hard to find any ethnic group not substantially represented here. People come to Ocean City mostly from Washington, DC, Baltimore, Wilmington, and Philadelphia, with some from Richmond and even from New York City. As Ocean City is less than a two hour drive from our home on Maryland's Eastern Shore, we make day trips to it from time to time to enjoy the sun, the surf, the breeze, and the ultra-casual ambience.

As we strolled along the boardwalk and scanned the T-shirts and decals hung in front of its many shops, we were struck by something quite amazing. There were hundreds of them carrying the name of Trump, often accompanied by representations of the American flag, some saying "Make America Great Again" or "Obama, You're Fired". There was NOT ONE shop that displayed EVEN ONE pro-Hillary shirt or other object. Nor did we see ANY worn by people during our several hours at Ocean City. The only Hillary display we observed, offered in several shops, featured an unflattering image of her face with the text "I suck too."

This Ocean City T-shirt poll taken in one of the most Democrat-leaning states in America, strongly suggested to us that Donald Trump would be the next President of the United States. Our observations there seemed consistent with what we sensed in many other parts of America when we drove cross country in 2016. Alas, we didn't bet on the election outcome despite seeing all this and understanding the statistical limits on the reliability of current methods of professional polling.

Let's Follow the Money

And let's use data and quotes from a September 21, 2016 Wall Street Journal article by reporter James Grimaldi. Bill Clinton gets paid $250,000 to give a one hour lecture at a U.S. charitable foundation set up by a business - Firmenich International SA. Clinton reports the income on his tax return as an honorarium, and assuming he pays about a 40% income tax rate nets about $150,000 for that one hour. The U.S. government receives close to $100,000 in tax.

Firmenich, like other corporations, can deduct from its income - as an expense on IRS form 1120 - the full amount of its donations to a charity (up to a limit of 10% of its earnings ignoring the effect of the deduction). $250,000 won't come close to exceeding that limit for "one of the world's largest fragrance and flavoring suppliers". Firmenich is a private company headquartered in Geneva, and according to Google Finance has an estimated 14 % of world market share for its products. It has annual revenues estimated by Hoover's at over $3 billion, and as a private company does not publicly report its income. It undoubtedly has a U.S. subsidiary whose earnings are offset by the deduction, or another means to claim the charitable deduction. Assume its corporate tax rate is about 35%, so the $250,000 that went to Firmenich's foundation and then on to Clinton cost Firmenich about $162,000 and cost the U.S. government nearly $88,000 in reduced tax receipts from Firmenich's U.S. operations.

In addition, Firmenich's foundation contributed "about $250,000" to "plant thousands of dollars of lime trees" in Haiti, "a project designed to help both the impoverished farmers and the perfume and beverage industries which had been hurt by a spike in lime prices". This money went partly to a Haitian unit of the Clinton Foundation and the remainder to "a charity recruited for the project that works with the Clinton Foundation in Haiti". Firmenich's second $250,000 is also deductible against its earnings costing the company about another $162,000, and the U.S. government another $88,000.

Of Firmenich's charitable donation, the part that went to the special Haitian unit of Clinton Foundation is unlikely to have been fully paid out to Haitian farmers - surely some was consumed in Foundation expenses, administration of the project, etc. It is virtually certain, given the endemic corruption in Haiti, that the other charities chosen ("recruited") to assist the project, the tree suppliers selected, even the workers and their bosses picked to get paid on the project kicked back some of the money to the Clinton Foundation or to Firmenich. How the money moved around in Haiti is currently unknown, so can only be guessed at. What is certain however is that Firmenich gained reputationally from its "help" to the "impoverished" Haitian lime farmers, and financially - though indirectly - by reducing the price of limes for its fragrances, etc. through creating thousands of new lime trees. In addition, when Firmenich needs a favor from the United States government in the future, the Clintons will be there to help.

So now let's do the math:

Clinton personally: +$250,000 - $100,000 = +$150,000 gain

Clinton Foundation: +$250,000 - $X (money expended on the project) + $Y (kickbacks). Best guess is that the foundation came out ahead by at least +$50,000. It also get praised for helping poor Haitians, and presumably it did help some of them though nobody knows who and by how much since the money can't be or in any case is not yet followable.

Firmenich's after-tax cost of its payments to their speaker plus its donations to his foundation total about $335,000. That is what the company paid for enhancing its reputation, cheapening the price of one of their necessary supplies (limes), and currying favor with U.S. politicians for help to their business now and in the future. My guess is they made a good investment, and in some manner they will ultimately recover at the least the cost of their payments. The most conservative number realistic for their long-term economics is probably a wash: = +$0. And they are almost sure to find a way to improve that number into a net benefit.

U.S. government: -$176,000 + $100,000 = -$76,000 loss, with no offsetting benefit unless Firmenich's earnings reported on future U.S. tax returns grow somewhat from the lime project.

So the politician personally comes out ahead by $150,000 for an hour of his time, instead of doing the unthinkable - simply giving his talk free as his personal contribution to the Firmenich Foundation. The Clinton Foundation grows. Firmenich SA is likely to benefit by at least as much as it expended. And the U.S. government loses money. Some Haitians were helped, but it may be doubted if the "poor farmers" actually received as much money as the U.S. government lost or by which Clinton got richer.

In contrast to all the above, Firmenich could simply have directly spent $250,000 for planting lime trees in

Haiti, deducted the cost as a business expense, and been out -$162,000 or so after taxes. But then the only offsetting benefit to them would have been lower cost for limes, without gaining U.S. political influence. Alternatively, in theory they could have done nothing in Haiti and just paid $250,000 to hear the speech and gain influence, and tried to deduct this as a business expense. But it is unlikely that such an extravagant fee would be considered by IRS to have a legitimate business purpose (hence potentially not be deductible against earnings), it would do nothing for Firmenich's reputation or their cost of limes, and of course it would be obvious to all that the ex-President was just being bought. So the foundation route appeared preferable to both of them.

This is just an instructive example of what goes in a society where individuals and corporations pay taxes, but foundations, universities, not-for-profit hospitals, and other tax-exempt organizations (some of which pay their CEOs several million dollars a year) do not. And it also illustrates how the game is played in Washington, DC through which flows about $3 TRILLION dollars of other people's money each year. To use the analogy from Tom Wolfe's immortal "Bonfire of the Vanities", when cutting a cake of that size many large crumbs fall off it. And some of those crumbs are used to pay, and pay well, for political influence.

The corrupt boss of a Mexican state was quoted a few years ago as saying: "A politician who is poor is a poor politician." How true it is!

The God of Free Trade

As a non-professional in economics I offer here some heterodox thoughts about free trade. These will doubtless be criticized by some "real" economists. But since the largest employer of "real" economists is the government and I don't work (except when I pay taxes) for the government, here goes anyway. My basic conclusion, to be amplified below, is that no country in the world practices complete free trade, and indeed most countries are very far from that conformist ideal. So to paraphrase Jean-Jacques Rousseau, whose unproven assertions caused major adverse consequences, "If trade is born free, why is it everywhere in chains?" The answer: there are many good reasons as well as some bad ones.

The economic theory of free trade was in large part developed by David Ricardo, born in 1772 in London, and Frederic Bastiat, a Frenchman born in Bayonne (France, not New Jersey) in 1801. Their several books are necessary reading for anyone interested in economics, and I have particularly enjoyed much of Bastiat. The basic idea behind free trade is "comparative advantage". Imagine country A, an island with a climate rather good for growing pineapples but almost entirely deficient in coal deposits, and country B which has lots of coal but is far too cold to farm pineapples. A has a comparative advantage in pineapples, and B is advantaged in coal. So it makes economic sense, according to Ricardo, Bastiat, and me too, that A should grow pineapples and exchange them with B for coal rather than for A and B to each attempt to become self-sufficient in the production of both pineapples and coal. The basic idea then is that each country should identify the mix of products best suited to its conditions, maximize their production, and utilize trade to exchange them for the needed products of other countries.

Of course, in the real world such a decision has limitations as well as advantages. What happens in country A if country C starts selling pineapples at half the price A offers? C may have a better climate or soil for pineapple production. Or C may be deep in the third world with extremely low labor costs. Or C may control its exchange rate to make its products cheaper for export, while limiting the buying power of its own people. What can A do to prevent a collapse of its economy? It's hard to find a good solution for its population. A can try to become more efficient in growing pineapples, perhaps by borrowing or using earnings to mechanize its pineapple plantations (this is called capital investment). A can educate its workers to make something else (this is called retraining) - although what that something else would be is not simple to figure out. Furthermore it will not be easy - and may be impossible - to retrain all of A's pineapple farm workers to become software engineers, or even coal miners. But, say the economists, they will figure something out since starvation is an unappealing alternative.

Furthermore, say the economists, even though A experiences a tragic contraction due to C's appearance in the pineapple market, the world's people are better off because they can buy pineapples, to quote Walmart, "for less". More precisely, they can shop for pineapples "for less" provided they have kept their own jobs. If not, they can get retrained in their turn, or maybe go on the dole and be supported by their lucky co-citizens who haven't (or haven't yet) lost their jobs to country D.

The point of this little thought experiment is not that free trade is good or bad, but that it's a very complicated issue with aspects both good and bad.

The economic orthodoxy in favor a free trade is based in part on a particular interpretation of history: mercantilism was wrong and needed to be replaced by an alternative. Mercantilism was the dominant trade system of the 19th century. Most history books describe mercantilism with its protectionist elements for domestic industries as an antiquated, flawed economic system now abandoned for something better. But Great Britain did very well indeed and became the world's leading manufacturer under mercantilism. Its best known economist, the Scotsman Adam Smith, actually earned a living as a supervisor of tariffs. The 19th century expansion of the American economy which embraced tariffs and many other mercantilist elements was breathtaking. Was mercantilism really the abject failure it is often considered today? Not in the opinion of many businessmen who, after all, earn their living in the real world. One of my friends, alas now deceased, who had been the head of European operations for a huge international company headquartered in the U.S. was strongly in favor of tariffs - and he was far from alone in this opinion.

The ghost of Smoot-Hawley is invoked whenever deviations from free trade are proposed. For those too young to remember, Smoot and Hawley were politicians who encouraged an expansion (not the inception) of American tariffs on imported goods to protect employment as jobs were lost during the first years of the Great Depression which began in 1929-1930. Reciprocal tariffs by other countries followed, and the dogma - and perhaps the reality - is that this made the Depression worse. But it is also worth remembering that America had reinstituted tariffs in 1922, well before Smoot-Hawley, and the subsequent Roaring Twenties were marked by major economic expansion in the U.S. and many other countries. Smoot and Hawley, nor Herbert Hoover, did not cause the stock market crash that started the Depression. The great American economist, Milton Friedman, and his eminent collaborator, Anna Schwartz, in their landmark "Monetary History of the United States" attribute the Depression primarily to mistaken monetary tightening by the Federal Reserve, an error that Ben Bernanke was determined not to repeat in 2009. Economist Barry Eichengreen considers the difficulties in the 1930s to be worsened by the gold standard which his book called "fetters of gold". Even today economists debate what caused and what ended the Great Depression. Some people attribute the amelioration of the Depression to the trial-and-error economic policies and government programs of the Roosevelt administration. In contrast, other students of the Depression feel that going off the gold standard and then expansion of production for World War II were the major factors which terminated America's worst decade of mass unemployment.

Still, free trade helps the American consumer. Many products now available at bargain prices from Walmart, Amazon.com, and elsewhere would surely cost more if a larger proportion of the products or their components were made in the U.S. So as a consumer with a reliable income I count myself among the free trade winners. Most of you reading this analysis are as well. But now let's ask: "How would you feel about paying lower prices for certain products if the same policies that facilitated this made you LOSE YOUR JOB?" Maybe a way to bring the importance of that question home is to imagine that ALL jobs in the United States were opened up completely to full foreign competition. Academicians would have to compete on an equal basis with professors in India teaching classes and granting identical undergraduate and graduate level degrees via internet education. Research grants from the National Institutes of Health, National Science Foundation, and all other funding sources would be offered to scientists from every country in the world on the identical basis to American university faculty. Using telemedicine and nursing assistants, American physicians would compete for their bread and butter (and their spouses' Gucci bags) with doctors in Europe, Asia, and elsewhere on an absolutely equal basis and American insurers including the U.S. government would pay American doctor just like such foreign doctors. Lawyers would compete with foreign lawyers trained abroad in American law and certified to practice law in the U.S. through the internet. Teachers in our secondary schools would be competing for employment with teachers in Australia or Ireland granting elementary and high school diplomas after internet classes. Obviously if such things happened and caused massive job losses and fee retrenchments in the professional classes, the revolt against free trade would go far beyond what some elitists call the Rust Belt. Millions of unemployed or barely employed doctors, lawyers, schoolteachers, professors, researchers, and their like might well change their minds about the glories of free trade.

What if the one-seventh of all U.S. jobs, those of government workers, were to be outsourced (except for a small number of very high security jobs like those at the CIA or the Pentagon) to foreign countries? Would government workers, including government economists, still vote for free trade?

What if the massive American defense industry was forced to deal with full foreign competition after careful security screening? How would so-called educated workers at General Dynamics or Boeing feel about having our nation's latest aircraft, both civilian and military, manufactured abroad by non-American companies?

Here's a real life story. One of my relatives is a gifted hardware engineer who worked for IBM. He supervised a large team of about 900 employees. Some years ago when Lou Gerstner was making IBM shareholders happy, the word came down that IBM management was going to fire all of his 900 U.S. workers and send my relative to China (with his family, and where he didn't want to go) to train hundreds of Chinese to take over their jobs. The result was that 900 Americans lost their jobs and my relative left IBM. How would you like it if you were one of the 900, while economists drawing stable salaries from Big Government and shareholders collecting dividends told you this was necessary for the greater good of the United States?

As for countries other than the United States supposedly embracing free trade, nothing could be farther from reality. France protects its agriculture, Germany its car industry. Airbus gets help from European governments. Do you think American companies can compete in Japan on a level playing field? As for China, it is a trade manipulator, a currency manipulator, confiscates businesses built in China by American companies ranging from giants like Chrysler to small entities, while abused foreign companies get no help from the Chinese legal system nor, for that matter, from our own government. As for China tariffs, if you want to import a $65,000 BMW into China you pay an import duty of 25%, VAT of 17%, consumption tax of 25%, and parcel tax rate of 30%, which aggregates with offsets to a landed cost of $85,500 for an effective tariff rate of 31%. As for currency manipulation, as China moved out of its Maoist period to greater development its currency should have appreciated against the dollar but the Chinese government instead depreciated its currency to help Chinese exporters sell "for less" while impoverishing the ability of its citizenry to acquire products from the United States and other countries.

Free trade worldwide doesn't exist, despite the myths about it to which many American reporters and press editors seem addicted. Expect to be exposed to more ignorant articles as well as intentional disinformation about free trade in the future.

Theorists in favor of free trade for goods often also favor free trade in people - unlimited migration across national borders, such as what is going on in the European Union. Sensibly controlled immigration is a huge advantage to the U.S. bringing into our society large numbers of the world's most energetic and talented people - nearly one million of them per year. But UNLIMITED immigration - what illegal U.S. immigration really is - is another story. My California plumber is Hispanic, about 40 years old, and recently started his own small business. He was born in the U.S. to parents who were legal immigrants from Mexico. He spoke to me spontaneously about immigration right after the November, 2016 elections. His view was that illegal immigration from Mexico must not be allowed to continue. Why would he say this? Actually most Americans have immigrant ancestors or are themselves legal immigrants and in my personal experience they generally oppose unlimited illegal immigration. Furthermore, illegal immigrants are potential competitors for Mr. Perez - they will work "for less", and are threats to his income and the very survival of his business. In addition, some of the illegal immigrants are criminals or otherwise destructive elements in the largely blue-collar desert community where he and his family can afford to live.

So who wins big from illegal immigration? It's people like me. When I hired a company to repair my driveway, I did it "for less" because some of the non-English-speaking workers used by the bilingual contractor doubtless were illegals. My gardening costs are reduced because of the mix of legal and illegal workers, and I don't and can't tell them apart. Same goes for taking care of my pool, and many other things too. And no illegals, criminal or otherwise, live anywhere near me. This is why many wealthy people vote for a continuation of the status quo. And the most cynical of them don't even care if illegals illegally vote or don't pay taxes as long as they are available for cheap labor.

A few years ago, my wife and I stayed at the Greenbrier resort in While Sulphur Springs, West Virginia. It's a large fancy place that claims to have its humble beginnings in 1778. A public room that used to be its library had become a display area showing a collection of photographs at the Greenbrier the 1930s. These hundred or so black and white images made an unforgettable impression on me. One showed GM's elegantly attired CEO, Albert P. Sloan, Jr., strolling with Henry Ford. There were pictures of large marriage parties, lovely women beautifully dressed in white outfits playing golf, tennis, or croquet, formal dinners and dances, fancy cars - all the many manifestations of affluence and happiness at the Greenbrier. And this was in the midst of the Great Depression! At the very same time nearly 25 % of Americans were unemployed. My own parents, coming out of college in about 1931, could not get a job and my mother waited 5 years - living in her parent's home - for a part-time position as an elementary school teacher in Brooklyn, NY. Meanwhile my father, with a law degree and an M.B.A., could not find steady work until AT&T hired him in 1940 after America's entry into World War II seemed inevitable.

Yes, it was doubtless wonderful to have a job, to have money, to be able to live the good life in the 1930s. Everything was cheap, whatever you wanted could be bought "for less" than during the booming 1920s. And why not enjoy yourself? How would it help if you didn't spend money having a good time at a hotel, a party, a speakeasy? You hadn't caused the depression and you couldn't make it go away. You felt sorry, at least a little, for the poor bastards who couldn't find work but at least you were helping to give some of them jobs while you lived well. What else should you do?

The next time you go shopping think about the man or woman who isn't there alongside you, who is out of work because of free trade. Free trade is a slogan, and despite the dogma it's both good and bad and can never be fully realized. Trade, as its very name suggests, necessarily involves tradeoffs and negotiated deals. Robert Heinlein famously acronymed TINSTAAFL - "there is no such thing as a free lunch". I now suggest TINSTAAFL - "there is no such thing as all free trade."

To get a further perspective on this issue and on our country, I suggest taking some time to leave your coastal suburb or university community and visit the real America, that oft-forgotten region occupying approximately 3,500,000 square miles between the eastern shores of San Francisco Bay or Puget Sound and the western edge of the Hudson River or Boston harbor. Coastal elites seem to believe that inhabitants in this negligible realm are mostly insignificant boobs, low information left-behind white males with dumpy half-enslaved wives, except for those who live in the small college towns where Obama 2012 bumper stickers still exist. It ain't so. The elites are wrong. Throughout America you will find millions and millions of people worthy of appreciation and respect. They aren't stupid just because they don't live within sight of the Atlantic or Pacific oceans or Lake Michigan, or don't read the New York Times. I've been privileged to personally visit all fifty of our United States and talk to folks who live there - ordinary people, people who work, people with families, people who pay their taxes, people who observe the law, people who worry about their jobs, people who love their kids, people who stand in line to vote, people who say "God Bless America".

Einstein is credited with stating that everything should be made as simple as possible, but not simpler. Trade, free or otherwise, is complicated. It cannot soundly be reduced to something simpler than it really is.

Comments at My 75th Birthday Party

Le Vallauris, Palm Springs, CA
December 20, 2016

Michel de Montaigne said 500 years ago, "We need a fecundity of conception, not a fertility of words." W. Somerset Maugham advised, "Say everything as simply as possible - then cut". So I will be brief.

I am deeply honored that you made the effort to be here tonight. Thank you. It is hard to imagine a more distinguished group of people including current or former professors in chemistry, biology, genetics, medicine, optics, astronomy, physics, psychiatry, political science, and more as well as one university president. Others of you have been successful in business, law, the arts, and other pursuits. Some of you have advanced degrees, others never went to college. The trait which unites all of you is the one most important to Dixie and me. It is not family, not learning, not success. It is the quality of your character.

I was born in Brooklyn 13 days after the attack on Pearl Harbor forced the United States into World War II. The long journey of my life since then would have been impossible had I not been born in America. I am really one of the luckiest men in the world. I am unable to fully express the depth of my appreciation for the love, kindness, generosity, and efforts of family, teachers, mentors, colleagues, companions, and friends who had faith in me along the way. I am saddened that many of them have already left us forever, and would like to request a moment of silence in their memory.

I would like to close with a few thoughts related to the little book on your table. "On Bullshit" was written by a professor of philosophy at Princeton University. Bullshit is the subject of the first story of mankind in the Bible. Eat of the apple said the serpent, "You will not surely die". He may have been lying, or maybe he just wanted to see what would happen - but that was bullshit. Eve ate of the apple, it tasted good, and she said to Adam, "Try it, you'll like it". Maybe she meant well, but that too was bullshit. And from this, so the Bible tells us, evolved the rest of man's troubles.

Bullshit is everywhere, and it causes immense harm. Every day we read, hear, and are expected to believe things that are false, bad advice, unsound thinking. This is a particularly obvious problem in movies, news and financial media, the internet, and politics. But - and I say this particularly to the younger members of our audience - the problem is far more universal. In my own life, and it can hardly be unique in this regard, I was often exposed to unsound ideas, advice, or thinking, most of which came from people who sincerely believed their own bullshit. Some of them were relatives, some were teachers, others were friends, colleagues, or companions who meant well but were wrong. Of course I was also exposed to sound ideas, good advice, and correct thinking. Distinguishing between the good and the bad was not and still is not easy, but it is critically important to do. Efforts to do this made a bigger difference in my life than perhaps anything else. Of course I made mistakes along the way, but mercifully avoided the worst ones. I often heard a little warning bell inside my head reminding me to think harder, to take my time deciding, to again weigh alternatives carefully. It is tragic that so many good people I know have been seriously misdirected, damaged, or even destroyed by their failure to recognize bullshit.

I wish all of you many years of health and happiness, and hope that you will, along with me, successfully keep your bullshit detectors fully operational and in the learning mode in the years to come.

Thank you, and now relax, have another drink, and take a bite of dessert. As Eve said, "Try it, you'll like it!

Orange Cadillac

"Return with us now to those thrilling days of yesteryear" as General Mills advised when introducing the television Lone Ranger. We won't go farther back than the late 1960s. Instead of the Wild West we journey eastward to a remote corner of Israel. Our hero, if there is one in this little tale, isn't a cowboy with an Indian companion but a young American geneticist. And instead of riding the horse, "Silver", he rode an orange Cadillac - really!

Many things happen at academic conferences like the genetics meeting I was attending in Jerusalem. Information on the latest scientific advances is acquired, at least at the better conferences. Collegiality is established and reinforced. Serious discussions follow major breakthroughs. New ideas may be initiated. But outside of working hours much happens that doesn't appear in abstracts or official summaries: alcohol is generously imbibed, new extra-marital affairs are begun and old ones refreshed, side trips are undertaken in lieu of attending one more special session. I'm not going to tell you here about anyone's drinking or sexual behavior, so if either is your special interest you can stop reading now. But I will relate what happened to three guys who decided to play hooky, cut classes for one day, and take a little journey together.

Rod, the oldest, was a professor of genetics and competent administrator who had become a pediatric department chairman in Texas. Rod and I were friends, and he once correctly diagnosed my one and only experience of nightmare hallucinations as poisoning from contaminating alcohols in cheap tequila consumed at a bar in Mexico City during another international meeting. Over dinner in Jerusalem, Rod explained that he wanted to visit the Golan

Heights and had rented a car for this purpose. He asked if I'd like to come along, and it sounded more interesting than the next day of conferencing. Indeed it was.

Some background is needed. The Golan Heights was then much in the news. It is a hilly region to the east of the Jordan River valley and the Sea of Galilee. The latter are part of Israel, while the Golan had belonged to Syria for many years. Syrian artillery and rockets on the Golan hills repeatedly bombarded Israeli settlements, mostly farming communities in the valley below, and from the Golan murderous cross-border infiltrations were launched. Israel captured the Golan Heights in the Six Day war of 1967, swore it would never be returned, and occupied and extensively fortified it.

Now why would anyone want to visit this area as a tourist just a few years after its conquest? I still don't know why Rod wanted to do it - bragging rights probably at cocktail parties or poker games back in Texas. I had a mild curiosity to see what the fuss was all about in the newspapers and the U.N., I liked Rod, and the adventure promised a one day escape from a part of the meeting that lacked interest for me.

Next morning as I waited in front of our hotel an apparition arrived - a gigantic, 4-door, bright orange Cadillac with big fins, lots of chrome, and showing its age. It was far larger than any car I had seen in Israel, and in fact it probably was THE largest car in Israel at that time. Rod was behind the wheel. Next to me was Tony, another acquaintance of Rod's; Tony didn't talk much and later built his career writing useless articles on genetic bioethics. Tony got into the remaining front seat, and I clambered in back. The plan was that Tony and I would switch positions on the return trip, which had a fortuitous significance I will soon describe.

As we drove out of Jerusalem toward the north, I asked Rod why he had rented an oversized orange Caddy for our trip. He replied that it was the only car he could rent after he told people he was going to the Golan Heights. That did not seem to me to be a good omen. And as I considered that we had all agreed to "chip in" for gas, gas in Israel cost several times the U.S. price, and I was traveling on a tight academic budget, my limited affection for the Cadillac further decreased. To this day I cannot understand why there was even one orange Cadillac in Israel. Israelis drove fast on narrow roads in tiny cars that could get 30 miles or more to the gallon, many of their vehicles seemed to lack brakes, and deaths from auto accidents greatly outnumbered those from Arab attacks. Perhaps the orange Caddy had been a tax-deductible gift from a wealthy American Jew to a Hebrew charity which disposed of the vehicle as part of its donations to the State of Israel. But why orange? Maybe it had belonged to a beauty contest winner like Bess Myerson, the first (and I believe still the only) Jewish Miss America. Maybe it had been a gift from Hugh Hefner to a mammiferous Semitic Playboy bunny. Maybe the car had had an accident in Israel and orange paint was cheaper. Don't laugh. Israelis don't waste money. Remember the joke about the new Israeli car that stops on a dime, and also picks it up?

Rod said it would take only a "few hours" to complete the round trip. Presumably he thought that because Israel is so much smaller than Texas. He had seemingly worked out the route by himself or maybe with advice from an Israeli tank commander. Rod believed that, in Israel as in Texas, the shortest distance between two points is a straight line. A problem with this theory quickly became apparent as our route soon became a dirt road. We advanced north and east trailing a gigantic dust cloud, and soon were in open desert. In fact, we were not only in the desert but were innocently driving across the Arab-populated West Bank which, like the Golan, had been acquired by Israel in 1967. After an hour or more we approached a kind of village. It was Jericho.

Jericho then, and even today, is a poor town with a few thousand Arab occupants. As our Cadillac swept along the unpaved main street, little children ran to see it followed by their elders. The crowd grew very fast. The people did not seem hostile, just amazed. They stared in disbelief, laughed, pointed, jumped up and down like a circus had arrived. Presumably none of them had ever seen an orange Cadillac occupied by three crazed Caucasians, and I'm pretty sure none of them ever saw an orange Cadillac again. Actually, neither have I. From the back seat I urged Rod not to stop, but he had figured this out on his own and increased speed. Fortunately no group formed in front of our car and we soon escaped past the outskirts of Jericho. My guess is that nothing this interesting happened in Jericho until 1998 when Yasser Arafat opened a casino-hotel there which, says Wikipedia, cost $150 million. The casino then failed, but, according to the same source, "the hotel on the premises is [currently] open to guests" - which won't include me.

Much of the subsequent afternoon is a blur in memory. I spent part of the time asleep in the back. The car bounced around on dirt road after dirt road. The trip never seemed to end. Road signs did not exist, and there was no way to be sure we were going the right way except for guidance by the sun which, after some hours, began to sink toward the western horizon. At long last we found ourselves back in Israeli territory and on paved roads. Rod sought directions to "the best place to see the Golan Heights" and was told there is no such thing. Finally an Israeli soldier guarding a transit check point explained how to reach a vantage point on the Heights with an overlook of the Jordan Valley - and if we hurried we might get there before dark. The wisdom of abandoning our goal did occur to us, but we felt committed and pressed on. In deep twilight we reached the viewpoint. All I could see were dark hills, a few trees silhouetted against the pale sky, and down below a black space that - presumably - had the Jordan River at its bottom. That was my one and only view, ever, from the Golan Heights.

Night had fallen. Returning to Jerusalem by the route we had taken was out of the question. Rod's map showed that by going west toward the coast and then south we should be able to make it back to our hotel over paved roads while remaining within Israel proper. I switched seats with Tony, and joked about riding in the death seat next to Rod. This was an appropriate sobriquet. By now Rod was tired and driving as fast as possible, since at best we would be very late returning and it was believed - probably erroneously - that some people might start to worry about us. Tony fell sleep in the back. There were no lights, no signs, and in the moonless night nothing could be seen except the road twisting in our headlights. And then, as we whizzed along at over 50 miles an hour, I suddenly observed something else. By the right edge of the road was a small red lantern which we ignored. My window must have been open because a moment later I heard shouting as dark human shapes raced toward our car. Rod seemed oblivious, but I yelled to him to stop - several times - and he finally did. Twenty or more Israeli soldiers carrying Uzis and flashlights - all of which were pointed at us - had emerged from the black woods and surrounded our car. Their leader spoke English, and as he ran up breathing hard shouted at me, "What are you doing? You nearly got shot! We didn't shoot because you were in this big car so someone thought you might be Americans. You ran a checkpoint at that red light. You are near Afula, the military headquarters for the Golan. This is a high security zone. Red means stop!!" It was clear we had had a very close call. Another soldier asked what we were doing in Afula at night, and we replied we were tourists returning from the Golan Heights. The idiocy implied by our stated motivation for being where we were, our nearly fatal ignoring of the checkpoint, and the absurd vehicle we occupied apparently convinced the soldiers that we were just harmless lunatics, not attackers from Syria, and after examining the car they allowed us to proceed.

We drove much more slowly on the long way back to Jerusalem, arriving near midnight. I went to bed immediately. I kept seeing the orange Cadillac in my dreams, but never again in real life. The next day Rod didn't even hit me up for gas money. Then the meeting ended and we all flew home.

If I ever see another orange Caddy from the 1950-60s I just might buy it, caress it for a few months in my garage, and finally donate it to some car museum. I am convinced that giant Cadillac with its unmistakable tail fins saved our lives that night near Afula. You may feel this is an exaggeration, that the soldiers really wouldn't have shot us even if we had been driving something more conventional. You could be right, but I was there and believe otherwise. We did several incredibly stupid things and had a real close call. The Golan Heights in those days experienced nightly sneak attacks, guerrilla raids, murders, massacres, and retaliations. We were mindlessly wandering in an active war zone. To do something that dumb you have to be not just an ordinary fool but - I may as well admit it - you have to be a professor.

Interstate Water System for the American West

American does not have a water supply problem. It has a water distribution problem. California, Arizona, and many western states currently suffer water shortages. A major new infrastructure project could revolutionize water distribution in the United States and further development of the western half of our country.

John Wesley Powell - explorer of the Colorado and other western rivers and second head of the U.S. Geological Survey - correctly recognized in the 19th century that west of the 100th meridian water supply limits agriculture, ranching, and settlement. Initially he was not believed, since most Americans, including farmers, lived in the humid East with its frequent rains, large rivers and lakes, and periodic flooding. But from the Sierras to the Rockies rain is sparse and except for the Pacific Northwest water comes from just one major source - the Colorado River. The largest eastern river, the Mississippi, has about 30 times the average annual flow of the Colorado, and the Columbia close to 10 times. Water from these and other large rivers pours unused into the sea. In addition, the Great Lakes are an enormous fresh water reservoir shared with Canada.

So America does not have a water supply problem, but rather a distribution problem. The West's chronic water shortages result from failure to appropriately redistribute our nation's abundant total water resources.

Water can move through pipelines, tunnels, and aqueducts with perfect safety over long distances on a virtually limitless scale. Why do we transport oil, but not water, across America avoiding an oil glut in Texas and an oil drought in, say, Florida? Oil and gas distribution evolved through private enterprise. In contrast, water supplies are managed by state and local governments. Each state aims to control its own water. Water has long been a source of western interstate and intrastate conflict.

I envision in the near future a combined Federal and private hallmark program for our nation – an Interstate Water System. This IWS would rival in importance and transforming potential the Interstate Highway System whose formation was championed by President Dwight Eisenhower. The IWS would be designed to expand America's water-related infrastructure by crossing state boundaries to transport water from where America has too much of it to where it is wanted. With modifications and expansions in the future, no part of America need find itself short of water as this program is developed.

The basics of why the IWS is currently practical are not hard to grasp. Assume an initial goal might be doubling the water flow, averaging about 20,000 cubic feet per second, to Colorado River system reservoirs. Raising Mississippi River water to about 4,000 - 5,000 feet altitude would likely be needed to supply Lake Mead (altitude 1,100 feet) or Lake Powell (altitude 3,600 feet). We estimate that fewer than 10 power plants of typical 1 Gigawatt size could provide the energy to move water half-way across our nation to double the flow of the Colorado, while turbines in dams below its lakes would eventually regenerate a significant part of the pumping energy.

The implications, if feasibility studies confirm the basic assumptions, are enormous. America already moves water in pipelines, tunnels, and aqueducts, and stores it in man-made lakes. Interstate highway and railroad routes suggest cross-country paths for an IWS. Power supply is not limiting. It is suggested that what is needed is recognition of the great long-term importance of the fundamental idea and determination at the highest levels of government and industry to make it happen. The proposed IWS would evolve over years, create many jobs, provide numerous construction and other business opportunities, and facilitate national growth and development. An IWS should be done and eventually will be done. Why not start now?

The above idea is supported by several scientists including a former President of the University of Arizona. I hope it will reach persons influential enough to organize a further detailed analysis of its feasibility. A spreadsheet with energy calculations by the writer is available upon request.

On the Future

Not long ago I was drinking late at night with two friends who are (or were) social science professors at top California universities. Banter, bullshit, political opinionating, and different perspectives on the future of America and the world were offered by each of us and our far-from-mute spouses. As he finished his cognac, one of the professors proposed a homework assignment. "Please write down", he said, "what you think is going to happen over the next 4 years, and the next 10 years. Then we'll take a look."

When young I was one of those nerds who almost always did his homework. Now older and hopefully wiser, I probably should not have taken the bait. But the challenge was intriguing. What follows is done with fear-filled awareness of the fallibility of human judgment (mine very much included), inevitable occurrences of the unforeseeable, and the proven unreliability of most predictions about what will happen and when. Predicting the future of the whole world is impossible in my opinion. So I beg liberty from the assigning professor to focus my efforts on the future of America.

Why might I hope there is some possibility of getting right at least part of the American future? I have some intelligence and many years of formal education, but these are just basic tools for attempting to understand what may lie ahead for a nation of about 350 million people. I am a second generation native-born American, and that really helps. As an American in my very marrow, I have spent my whole life immersed in the American milieu, in American culture, and this helps me to think like an American. I visit France almost every year and speak

French tolerably well, but I cannot enter into the soul, the intimate conscious and unconscious thought processes, of the native-born Frenchman. Nor can I hope to do this even for Great Britain where they speak my native language, I also regularly visit, and even spent a whole year doing research at Cambridge University. I am not sufficiently chauvinistic to maintain that only Americans can understand America, and rare geniuses like Alexis de Tocqueville surely disprove such an assertion, but I do suggest that being a native born, fully acculturated American increases the possibility that I might be be right about at least a part of America's future.

There is an also a special advantage that I feel I bring to the task. For a period of over 20 years I was one of America's more prominent physicians and medical researchers and was heavily involved helping parents and children. My professional role provided an unusual and advantageous setting for getting to know many, many different people. During a typical encounter with a new patient, a full hour was set aside to discuss various aspects of the patient's medical and personal situations. This was then generally followed by at least another 30 minutes of discussion after preliminary testing was completed. Thus I spent about 1.5 hours talking to each new patient or couple. I engaged in this process with an average of 4-5 new patients per day, 5-6 days per week, for a total of about 1,000 weeks over this long period. This then involved intimate, confidential, and often wide-ranging discussions with well over 20,000 couples and - even allowing for the single status of some of my patients - not less than 40,000 different people. In addition, I got to spend additional time with my patients during telephone discussions, actual medical procedures, etc. Even excluding that additional time, I had the rare lifetime privilege of at least 50,000 hours talking heart-to-heart to a wide variety of people about many things. I learned a lot from them about who they were, and what their hopes and dreams were for themselves, their future children, and the future of America.

Who were these patients? They were usually between the ages of 30 and 50, and over 90% were Americans. Maybe 80% were from Maryland, Virginia, West Virginia, or DC, perhaps 15% from elsewhere in the U.S. coming from as far away as Idaho or Oregon, about 5% were from other countries. Many were married but not all. Patients were of numerous races and backgrounds. Most wanted help with having children. Some had factors predisposing to genetic disorders and wished to avoid them in offspring if possible. Some of my patients were rich and famous, and included billionaires, Presidents of countries, US senators and congressional representatives, media personalities, career government workers, prominent newspaper columnists and editors, lawyers, and doctors. Some were highly unusual - men from the Middle East who would bring a wife for treatment, and when it failed, go home, clap their hands three times, and come back a year later with a younger, hopefully more fertile wife; men who came to father children by women who were not their wives; a concubine who flew from London to have a child at the request of her millionaire lover; a woman from Iran who traveled around the world, had a baby with our help, and vanished without paying us but sent me annual postcards on the progress of her child. But most were middle class Americans drawn from almost all walks of life. And there were some poor patients too. And some patients became future friends I got to know very well indeed. The key point for our current purposes is that my patients were in no way selected politically or by criteria other than needing help with having children. I believe that I was thus privileged to know an exceptionally large number of my fellow Americans and what they cared about, and thus learned about human nature and aspirations from these interactions.

I have also had the privilege of being comparatively healthy and mentally alert while being mostly retired for several years, enabling me to read widely in such fields as economics, finance, political science, and history while continuing to track biological science and medical progress. I was also able to ponder what I had learned from my years of running a closely held business with many employees. Beyond that, my wife and I enjoy traveling by automobile throughout the United States and have actually visited all 50 states. And when we travel around our country we talk to people, plain "ordinary" people, the folks who stay at Comfort Inns and Holiday Inns with us, the people who work in such places, the kids who work at McDonalds and Pizza Hut. In cities we talk to desk clerks, bell hops, people who park cars, waiters, chefs, bartenders, baristas, salespeople in retail outlets large and small, collectors, and artists. At our homes and the homes of some of our relatives we employ immigrants (legal and indirectly some perhaps illegal), many of them Hispanic or Black, as gardeners, plumbers, roofers, and more and we talk to them too. We also meet a fair number of retired persons, some with money to burn but other getting by on tight budgets. So these experiences facilitate perspectives based on meeting and talking with a large and varied number of what one politician liked to call, "My Fellow Americans".

The most important point is that the people in all the above groups are in only to a minimal degree a selected population of "the elite". Yes, I have a number of friends who were professors, others who were or are university, think tank, or business leaders, even some colleagues who are Nobel Laureates. We do know a fair number of lawyers and doctors. But their proportion in the total range of our contacts is small. We have almost nothing to do with media stars, administrators, journalists, Hollywood, bureaucrats, professional politicians. We don't watch television, and above all, we don't rely on elites and newspapers or other secondary sources to tell us what "ordinary" people are really thinking. We get out there, see for ourselves, and make up our own minds. Examples that illustrate this key point may be of interest.

After the large economic downturn that began in 2008, during a mid-week afternoon in March, 2009 I went to a mall about 30 miles west of Palm Springs. Centered in this mall were parking places for at least 600 cars. Only three cars were there including mine. I went into the Movado store to look at a watch. The lady working there told me I was the only customer who had been in there all day. She sold me the watch I wanted at a heavy discount to its marked price. In August, 2009, my wife and I went to buy furniture and household equipment for a condominium we had just acquired in Florida, the seller being a victim of both the real estate downturn and Bernard Madoff. We shopped at a nearby Macy's which was essentially empty, and on one huge floor we were the only customers. Everything was for sale at 50% off, 70% off, and if you took out a Macy's credit card they took another 15% off the discounted price. Another furniture store we used offered everything at half price and still was nearly empty. Now, let's fast forward one year later to March, 2010. I was participating in an investment and economics group at the California Club, and most people there were very worried and seemed to rely heavily on secondary sources for much of their economic information. Newspapers were filled with predictions that the Great Depression was happening again and there was no evidence of things getting better in the economy. But that secondary information was false.

All you had to do to know it was wrong was to visit the same mall I visited one year before, and you found there not 3 cars but maybe 300. All you had to do was drive from Palm Springs to downtown Los Angeles along Interstate 10 and look out of your car window - without stopping - and you could see other malls with a substantial number of cars parked in them. The media, the elites, the professional economists, the professors, the bankers, the reporters, the financial analysts, were almost all wrong. An economic recovery was obviously underway, and you could see it if you just opened your eyes. Not a full recovery, but a recovery. A trend. An improvement. Meanwhile, most investors were still fleeing the stock market. But anyone who saw the malls and thought about what they saw could have figured out that the future direction of the market was going to be up, and now was the time - if you could - to hold or to buy if possible, not to sell. All you had to do to reach that conclusion was to go out in the real world and look around and think for yourself.

Now to a more recent example of the advantages of relying on first hand data. In September, 2016 my wife and I drove to Vancouver, Canada on the Trans Canadian Highway. We drove north through Minnesota to enter Canada at the isolated border crossing in Warroad MN. Now, we were traveling in one of the "bluest" states in America and the November election was not far off. The only bumper stickers and the only political signs we saw along the highways in Minnesota were for Trump. At tiny Warroad, we stopped to get gas and eat some fried chicken. The station had wooden benches, tables, and a TV to accommodate its "diners". Hillary Clinton was speaking on the TV and explaining how when she became President every kid in America was going to get a free college education. A truck driver sitting with his wife at an adjacent booth yelled out, "Yeah, lady, and who's going to pay for it? ME!" He later gratefully accepted a gift of Trump bumper stickers from some travelers. Shortly thereafter we were visiting super-liberal Montgomery County, Maryland where before any election one usually sees maybe 100 lawn signs for whoever is a Democratic candidate vs. one or two for any Republican candidate; but in 2016 the ratio was about 4 to 1 because of the absence of Hillary signs. If you drove from Washington, DC to Ocean City, Maryland - again, in one of the "bluest" states in America - all you saw along Highway 50 were Trump signs and billboards. Meanwhile, the elites, the pollsters, and the media were all so sure who would win that Newsweek magazine actually distributed on election eve about 100,000 copies of a full special issue (later recalled) with a cover picture of a smiling Mrs. Clinton coronated as "Madame President". But those of us who used our eyes and thought about what we saw had earlier said to ourselves and to our friends, "Wait a minute. The average poll is based on interviews with about 500-700 people. These are an infinitesimal percentage of our population. How do we know they've picked the right people? What about the road signs? What about the tee shirt shops in Ocean City, MD which sell to a substantially working class and black population all showing only Trump shirts except one featuring "Hillary for Prison"? Doesn't that tell you something? Might all the stuff we saw firsthand in Minnesota, in Maryland, and in other states suggest that maybe - just maybe - Trump could win?" To be clear, we did not then go out and bet (unfortunately) a pile of money on the election outcome. We didn't know what it would be, and we figured too that America would survive whoever won. But we did consider it incredible how the pollsters and the media - with a very rare exceptions - maintained that a Clinton victory was inevitable and no other outcome was sanely imaginable.

So after this long introduction which is offered as background and not boasting, what about the future? Before we get there, permit me to summarize a few interpretations which form the underpinning of the predictions. You may not agree with some or all of these interpretations, but it seems fair to put honestly before you what I personally feel are the current core of beliefs and values influencing the behavior of most Americans. These profoundly impact the short term future, and likely also the longer term future, of our nation.

To most Americans, Thomas Jefferson's oft-quoted statement that "all men are created equal" seems absurd. The average man or woman knows by instinct and experience that every individual is unique from the moment of birth. Better toilet training, preschool or other education, better parenting, more government programs, religion, humanism, socialism, communism - none of these or anything else can make all of us equal. Not everyone can be a great mathematician, fine athlete, or wonderful musician. We are each different and most of us who have been a parent of more than one child, who has siblings, who look at their grandchildren with open eyes know in their heart-of-hearts that we are all born different. And Americans mostly know too that English poet laureate Philip Larkin's famous line about who's to blame for messed-up children, "They f_ck you up your mom and dad, they don't mean to but they do", is false. Many more agree with the response to Larkin offered by Judith Rich Harris who, partly paraphrasing King Lear, answered on behalf of parents: "How sharper than a serpent's tooth, to hear your child make such a fuss. It isn't fair, it's not the truth, he's f_cked up yes, but not by us."

Americans by and large value liberty far more than equality. John Adams, America's second President, was one of many who explained that liberty is impossible if government attempts to produce equality of outcomes. Most Americans do not want to give up their liberty in the name of someone else's equality.

Paradoxically perhaps to the above interpretations of what most American's seem to believe we note de Tocqueville's observations - echoed by many other authors - that Americans nevertheless are susceptible to group pressures and herd-like behavior. We agree, and it means that predicting behavior by studying isolated Americans (say a pollster seeking your opinion) fails to take adequate account of the innate and often unconscious factors that can influence mass behavior, including the "madness of crowds".

Americans largely accept the truth, reinforced by interpretations derived from both evolution and religion, that human beings are deeply flawed. Greed, lying, cheating, stealing, coveting what is thy neighbor's, adultery, are widespread, incurable and ineradicable. Human error and misjudgment cannot be fixed or prevented by government. But a government based on law must restrain and punish the worst among us who would murder and torture with impunity, while not forgetting that an accused person should be considered innocent until proven guilty.

Americans overwhelmingly love our form of government - a mixture of local, state, and federal laws and Constitutional division of powers (legislature with two components, executive, and judicial) - which has survived and evolved over nearly 250 years. They respect the Constitution of the United States. They have no interest in being governed by a League of Nations or a United Nations. A North American, let alone a North and South American, Union modeled after the EU with its remote bureaucracy not in Brussels but in, say, Toronto, would have no chance of being accepted by most Americans.

The average American, who never uses the word "multiculturalism", has little problem with marriage between people of different religions, races, and backgrounds. And he knows that the culture of America, and what it means to become an American, is not damaged or destroyed by immigrants integrating into American society while retaining ties to their own familial backgrounds. But Americans will not accept the substitution of another nation's culture, or some kind of "world culture" for their own.

Americans mostly believe, even though they may not know Calvin Coolidge said it, that "the business of America is business." Jobs matter. On economic matters, government should mostly get out of the way. Americans almost all hate paying their taxes and would like them to be lowered, but pay them nevertheless with a remarkable degree of honesty. Most Americans are instinctively opposed to regulation of their businesses or their lives.

In summary, I believe that a preponderance of Americans hold the above views. The following predictions are in large part based on them.

One may consider the short term future of America and its longer term future. The "homework assignment" of 4 years is pretty short term while 10 years is neither really short nor long. Cyclical occurrences such as economic downturns and "irrational exuberance" can take a decade or more to happen. And one never can really predict when a cycle will start or end. So I will offer predictions about the 4 year period and, instead of 10 years, the longer period of 50 years. As for the second set of predictions, my grandchildren will hopefully be able to check out its veracity.

In 4 years, I predict for America:

Economic growth will have increased by 1% or more per year over current levels.

Unemployment will be modestly lower.

Corporate and some personal tax rates will be lower.

Inflation will be higher, but not much higher than it really is today (I feel the official figures on inflation substantially underestimate it).

The intrinsic value of all American enterprises in aggregate will increase.

Bursting of a stock market bubble is possible, but more likely after 4 years than before.

Intermarriage will continue to increase.

There will neither a striking increase or decrease in religious influence in politics or American life in general.

Abortion and reproductive rights will remain unchanged.

Crime will be better contained, but there will still far more of it than law-abiding citizens want. Strong support will re-emerge for proactive local police.

Regulation will decrease in many areas but will remain much more than most Americans want. There will be fierce resistance to down-regulation from government bureaucrats.

K-12 school choice, vouchers, charter schools will increase. This may or may not result in a decline of students in Catholic and other religious-based schooling.

Health insurance will offer a wider range of choices, although average cost may not decline from current levels and could continue to rise significantly.

There will evolve a greater tolerance and protection for "free speech" on college campuses.

There will be a decline without full elimination of race preferences in education and jobs.

Vocational education will increase.

Total immigration to the U.S. will continue at about current levels, and may increase for highly educated immigrants. Illegal immigration will be reduced. The southern barrier to illegal immigration will be substantially improved. The status of current long-term illegal immigrants is likely to be resolved in favor of "grandfathering" them in to legal participation in American society, though this may not be completed within 4 years.

Voting registration and participation will involve greater safeguards against fraud.

Aggregate welfare payments will likely remain similar to current when adjusted for inflation, with a shift to more support for the really needy and handicapped and less to people who decline to work or take unpleasant jobs.

Terrorism will be contained but not eliminated. The same will be true of the occasional mass murders by insane persons. A nuclear terrorist event will not occur.

America will not engage in a new major foreign war. There will be no war with Russia or China.

Terms for international trade with America will be modified to include some protectionist and mercantilist elements. This will work better than many economists currently believe. There will be increasing development of factories in America by American and non-American companies.

The influence of conventional media - newspapers, TV, movies - on the average American will continue to decrease.

The importance of the internet will continue to increase.

There will be an acceleration of innovation in American private, university, and public science.

Medical research and treatments will make many advances, but "the cure for cancer" will not be found within the next 4 years. The role of the FDA in controlling drugs, devices, and medical methods will be curtailed, but not as much as some would wish.

The rich will get richer, the middle class will get richer. Being poor isn't fun now and won't be fun in 4 years either.

Many more predictions are possible, but perhaps the professor who assigned this homework will consider the above sufficient to test the predictive ability of the author. I decline the 10 year timeline predictions because of my inability to time cyclic events which are intrinsic to human nature, all economies, and free peoples. But I will make some longer term predictions for 50 years or more that are similar in some ways to those expressed by businessman-investor Warren Buffett. I am a long-term optimist. Americans will be far richer on average (in real terms) than today. They will work less and have far more leisure time. They will benefit from countless new inventions. There will still be some poor people. World war and nuclear war will be avoided. There will be no American submission to a world government. Crime and terrorism will not be fully eradicated, but will be viewed more like automobile accidents are today - unpleasant and sometimes deadly, to be prevented if possible, and otherwise accepted as a fact of life. There will be enormous advances in medical science and people will on average live longer and healthier lives. America will still be the country of choice for many of the world's smartest people. Our nation's population will likely approach or exceed 400 million. Water will be transported, like oil and gas, in pipelines, aqueducts, and other conduits throughout the U.S. Cheap solar energy will be widely utilized, especially in the southwest, and there will be many perfectly safe nuclear power plants. And despite all these blessings Americans will still commonly break one or more of the Ten Commandments, and still find things to disagree about including debating whether or not the world is going to hell.

My homework assignment is now finished.

Friedman on Freedom

Milton Friedman was an intellectual giant of the 20th century. Born in 1912 in Brooklyn, New York (my place of birth), he was a great economist whose most famous work with Anna J. Schwartz, "A Monetary History of the United States, 1867 - 1960", provides the best explanation of the causes for the Great Depression. He was also a brilliant teacher who participated at the University of Chicago in mentoring many prominent economists including Gary Becker (who like Friedman became a Nobel Laureate) and Thomas Sowell. And his books for the general public, like "Capitalism and Freedom" and "Free to Choose" helped to educate millions of people.

It was my great privilege to meet Friedman personally and hear him lecture at the Hoover Institution in California. He was physically unprepossessing, a little over 5 feet tall and with a very crooked spine (the medical term is kyphoscoliosis if you want to use that in Scrabble). But his eloquence and clarity of thinking were almost unbelievable. He was also a gentleman kind enough to agree to read some thoughts I had written down (unpublished) about the magnitude of the government's expenditure in healthcare vs. education and he wrote back a response, which I treasure, that I might be right in suggesting that if the tax deductions for employer-paid health insurance as well as Medicare, Medicaid, and other programs were included then health rather than education might already be America's largest socialized industry.

Friedman is one of my heroes above all for his views about freedom. Assisted by his fellow economist and wife, Rose, he was a leading - some would say the leading - spokesman for presenting the case that individual freedom forms the soundest basis for structuring society.

Maximizing freedom as Friedman explains it means capitalism instead of socialism or communism, and it also means limiting the role of government to its essential tasks - supporting a volunteer military force, operating the legal system, maintaining a currency. Since everything that government does involves taking money from individuals or organizations by coercion through taxation, the bigger government gets the more it interferes with freedom. At the time of Friedman's most important writings - broadly from about 1960 to 1990 - government in all forms (federal, state, and local) absorbed about 40% of national income (gross domestic product, GDP). Today that percentage is slightly lower (at about 34%) than when Friedman wrote, but the modest percentage reduction does not represent a decrease in government expenditure - now exceeding 7 trillion dollars per year of which about 4 trillion is Federal - but a slightly slower rate of growth of such expenditure compared to the more substantial expansion of the total U.S. economy.

The Hoover Institution recently reprinted a carefully selected group of Friedman's writings entitled "Milton Friedman and Freedom", compiled and edited by Robert Leeson and Charles Palm. The latest of these writings is dated 1988. Reading and in many cases rereading essays I had discovered years ago stimulated this effort to offer thoughts about Friedman's view of freedom, his stated reasons for valuing freedom so highly, and with temerity suggest caveats about some of his interpretations. Some of my comments also appear applicable to views about freedom articulated by Ayn Rand in "Atlas Shrugged" and her other writings.

Friedman of course emphasizes that personal freedom and capitalism are inextricably linked. And he argues that there are basically only two ways to organize

393

society. A capitalist system involves non-coerced exchanges between parties who voluntarily participate in these transactions. The alternative is government control (whether dictatorship, socialism, or other) in which government forces people to give up resources to be used not between themselves in a free exchange, but by bureaucrats and others for purposes which government decides are best. He believes that many people inappropriately derive special benefits from any system of government control, but that the capitalistic system survives nevertheless because it is far more productive than alternatives even though the bias against it is great. It is thus not a coincidence that the scale of government grows not only in times of war - when it is necessary for survival - but whenever the economic promise of capitalism seems disappointing to a larger proportion of the population, as witness the large expansion of government during the Great Depression or the more recent Great Recession which began in 2008, two years after Friedman died.

So per Friedman capitalism survives in large part because it delivers the goods. And he posits that it is hard to imagine real capitalism without personal freedom, although the modern Chinese state is essentially trying to manage such a system. (Friedman would presumably argue that this is unsustainable in the long run and he optimistically predicted in an interview a few years before his death that "China will move increasingly toward political freedom if it continues its successful movement for economic freedom.") Very importantly, Friedman's positive views on capitalism are founded on more that its economic success - they are based on what he perceives as the primary importance of freedom. What is his justification for endorsing freedom as a core value? He has offered his own explanation many times: at a philosophical level it is because no individual can reliably claim that he is right. To quote from his informative interview with the editors of Reason in 1974, "I start, I guess, from a belief in individual freedom that derives fundamentally from a belief in the limitations of our knowledge - from a belief in the idea that nobody can be sure that what he believes is right, is really right." And later in the same interview, "So the question everyone must ask himself is, here I am; I'm an imperfect human being who cannot be certain of anything, so what position can I take? Which involves the least intolerance on my part, the least arrogance, the least expression of belief in my own superior wisdom or knowledge? And it's in this sense that I say that the most attractive position, or the least unattractive position - these are identical - is putting individual freedom first. Because that involves placing least weight on personal views of what's right or wrong. It says that every other man has just as much right to his opinions as I have, provided he doesn't try to interfere with my having my opinion, and that I don't interfere with him". And freedom involves not just speech: "The positive case for freedom has to do with individual behavior and with the argument that in a free society each individual will have to formulate, and act in accordance with, his own person values and beliefs and ethics. That is the positive case for freedom."

Readers of Ayn Rand will find this argument familiar. She basically believed that the rules of the games should be that people may say and do anything they wish as long as all agree that violence against others is off limits. How that agreement is to be reached, however, is less clearly explained. Furthermore, the far less frequent readers of the masterpiece by British jurist, A. V. Dicey, "Lectures on the Relation between Law and Public Opinion in England during the Nineteenth Century" will appreciate how really "not new" these formulations of government emphasizing individual freedom are; for during approximately 1830 - 1860 British laws were heavily modified under the influence of Jeremy Bentham and others to reflect this primacy in an almost pure form, a combination of laissez-faire governance and free trade economics. Needless to add, neither in England nor America, nor to my knowledge in any present modern society, can one identify government that is structured in anything like such a pure form today.

I first read Friedman over 50 years ago. The power of his arguments and clarity of his reasoning were, and remain, deeply impressive. And Friedman of course acknowledges that there is - and there must be - a role of government in punishing violence and other serious crimes, and in acting against what economists call adverse "neighborhood effects" such as the unquantifiable damages to parties downstream from the polluter of a river. But I am not fully persuaded that the underlying philosophical basis for loving freedom should be self-doubt. It is possible to reach a similar conclusion, as Bentham did, by positing that maximizing of individual "utility" should be the fundamental principle of government. Beyond that, I am not convinced that freedom of expression and harmful actions to others can be cleanly separated because it is my conviction that human beings are hardwired to instinctively link words, thoughts, and actions, and perhaps even more fundamentally because evil exists.

Perhaps Friedman would say, "How can you be certain that evil exists?" My answer would be simple. "Just look around." Was a Stalin not evil? Was a Hitler not evil? Ordinary murderers in California gets to live at government expense (really the expense of other people paying taxes) for the rest of their lives, as did the late Charles Manson. Stalin and Hitler murdered millions and lived very well at the expense of others for many years, and

Stalin and many like him died with their boots on. The Hoover Institution's mantra is "ideas have consequences". They do. Is it then an absolute truth that bad ideas deserve the fullest possible freedom of expression? If such ideas remained purely in the realm of thought and never resulted in actions that harmed anyone else that might be a justifiable position. But surely that does not always happen. As history and everyday experience both teach us, bad ideas, even evil ideas, can and often do lead to results causing great harm to others.

It is easy to think of numerous ways in which words can lead to serious damage in the real world. Moslem extremism has influenced the minds of millions. Communist ideas misled countless people. These are obvious cases. Not everyone exposed to bad ideas remains inactive. They don't necessarily commit violent crimes, although some of them do and some of those get punished. Some excite others to do harmful things. And there are many harmful actions that are not crimes and that are not punishable. Furthermore, the likelihood of harmful ideas leading to bad actions may be worsened by drugs, alcohol, mental illness, limited intelligence, and more.

Let us imagine the simple case of a man who decides to articulate that slavery of blacks should be restored in the United States. He stands in a public park and starts saying this. His right to freedom of expression, disgusting as his ideas may be, would be defended by those who value individual freedom most highly. Undoubtedly he would be hooted at and have things screamed at him by some in the audience. They too are expressing their different ideas. But how long, in the real world, would it be before someone started to pelt that man with rocks, or shoved him, punched him, or worse? Words, ideas, and actions are complexly entangled in the real world. A world in which everybody is perfectly free to say anything they want without resultant violence is difficult to imagine. It may be possible to limit disagreement to words between antagonists in a debate or professors on a university campus. But in much of the rest of the world it will not always prove true, to use a famous quote, that "Your liberty to swing your fist ends just where the other man's nose begins". The fist may not stop there.

Ideas, good or bad or maybe even unproven and not so easy to classify, have consequences involving actions that impact others. Friedman and most economists favor free trade as part of a free economy. There is no doubt that many people, perhaps most of us, benefit significantly in economic terms from free trade, lower prices for imported products being just one obvious example. Free trade maximizes aggregate productivity. But it also throws some people out of work, and not all of them will be able to be retrained or are even capable of holding another job. The "idea" of free trade helps many, but harms some severely. Ideas don't just exist without doing harm, even ideas that have a predominance of good in them.

All this is meant to say that much as I enormously admire Friedman and appreciate the brilliant eloquence and idealistic passion he consistently possessed, I find I am unable to fully agree with him in defending the absolute freedom to disseminate - in many different ways - all kinds of ideas however good or bad, however true or untrue, however beneficial or harmful. Ideas often get turned into actions which can be extremely harmful to other people, and sometimes to many other people. Yet censorship, regulation, or the like are at least as unappealing and also, in many ways, even unenforceable.

I strongly hold that freedom merits being a primary value, even if in practice it should not in all cases be unbounded. To modify a phrase from Abraham Lincoln, "I hold this truth to be self-evident, that freedom is better than slavery". That is not simply because the advocate for slavery might be right and I might be wrong. Freedom is good, and slavery is bad. It's that simple, unless one denies - as some do - that the very concepts of good and evil are flawed, in part because they are so difficult to define and bound.

Yet we all must compromise between freedom and its opposite in some ways. The man working for 4 months each year to pay taxes under coercion to his political masters is to that extent a slave. It matters not that he, like almost all slaves in the world of the past when slavery was universal, receives some benefits in return. He is not free to choose, as an individual, what his extracted money shall be used for. But most of us pay our taxes without open rebellion. We mostly accept this partial limitation on our freedom. And while we cannot rely on the the the Bill of Rights and the rule of law to protect us from confiscation through taxation of income "from whatever source derived" (from the 16th Amendment to the U.S. Constitution), they do offer important protections from other forms of control by government in the United States.

Dicey's "History" brilliantly summarizes what happened in England after the high point of laissez-faire economics in the middle of the 19th century. Laws began to be passed in response to injustices widespread in that era - or at least what many members of the increasingly enfranchised population came to view as injustices. The first major limitation took the form of laws prohibiting the labor of children in factories, even when such labor followed contractual agreements between employer and parent. This was closely associated with a movement for free and universal basic education of children, modeled after the example of Germany. Many other modifications to full economic personal freedom (and individual responsibility) followed thereafter including government support for the elderly, the mentally ill, and the "deserving poor" (a category indeed hard to define). The British regulatory state began with an agency to protect the public from adulterated foods. Free trade gave way to elements of protectionism, and even to outright colonialism. All of these changes are correctly classified by Dicey as examples of "collectivism" and in some cases as reflecting socialist ideas. But they were increasingly favored by large segments, and in many cases absolute majorities, of the British electorate.

It is perhaps needless to add that since the second edition of Dicey's book appeared 1914, there has been a vast increase in the power, economic grasp, and regulatory reach of government in both England and America. To many of us, the degree of government intrusion in our lives seems excessive. Yet today almost nobody, and certainly not Friedman, would advocate abandonment of all government involvement in providing a safety net - beyond the military, a legal system, and policing - to our citizenry. The difficulty comes in defining the optimum balance between individual liberty and government control. It is not so much a matter of "either/or" but of specific elements and overall degree of influence. And it is difficult to imagine anything like a perfect solution that will satisfy me, you, and all our fellow citizens. With regard to taxes alone, the major enabler of government action, almost every American would oppose the complete elimination of all taxation. On the other hand, almost all would oppose tax rates on the population - or indeed any segment thereof - approximating 100%. We must compromise on something in between. And the specifics of a reasonably satisfactory compromise today, may or may not suffice - and almost surely will not suffice - for future generations of Americans.

So should one place supreme value upon freedom as the overriding principle in a society? My answer is, "Yes, but....." since while freedom is of extreme importance, it is doubtful if any one ideal exists that should never ever be subject to some limitations. I value freedom for me and for others very highly, and also voluntarily try to help others. But not everyone shares my particular principles. So I and most of my fellow citizens find it necessary to accommodate to innumerable deviations by others from our favored value or set of values. Most of us learn to accept such compromises and to coexist and tolerate each other in that vast grey zone between the poles of complete personal freedom and absolute government power.

Each of us differs in our preferred shade of grey. Compromise and mutual toleration is what we must accept to maintain a civil and productive society, and ultimately to keep blood off the streets. So I believe, but as Milton Friedman might say, "Maybe I am wrong."

D-Day

I awoke this morning and the first thing I said to my wife was "It's D-Day". Half asleep, for a moment she was puzzled. Then, together, we remembered.

On June 6, 1944 I was less than 3 years old in a playpen safely in the center of Brooklyn, New York. Across the Atlantic on the northwest shore of France thousands of fellow Americans already lay dead - drowned, blown up by mines, machine gunned on the beaches, massacred beneath their parachutes, torn apart gliding into hedgerows. They died so that Nazism would not conquer the world, so that mankind would not be ground down under the heel of the German boot, so that as Winston Churchill said we would not all be ruled by the light of "perverted science". One of my mother's cousins survived in the D-Day invasion, my wife's first father-in-law was one of the surviving parachutists. My mother's cousin refused to talk to anyone about the horror of that day. The unforgettable words of Abraham Lincoln's Gettysburg address surely also apply to D-Day: "But in a larger sense we cannot dedicate—we cannot consecrate—we cannot hallow—this ground. The brave men, living and dead, who struggled here, have consecrated it, far above our poor power to add or detract. The world will little note, nor long remember what we say here, but it can never forget what they did here. It is for us the living, rather, to be dedicated here to the unfinished work which they who fought here have thus far so nobly advanced. It is rather for us to be here dedicated to the great task remaining before us—that from these honored dead we take increased devotion to that cause for which they gave the last full measure of devotion—that we here highly resolve that these dead shall not have died in vain—that this nation, under God, shall have a new birth of freedom—and that government of the people, by the people, for the people, shall not perish from the earth."

The subsequent destruction of Nazism and then of Japanese military imperialism created renewed opportunities for Lincoln's "new birth of freedom". That freedom included the advocacy and development of many other "isms" including communism, socialism, and Moslem extremism to name just a few egregious examples. That same freedom also led to innumerable scientific and economic advances for mankind, and made possible the America we all - or mostly all - enjoy today. America is a nation where, as I saw just yesterday on Route 50 in Easton, MD one person can be driving with a bumper sticker on the back of his car saying "TRUMP Make American Great Again" while in the next lane someone else's bumper stickers say "HILLARY" and "Love Trumps Hate". And these people live in peace together. That's what I call freedom of expression.

And if you can, please make the effort to visit the American cemetery above Omaha Beach at Colleville-sur-Mer in Normandy, look at the many rows of crosses punctuated by an occasional Star of David, and try not to cry. I tried and failed.

A Very Short Story

"As you know, Dad is good enough at tennis that he once even won at Wimbledon, and carried off all sorts of other prizes. And Mom is also a great player, not as good as Dad but still outstanding. And they want me to play tennis, and I'm being forced to take lessons in it. But I don't like tennis, and I have no talent for it. I can tell. I'll never be a good player. And I'm miserable over it.

Sure, I'm old enough to know that there are lots of people with worse problems. Some of the kids in my school aren't even smart enough to get average grades, and a few of them are really dumb. Some can't understand simple math, or learn how a battery works. They have brains that don't do what they want them to do. And they know it too, and that's sad.

And there are kids worse off than that. I've read about some who can't grow to normal size because something is wrong with one of their genes, other kids that can never learn to speak or hear. Or they can even be born blind. Some can hardly think at all. And they can die very young. Maybe some of them know what is happening to them. They are terribly worse off than me.

Me, I'm more like a 300 pound woman who looks in the mirror and wishes she weighed 130 and was beautiful instead of being fat and ugly. All the while she knows she's never going to be what she wants to be.

Mom and Dad keep telling me that there is a God. And if there is a God he must have a reason for what he does. Do you think there's a God? I hope so. But if He is there, why does all this happen?

Please explain it to me, Grandpa."

Two Old Men

Hoover Institution, Stanford, April 1998

He was a very old, very small man in a black suit, seated in the front row. His eyes were closed. He had large bushy eyebrows and a hawk nose. Age had bent his shoulders, and his hair was thinned and gray. In his right hand he grasped a massive, club-like walking stick of white ash.

The 5 faculty on the stage had finished discussing American foreign policy. They asked for questions from the audience. The old man opened his eyes, slowly transferred his cane from right hand to left, and waved slowly for the microphone.

"I am concerned", he said. His voice was remarkably deep and strong, with just the smallest trace of a European heritage. "I am concerned about missiles." He pronounced the word like Miss Syles.

"We must have a way to protect against them. There is the technology to build them in several countries. They will become a great threat to this country if we do not have this protection. I am trying to think, what can we do about missiles? We cannot ignore the issue they represent. We cannot pretend that this issue will go away."

He rested.

"Thank you, Dr. Teller", said the moderator. So it was Teller! Teller, the great physicist, the father of the hydrogen bomb. The man who had persuaded the American government that they had better build "Mike" before Stalin did, who had correctly seen the bomb as a vital protection for peace and security. The patriot who had argued against unilateral nuclear disarmament, who had testified that Oppenheimer - the scientific director of the Manhattan Project - might be a security risk, who had had the courage to withstand the brutal ostracism of his fellow physicists and intellectuals. And here was Teller. His few words had been so powerful, focused on a simple idea of overwhelming importance. They swept out of my mind the trivial panel discussion that had preceded his comment.

The men on the stage fielded some questions from the audience, but none were about missiles. They concerned the "new world order" in which America was "the only superpower". NATO came up.

Looking at the old man, the moderator said, "Dr. Teller, perhaps you would care to tell us what you think the future role of NATO should be."

A woman handed Teller the microphone. "I am trying to think", he said. "I am trying to think, 'What can you do about the missiles'.

It was electrifying. His mind had cut right through to the essential, it had stayed on the essential. NATO did not matter to Teller.

"Many countries can now launch missiles. And you cannot say to them that they cannot develop missiles for peaceful means, for satellites, for other reasons. Other countries will not accept this. It does not include them, it would limit their legitimate development. And for technical reasons, if a miss-syle were to be launched with destructive intent, it is much harder to destroy it the longer the delay after it is launched. There would be no time to consult about what to do if it seemed like a missile strike were underway. So, I am trying to think, what can you do about this? I am trying to think. We must have an agreement. The agreement would say that anyone can launch any missiles for peaceful purposes. And any country that is planning to do so must announce to the world, say at least one week in advance, that they are going to send up missiles and where they will go and what the purpose of the launch will be. But if any country launches missiles that are not pre-announced in this way, then the rule must be that action can be taken immediately against these missiles."

Of course! Simple, profound, and unforgettable. This powerful example of genius, Teller near the end of a long life of service, bent and feeble and barely able to walk, still struggling, still pondering, still teaching, still persuading, focused intently on what he knew REALLY mattered.

Later, a conversation with Milton Friedman, one of my heroes, a great economist with a deep love for personal freedom, a Nobel Laureate able to simplify complex issues for broader understanding. It was Friedman who documented the critical error in monetary policy ("tight money") that effectively caused the Great Depression in the 1930s. I had read most of his popular works, and also some technical ones. He is now almost 85. Age has been kinder to him than Teller although he cannot be more than 5 feet tall and his upper body is shortened and twisted by scoliosis. He smiled a lot during his discussion with about twenty of us, comfortably seated alone on the stage, explaining his visions of economic issues and liberty.

I ask a complex question of him when the session is over. It concerns Ludwig von Mises and Friedrich Hayek, the greatest leaders of the so-called Austrian school of economics. They are pillars, and rightly so, of the libertarian (classical liberal) movement. Mises had argued that socialism could not survive because it had no rationale pricing mechanism. History proved him right. Hayek had written, among many other fine books, the prescient classic, "The Road to Serfdom". Yet on coming to America, neither had been accepted into the mainstream of free market economists. Von Mises in fact barely managed an affiliate academic appointment in New York University. Hayek's ideas had been defeated in England by Keynesianism, which had provided an intellectual base for decades of leftist economic developments. Why?

I had two clues. I had read Mises theory of the time-value of money as the basis for interest, and it did not seem to make sense to me. But I am not an economist. Another was a footnote in one of Friedman's books, in which he mentioned that the Austrians had argued that the depression had to be left to cure itself, that inflation had caused it and that government intervention would only make it worse; this noninterventionist approach had been loathed by other economists wanting to "do something".

At first Friedman did not follow where my question was leading, but then he smiled. "Oh, of course, now I see what you mean. The answer is that the Austrian theory of the business cycle is simply all wrong." A clear, simple answer, based on a lifetime of study and experience, and a profound reminder that great men like Hayek and von Mises can be right about some things and wrong about others, that we can never automatically accept as true the assertions of our heroes.

Teller. Friedman. A chance to learn from the greatest among us. Now they are gone.

Moments in France, 1999

Here are samples of amusing moments in France.

One morning Dixie emerged to have breakfast on our hotel balcony above Vence. She looked radiant in her robe. Below, a crowd began to cheer. For a few moments she was flattered, until she realized that a bicycle race was taking place just below our window.

The French language poses interesting challenges:
The message light is on in my room. I call the operator.
"Il y'a des messages pour moi?" I say.
A sexy female voice answers. "Monsieur desire un massage?"
"No, pas un massage, mes messages"
"Oh, vous n'avez pas des messages!" The message light was defective.
And it is possible the operator was disappointed.

Yesterday we were in Aix-en-Provence (pronounced X). We had just finished waiting in line to leave our car in a "parking" near the huge fountain at the foot of a famous tree-lined boulevard, the Cours Mirabeau. The street is heavily populated by pretty French university students who sit under the trees in cafes much of the day while spending their parent's money on coffee and cigarettes and pretending to study. As we emerge from the parking I am greeted by an anxious bleach blonde of about 50 clutching a guide book.
"Excuse me, do you speak English?"
"Yes, I do."
"Oh, thank God!!! Thank God!! Do you know where's the Coors Mirabeau?" (spoken as in Coors Light).

"There it is right just ahead of you."

"Oh, thank you, thank you!!" and then she calls loudly to her wandering husband, "Honey, I found it!"

After this, I decided to camouflage myself as a Frenchman or an Italian who speaks little English. So I went into a store to buy a black shirt and found the only one in my size. The electronic register displayed the name of the product I had bought: "Chemise Sinatra". Amusant! I wore it out as my disguise and with sunglasses could now pass for a Mafioso.

A few days later in the small Alpes above the Riviera we observed a remarkable vertical curtain of rocks which the guide books call the Rochers de Mees. Dixie pointed them out as the "Roachers of Mees". I nearly lost control of the car, and made imaginary plans to call Orkin.

And later at dinner, a chariot de fromage bearing about 10 square feet of different French cheeses was rolled over to our table. We both like Epoisse, a very strong cheese that make Limburger seem mild. My wife asks for the "epuissee", which mean "exhausted" in French. Because she is so pretty the waiter seemed nevertheless to understand her perfectly and politely, and almost forgot to offer cheese to me.

I speak French fairly well and must confess that it drives me crazy that Dixie, who speaks almost no French, is everywhere treated better than I am by all these randy Frenchmen. For example, when we returned to our hotel after a couple of day's absence, it was "Oh, how nice to see you back, Mrs. King", etc., etc. while I was totally ignored, in fact left to carry the bags. Oh well, what can you expect from a bunch of frogs.

Skagway, Alaska - July 4, 2006

From autumn 1897 through the summer of 1898 approximately 25,000 gold seekers, mostly Americans, arrived by ship at the twin towns of Dyea and Skagway at the head of the Lynn Canal, a fjord in the panhandle of Alaska. From there, they clambered over the Chilkoot and White passes, repeatedly shuttling 4,000 feet up into clouds, rain, wind, and snow to tow and carry the half-ton of supplies per man required for entry into Canada. At the top of the passes, they entered the Yukon Territory, the border guarded day and night and all winter long by Northwest Mounted Police. After reaching Lake Bennett or other headwaters of the Yukon River, they built rafts, boats, boxes, modified coffins, or other contrivances to float down the Yukon River and its dangerous rapids hundreds of miles to Dawson. Here, by the junction of the Yukon and Klondike rivers, they sought gold under the permafrost near streams called Eldorado and Bonanza. A few found wealth, many were ruined, but most survived.

Those who attempted to reach Dawson and its Klondike gold by other routes were still less lucky, and had been more ill advised by the outrageously inaccurate guidebooks and booster literature promoted from potential "departure" cities like Seattle, Edmonton, and San Francisco. They died from cholera in overcrowded ships sailing for the mouth of the Yukon near St. Michaels, collapsed from exhaustion and scurvy and committed suicide in the mountains above Wrangall and the Stikine River, went mad and snow-blind and froze to death crossing the glaciers from Valdez and the vast Malaspina icefields and the high passes over the main body of the Canadian Rockies. Only a small minority who ventured on alternative routes to reach the Yukon made it through, and these usually arrived at the end of the gold rush in 1899 after the unimaginable suffering of wintering out for two years in the arctic wilderness.

The miners rarely found any gold, except for the fortunate few who discovered and staked the original claims in 1896. But there were plenty of folks who got rich off the miners. This is one of the lessons of which we write here. We shall not try even to summarize the history of the gold rush to the banks of the Klondike. This has been done many times, and perhaps best in "Klondike Fever," written in the 1950s by Canadian writer and entertainer, Pierre Benton, a man who actually grew up in Dawson and whose father came over the Chilkoot in '98. Still available in paperback, Benton's is one of the most informative and entertaining popular histories ever written.

There was real gold discovered in the Klondike region, just as there had been 50 years before near Sacramento. A new source of wealth had indeed been found. Let's review who captured most of the consequent economic value.

It certainly wasn't the emigrant miners themselves. The richest gold fields had been claimed before the summer of 1897 when the first ships, each carrying a ton of Klondike gold, landed at San Francisco and Seattle. News of the arrival of these ships started the stampede to the Far North. Breton estimates that about 50,000 persons spent an average of about $1,000 of their own money to go north to get rich, often abandoning their jobs and sometimes their families in the process. The purchasing power of a dollar one hundred years ago was about thirty fold that of today. So the $50 million so "invested" and subsequently lost by the would-be miners is the rough equivalent of $1.5 billion today. And the seekers not rarely gave up their lives as well in the craze for gold. Yet Breton estimates that the total value of all the gold obtained from all the Yukon mines through 1958, including their reworking by modern methods, was less than $50 million.

In general it was not the miners who got rich but those who went where the money was and took from those who had it. One man carried a grinding stone over to Dawson and sharpened miners' picks at a price of one ounce of gold per sharpening. One far-sighted fellow carried in boxes of nails, which later sold during the construction boom for prices higher than an equal weight of gold dust. Another carried in two hundred dozen eggs bought for a dollar a dozen, and sold them all in a day for $16 per dozen. Another entrepreneur brought in a chicken, and it laid $5 of fresh eggs per day. One man dragged several canvas bags full of live cats into Dawson, and the animals were immediately sold at astronomical prices to lonely miners.

Some of the biggest money was made by whores, the going rate being about $5 per throw for the ugly ones, and all the traffic could bear for the classier variety. Some of the most appealing of these women wore belts of large gold nuggets as their sole working attire. These and other ladies ran roadside hotels, cooked, danced with, and sometimes married the men with the most gold. Dance hall girls got a dollar a dance, and that dance usually lasted less than a minute. A very smart and tough Irish woman set up one of the fanciest hotels in Dawson, collected a fortune, married a French count, and lived out the rest of her life on a ranch near Yakima and had a second home in Seattle. Wilson Mizner imported a hooker from San Francisco, who pimped for him in Dawson and helped pay for his opium; he later became a Broadway playwright and owner of the Brown Derby in Hollywood. His brother, Addison, also thrived in the back alleys of the Klondike and later became a well-known real estate speculator and architect in the Florida land boom of the 1920s.

Shopkeepers, saloon owners, butchers, gamblers, lumber mill owners made fortunes from the gold seekers. Card sharps, swindlers, and crooks flourished. Skagway was ruled by a Mafia of confidence men and murderers controlled by Soapy Smith - the Al Capone of Alaska.

In Dyea and Skagway, almost every man carried a gun and killings occurred nightly. But across the border in the Canadian Yukon, the possession of guns was illegal, gun control was rigorously enforced by the Mounties, and murder and even theft were rare. So a gun was nearly worthless once a miner reached the Klondike. Someone started buying guns there for a dollar or less, and shipped them to the Outside where they sold for far more.

Lots of money was made by those who serviced the gold seekers with borrowed funds or via syndicates - in other words, with other people's money. Investor pools were created in New York, London, and other cities; these pools capitalized the banks, hotels, lumber yards, ships, tramways, and railroads that followed the gold to Dawson. The syndicators, managers, bankers, and organizers mostly got rich quick, got out fast, and lived well during and after the bust which came quickly in 1899. The distant investors usually lost their investments, and some presumably were left with debts.

The Klondike gold stampede produced only a limited creation, and perhaps even an aggregate destruction, of wealth, but a very large transfer of wealth. The madness provided the setting in which fortunes were made from the gullible. One hundred years later, similar lessons of history continue to repeat themselves.

Consider modern biotechnology, where investors have sunk tens of billions of dollars into an industry which, taken as a whole, has yet to earn a net dollar of profit. In the famous internet and telecommunications craze of the 1990s, almost precisely a century after the Klondike bubble burst, we witnessed what may have been the largest wealth transfer in history. Millions of investors lost many billions of total dollars, while net wealth creation was far smaller and likely negative. But some winners captured gobs and gobs of transferred money. These included VCs, bankers, financial advisors, stock brokers, accounting firms, conference organizers, business writers, analysts, syndicators, insiders. Executives, officers, and even ordinary employees of bubble companies made fortunes from risk-free stock options.

Human nature remains unchanged while the world economy grows. We hence assume that the magnitude of the zero or negative sum wealth transfers of the past will be exceeded in the future. Economic and other follies show little sign of vanishing from the earth.

Indeed, there is eyewitness evidence that the wealth transfer started a century ago in Alaska continues there today on a grand scale. When we visited Skagway on July 4, 2006 the town was hosting tourists from at least five large cruise ships, an estimated 10,000 people in that single day. The money spent per tourist on each ship may be roughly estimated at $500 per day, or say $5 million in total just to get to Skagway on that one day and view some cliffs and waterfalls along its fjord. The picturesque train ride to the top of the White Pass cost $100 per person, not counting the tariffs for hats and other souvenirs, and several thousand people rode the rails above Skagway on the 4th. Barmaids in low cut dresses sold watered ale at outrageous prices, stuffed twenty dollar tips between their large and largely exposed breasts, and had a great 4th. Near Sitka, Alaska during a salmon fishing trip on July 2, four of us caught two salmon. We subsequently calculated that we had paid about $250 per pound for edible seafood, not counting the lost "opportunity cost" of the day's work of four employable adults while catching two fish.

Don't get me wrong. In Alaska on the rare days when the sky is blue the scenery really can be terrific, and few tourists lose everything to cruise line operators and barmaids. The scenery doubtless seemed even more novel and spectacular for the gold rushers to the Klondike, and one hopes it provided partial compensation to some of the many who really went bust there.

A last comment on an interesting historical coincidence. One of the few men who got rich by finding gold in the Klondike was named William Gates. Breton's book says much about him. "Stillwater Bill" Gates made an early strike at Eldorado, but lost his fortune through an unfortunate propensity for gambling and chronic involvement with young women, whom he sometimes married concurrently. This Bill Gates died poor. The modern Bill Gates is much too smart and much too rich to meet the economic fate of his namesake, and much of his money is being used to prevent diseases in underdeveloped countries. He arguably even has usefully created real wealth, rather than just shuffled the economic deck or dug yellow metal from the ground. Maybe we are making some progress after all.

On Stupid

As you may know I sometimes create little sketches about topics that have attracted my attention, and some of these have been quite serious like writing about freedom and international trade while others have been more humorous, and the truth is that my friends almost all seem to prefer being amused and laughing to getting serious about anything with the result that the feedback I get from my audience suggests that maybe I should try to make them laugh more and leave the serious stuff to others like politicians, social scientists, economists, and philosophers and actually I'm happy to do this, and the current example may convince you that I am persuaded and furthermore I am writing it in the style of one of my most popular stories which was about Jackie Mason in West Palm Beach entertaining a large bunch of mostly Jewish people, and which is called "Mason and More" and you can read it if you bought the first edition of "Essays, Stories, and Poems" on Amazon.com and paid for it or you can read it some pages back in the current volume, but in any case it's your problem and not mine if and how you read it but in the Mason story I said everything I had to say in one very long sentence and it turns out that everyone liked it that way so now I am going to do the same thing here but on a different subject and that subject is "stupid", and for me and my wife too we see a lot of stupid stuff going on in the world around us almost every day if not more often and we laugh about it because what else can you do except cry, and it really is a sobering fact that the average IQ in the United States and everywhere else too is by definition 100 (whether you believe me or not it's true) and so for every person with an IQ above 100 and whose intelligence is above average there are an approximately equal number of people whose smarts are below average, and while smart people can sometimes do stupid things it seems obvious that less smart people will generally do more stupid things, and since except at Lake Wobegon about half of people are below average and there are now officially 323.1 million people in America (currently the third most populous nation in the world) and actually more, that provides loads of opportunity for stupid things to happen right here in the good old U.S.A. and so maybe you would like to hear a few real life examples, but to give you an idea of what I mean we can start with the apocryphal story of the three dumb guys who are drinking in a bar and one says let's go to another place I know where you can get two drinks for the price of one, and the second guy says I know where you can get three drinks for the price of one, and the third says I know a place where you can get three drinks free and get laid in the parking lot and the other two say wow, who told you about that? and the guy answers my wife, that's sort of what I'm getting at but now let's move on to personal experiences such as a few months ago when we were driving cross country and we stop at a gas station in the Texas panhandle and all the gas pumps have a yellow thing over the pump handles that say NO GAS and so I go inside and ask the girl behind the counter why are you out of gas and she says we didn't think we'd need that much, which I thought was pretty funny, and then the next day we are in Oklahoma where our experiences proved that the old saw might be right that in the 1930s when some of the Okies left Oklahoma for California they simultaneously lowered the IQ in two states, because what happened there was we got on a road between Oklahoma City and Tulsa and it turns out that it's a toll road with no indication before you got on it that it was a toll road and it is 75 miles to Tulsa and no place to turn around and we start passing exits with barriers and signs that say exact change coins only and so we are going to need a lot of coins by the time we get to Tulsa or so it seems and I ask Dixie if she has quarters in her purse and of course she doesn't they weigh too much and we don't have any in the car either and so we just keep going, after all what else could we do, and after maybe 35 miles we pull into the only gas station actually on the highway and I pump gas while Dixie goes inside to get change and a few minutes later she comes back and says the woman there was asked for change by the man in front of me and she just said Tulsa four-fifty no coins and there is a sign over her head that says exactly the same thing and she kept saying it and the guy left in disgust and I tried and couldn't get a straight answer out of her either, so I said let me try and I walk in there is this middle-aged white woman with a handwritten sign near her Tulsa four-fifty no coins and I say to her how do I get off the road and she says you want to get off the road? and I say yes I do I am going to Tulsa, and she says its four-fifty no coins and I say how can I pay four-fifty with no coins and she says again it's four-fifty no coins and then finally a light bulb goes on in my head and I say wait a minute is there maybe a person at the toll booth at the Tulsa end of this road and she says yes and I say can you pay with a five or a twenty and she says you can pay with anything it's four-fifty no coins, and sure enough when we got near Tulsa it was four-fifty no coins and we escaped with two quarters change, but really this is only one of many examples, something just happened yesterday where we have a man who drives our car to other cities from time to time and his last name is Hartmeyer and Dixie decided to get a credit card from Chase Visa for him to use on such trips and so she called the bank and gave them the information she was asked for and carefully spelled out the last name HARTMEYER and yesterday the card arrived and the full name embossed on it was HEART MEYER and of course we needed to get another card for him and it reminded us of the time when a letter to Dixie was addressed to Mr. Dick C. King, and another to Dicksey King, no I am not making this up it's all true, and there is the time when a friend of mine called another bank about a possibly incorrect interest calculation and was told that it's OK we do our interest in the rear, and there are many other things like how a few years ago we had some guests coming to our home and they came all the way from China so we wanted things to look nice for them so we had our housekeeper carefully clean the front windows and door before they arrived and he did it very well except that after he finished and left, five minutes before our guests arrived I walked out onto the patio by our front door and discovered a large pile of dirty rags which the housekeeper had forgotten to remove, and then later that same day while the Chinese were inside our home all the lights went out and simultaneously we heard a kind of explosion near the house that comes between us and the street and so I went over there and see that a backhoe was being used to dig up a big shrub and I was told that when the hoe went in there were a lot of sparks and the lawn had been marked out for the removal by employees of the power company branch called Miss Utility and it seemed that Miss Utility had missed the correct location of the power line under the lawn, and we all agreed it should be renamed Misutility and the neighbor who hired them offered to pass on the suggestion for the new name to Delmarva Power but I don't know if he ever did, but it probably wouldn't have made any difference anyway because stupid is limitless, and this reminds me also of when Dixie and I stopped at a McDonalds in Middletown, Delaware that offered espresso as well as regular coffee and so I ordered an espresso and watched as the employee put the espresso into a large cup, looked sort of puzzled, and then filled it up with coffee from the nearby pot and when she handed it to me I asked her why did you put the coffee in my espresso and she said she didn't think it looked right so empty, but really that is nothing compared to a videotape I saw taken by a McDonalds security camera at about 4 am where a guy comes in, points

a gun at the lady behind the counter and says open the
register and give me the money, and she says I can't open
the register unless you order something, and instead of
shooting her the guy says OK give me a hamburger and she
says we don't sell hamburgers until after 10 o'clock and the
guy gives up and leaves and of course he was caught later
and it's good for him that he didn't shoot her and good for
her too but whether or not it was good to society you can
decide for yourself, but even that can't compare with the
real case of the man who bought a new Winnebago, started
driving it down a highway, set the autopilot, and then left
the driver's seat and went to the back to make himself a cup
of coffee and while he was doing this the Winnebago left
the road and crashed into some bushes wrecking them and
the motor home, and if that is not enough the guy who was
miraculously uninjured sued Winnebago because the
instructions didn't say you should stay at the wheel even
when the autopilot was on, and a jury of his peers awarded
him one million dollars and the company had to change its
ownership manual to remind new owners of this important
information, so maybe I should stop here because really I
could go on almost forever with examples of stupid and
you probably don't want me to so I won't but just remind
you that you can probably think of many instances from
your own experiences and if you don't laugh at them I
promise that I will so let me know and maybe someday I
will include them in another one of my ruminations, and
remember also that I laugh at this stuff because the only
alternative is despair and to let it really sink in that so
much of what is wrong in the world is due to plain old
stupidity and that it has always been abundant in mankind
and always will be, and maybe it's better to laugh about it if
you can.

Why Polls Get It Wrong

This morning my wife said to me, "They were wrong on Hogan by 18 points". Thinking about an entirely different thing, I replied, "What?" She explained, "The polls for Governor in Maryland predicted on the night before the election that Hogan would lose by 18 points, but he won." How true it is. And of course we all saw a similar situation in the 2016 Presidential election where the election-eve odds in Vegas, based in large part on extensive polling, were about 5:1 in favor of the person who lost. Lots of my friends ask me, presumably in part because I'm a scientist, "How can they get it so wrong?"

Pollsters are not stupid and there is an extensive and mathematically sophisticated literature, going back many years, on the sources of error in polling. Donald Rubin, a mathematician and a full professor at Harvard, has written a whole book on imputation methods for correcting polling errors, and a casual survey of the literature online will identify many other books and scholarly articles on attempts to make polling more accurate. Major polling organizations employ statisticians and marketing experts and use proprietary analytical methods (algorithms) to try to make their polls more reliable than their competitors' predictions. Yet polls, even when their results are averaged into presumably more reliable aggregate estimates, are often in error.

We've all read that polls are based on surveys of a few hundred to about one thousand people. These sample sizes are not chosen at random, but are taken to be of sufficient size to allow pollsters to claim in fine print that their "margin of error" in predicting voting proportions is about plus or minus 3%. That means that they are saying they offer a very great improvement on just plain guessing where with two possible choices there is only a 50% chance of being right, except in elections that are not going to be close where no polling is really needed even though the pollsters claim credit for being right. In my opinion, the reliability of polling predictions is even in theory far lower than claimed.

There is a fundamental, inescapable problem in polling. Estimated error rates in sampling a population depends mathematically on having a sufficiently large sample size and very importantly on the sample selection being a true representation of the population from which it is supposed to be drawn. And that kind of truly representative sampling simply can't be obtained by polling. Polling and sampling are not the same thing. Imagine that someone calls you up, introduces himself as from the XYZ Survey, and says something like "I would like to ask you a single question. Your answer will be kept confidential but will be included in our survey without anyone knowing who you are. My question is "How many times per month do you have sexual relations?" Most of us would just hang up, perhaps accompanying that action with an unprintable comment. But some subset, likely a small proportion, of the people would answer the question. And of those, some might tell the truth, some boastfully lie, some intentionally make up a number to confuse the nosey pollsters, and so on. Would the results of such a survey be a reliable determination of American sexual behavior? Of course not. There would be huge and unavoidable errors - called ascertainment bias or some other fancy scientific name - in any such survey.

The same would be true if pollsters called up people to ask about their incomes, their net worth, or any other significant personal information. Such surveys will necessarily have very large possible errors, and there is no way those errors can be accurately predicted or prospectively prevented. Lots of people just won't answer the question, and there is no way to ensure that those who do are representative of those who don't. Even when required by law to give answers, many people refused to fill out the "long form" if that was assigned to them in the 2010 census.

It seems intuitively obvious that the more important and personal the information being sought, the more likely it is that surveys will generate wrong conclusions since they will suffer from greater uncorrectable non-response bias. Uncorrectable without pollster guessing that is. In the recent Presidential election many people described experiences like losing friends over their vote, arguing about it with family (mostly with their children), being unable to express their opinion without being insulted, and so on. Whether or not an individual actually experienced this kind of thing, many people recognize that who you will or did vote for may be sufficiently significant to merit confidentiality. So it's only a non-random subset of the population who will honestly disclose their vote to strangers like pollsters, and maybe even to their friends or family.

And that's why - the major reason why - electoral pollsters cannot, even in theory, do accurate surveys. Their supposed +/- 3% predictions have far larger errors which they will not readily admit, since their livelihoods depend on getting people to pay attention to what they have to say and to sell. Shakespeare famously said that a rose by any other name would smell as sweet. Polling by any other name would smell as malodorous - and the more important the questions being asked, the worse the aroma.

All Cultures Are Equal?

About a decade ago I was invited by its director to join the Board of Claremont-McKenna College's small Holocaust Center. The director was a non-Jewish professor at this private college near Los Angeles, and had focused his research activities on art thefts by the Nazis during World War II. The Holocaust Center studied genocides and atrocities in many lands around the world, including of course the Nazi exterminations. I happened to be visiting the center on a day when my friend was hosting a special event for the undergraduates taking his course on Nazism: an elderly Jewish man now living in L.A. who had survived for several years in Auschwitz had agreed to relate the story of his imprisonment and escape from execution. I received permission to sit in on the class.

The speaker was a man in his eighties, compactly built and still vigorous for his age. He sat at the head of a rectangle of tables and almost 20 students listened in silence as, with an Eastern European accent, he told his horrifying story. He somehow managed to do this without shedding tears or otherwise betraying deep emotion. One of millions of Jews rounded up by Fascist agents, he had been stripped of his belongings, forced into a windowless cattle car, and brought to the death camp. Appearing sufficiently young and strong, was then triaged into a worker contingent. The other categories of men, women, and children were led into "showers" where they were asphyxiated by Zyklon B gas (hydrogen cyanide). This man's job was to extract the teeth from the corpses, pick out the gold from the teeth, and turn it over to his guardians. Resistance of any kind, theft of gold, working slowly, psychological breakdowns, and similar deviances were punished by immediate execution. He managed to perform these terrible tasks many hours each day for 2-3 years, and was then lucky enough to escape the extermination meted out to many of his compatriots as the Germans fled before the advancing Allies.

Like many others, I was sickened by the story he told and amazed at his ability to survive. It seemed to me that his tough innate personality had become even more hardened from his experiences, and that any outward manifestations of feeling were deeply restrained. He lived, he was there before us, and yet in another sense was almost not alive.

For a few moments after he finished, the stunned audience was silent. Then I turned to my friend the professor and asked if I could pose a question to his class. He nodded, and I said, "What you all just heard was a description of a culture - Nazi culture. After this, is there anyone who still believes - as some of you have been taught - that all cultures are equal, of equal value?" For a few moments, the students said nothing. Then a young man sitting in the chair just to the speaker's right spoke up. "I do." I replied, "Do you really mean that? You have just heard an eyewitness description of Nazi culture and you are the presence of a survivor of Auschwitz." And the kid said, "Yes, all cultures are equal". None of the other students contradicted him. And rather than taking this discussion further, the professor thanked the speaker, ducked the issue, and smoothly switched over to the subject of stolen art. Shortly thereafter I left the room.

This is an absolutely true story. It may be difficult for some of you to believe. Believe it. I was there.

Mashed Rambler

When I was at Harvard Medical School in the early '60s my dating was significantly inhibited by lack of a motor vehicle. Vanderbilt Hall, the student residence near the medical school campus in Boston, was some miles from the major aggregations of college women except for nearby Emanuel College, a Catholic school sometimes known as "Manual College", and Simmons College on the Fenway. To reach girls at Boston University, Radcliffe, Wellesley, Brandeis, and any of the really out of town schools like Holyoke, Smith, or Skidmore one had to have wheels. I determined to acquire them, and craftily announced to my financiers (otherwise known as my parents) that I was planning to buy a motor scooter. They caved, and agreed to pay for a used automobile rather than have me risk my life riding a scooter on Boston's ice streets.

Thus I acquired a light blue, boxy, and unsexy but useful Nash Rambler. Why this vehicle? Because it was very cheap. And it mostly worked. Its major limitation was frequent refusal to start in very cold weather, which Boston winters offered in abundance; several local garages were unable to fix the problem. But usually the Nash did start, and my dating possibilities increased. Of course with a car like this and a limited budget I could not hope to compete for women with one upperclassman who had a yellow Jaguar XKE convertible, was heir to a drug company fortune, and whose ever-changing girlfriends spent nights in his room. Still, things began to look up and I started to date girls from some of the above mentioned institutions.

Harvard Med provided no parking facilities for students, so one parked one's car on the street. One morning as I wolfed down a marginally edible breakfast in the dining room, a classmate suggested that I take a look at my car. I had found a seemingly lucky parking spot the previous evening on the edge of the traffic circle directly in front of the entrance to Vanderbilt Hall. Alas, as I emerged into daylight it was apparent that my Nash was a complete wreck. During the night someone had driven into it, knocked it up onto the sidewalk and into a large tree, and then disappeared. My little car was now U-shaped, deeply indented on its right flank, all its windows smashed in on that side, and almost completely wrapped around the tree - which had apparently withstood the impact quite successfully. The car was totaled.

I called my insurance company and asked how I could obtain a replacement vehicle, since my Nash was obviously unrepairable. The insurance person said they could give me only a temporary loaner until an adjuster had examined the car. While I felt this was a complete waste of time, the insurer insisted and later that day the car was examined at the scene of the accident.

Next day, I spoke to the insurance company's representative and was told the company intended to pay for repair of the vehicle and would not provide a replacement. They considered that the automobile could be fully restored. I protested but the company was unyielding. My hopelessly crumpled wreck was towed to a repair shop in one of the less agreeable neighborhoods of Boston. I went along in the tow truck determined to talk the repair people out of wasting their time.

I spoke with the owner, who communicated in English fairly well but with an accent I could not identify - he was from Armenia. I explained how the whole frame of the car was crushed in and I was sure that any repair would return to me a car whose front and rear wheels would never be in perfect alignment and that would move crablike over the road. The man told me not to worry. He very respectfully said, "Doctor (I was three years away from being a doctor), we have fixed cars worse than this. We have equipment for straightening the frame. It will take 2-3 weeks to return your car to perfect condition. I promise you will be happy when we are done." The insurance people had really left me no choice. And I was sure this guy was lying to keep their business. Disbelieving him quite completely, I departed angry about the whole situation.

A couple of weeks later, I got a call from "the Armenian". He said that my car was fixed and he asked me to come for it. I of course planned to examine the car in minute detail to identify its remaining, presumably irreparable, flaws. But when I went over the Rambler, to my amazement it truly appeared to be in perfect condition. I complimented the man on doing a great job, better than I had ever imagined could happen. He said to me, "Doctor, I knew you would be happy with our work. And by the way, did you ever have trouble starting the car in cold weather?" I told him that indeed I had. He went on, "This model of Nash has a design error. American Motors gave the car an ignition coil with inadequate power. I put in a more powerful one for you, and I don't think you will have starting problems anymore."

This guy was returning my car to me in better condition than it had been before the accident! It was obvious that behind the accent and soiled work clothes was a man of ability and intelligence. I began to talk with him about his personal history: how did he come to America, how did he get started repairing cars, how did he manage to eventually develop his own business? He willingly told me his story.

And then I asked him, "Do you have any children?" He had a son. And I asked if the son had joined him in the repair business, and he said no.

So I said, "Would you mind telling me what your son is doing now?"

And he replied, "Doctor, my son is a neurosurgeon at the Massachusetts General Hospital."

I was deeply moved. And I remembered that my own grandparents had been immigrant tailors who could barely speak English. That their children had become doctors, accountants, lawyers, and schoolteachers. And that two generations later, I was going to get an M.D. at Harvard Medical School and learn neurosurgery from this Armenian immigrant's son.

Years later I was at a discussion group at the Bohemian Grove, the famous men's summer camp in the woods near California's Russian River. And in response to a question from the moderator a middle-aged Frenchman who owned pearl farms in the South Pacific said, "As long as the smartest people in the world want to come to America, America will be just fine."

I couldn't agree more.

Fire - A Story

We were smoking Padron 45s and sipping our second snifters of XO. The flames in the fireplace glowed orange and warm. Our wives had long since gone to bed. Sunk deep in our chairs in perfect comfort, we talked with the frankness of trusted friends. Our conversation acquired a philosophical color.

"How sad it is", I said, "that it is impossible to live without hurting something or someone, no matter how hard one tries not to. The vegetarian deprives herself of animal meat. Then she drives her car to buy vegetables and hits a squirrel or rabbit or bird. And if that doesn't happen, dead insects still stick to the front of her car. You open a store because, after all, one must earn a living - and another man's shop loses business and fails, maybe he goes bankrupt, perhaps even becomes depressed or suicidal. We must outcompete others to obtain a good education, to get a scholarship. Boys and men, and now girls and women, are taught to engage in sports - and for every winner there is an unhappy loser. Beautiful women find husbands and lovers, ugly ones cannot. I have never understood how to live in a way that truly harms nothing or nobody. I want to but I can't. I can make no sense of it."

My friend took a long draw on his cigar. "Yes," he replied after a pause, "how true it is. Let me tell you a story from my distant past that illustrates perfectly what you are saying. Ah, it happened more than half a century ago, and it still troubles me. After all, one does not join the Boy Scouts to hurt others. Scouts are taught to be good kids. I still remember the attributes one was urged to develop: 'A Scout should be trustworthy, loyal, helpful, friendly, courteous, kind, obedient, cheerful, thrifty, brave, clean, and reverent.' And I really tried to be like that. Yet it was in the Scouts that I ruined a life.

Scouts were encouraged to acquire various skills, including those which might be useful under special conditions like being lost in a wilderness. Proven accomplishment allowed one to receive a merit badge in that skill. The more merit badges, the higher one's rank in the Scouts, the highest level of course being an Eagle Scout. One of my cousins became an Eagle Scout, which required, I seem to recall, about 20 merit badges. He later became a doctor and a drug addict, but that is another story. I never got close to Eagle level, just the much lower Star, and I quit the Scouts after the following happened."

My gray-haired friend paused and took another sip of cognac, somewhat larger than the last, and looked off into the distance. He again drew on his cigar, and we watched the smoke as it curled upward. After some time he continued.

"I was a lucky kid. I was born smart. Others were born to be athletes or musicians or artists. Success in almost anything involving science or math came easily to me and I was always at the top of my classes in school. Teachers adored me. My parents were proud of me. I had a low key pleasant personality and quite a few friends. In short, I was a happy and gifted child.

I don't remember why I joined the Scouts, probably because some of my friends did. And while I was not a real enthusiast, I followed the rules and worked, like the other kids, to acquire merit badges. One of them involved proving skill in fire-building with flint and steel.

Do you know how to do this? No? Then you probably were never a Scout. Well, the basic idea is that you start with the striker, a steel bar a few inches long and maybe a quarter of an inch thick and an inch wide. You hold a stone made of flint in your other hand and strike it sharply with the steel. This generates, some of the time, one or more sparks. At least one glowing spark will hopefully fall into a prepared nest of wood shavings. Then you drop the implements and whirl the nest at the end of your fully extended arm as quickly as possible through the air like a windmill. If done right, the shavings burst into flame. The burning nest can be used to start a campfire.

For some reason I found it easy to succeed with flint and steel although many kids couldn't. I got pretty good at striking sparks and getting my shavings to burst into flame. But the best at this in our troop was a boy named Jerry. He was a whiz at it, incredibly fast. Jerry was an odd little kid, smaller than the other boys, weak, ignored for sport teams, and a terrible student. He was the butt of jokes from some other kids and even a few mean teachers. His parents were poor, and he lived in the worst apartment building in our neighborhood. Jerry seemed good at nothing - except fire-building. That was his skill, his pride, his precious corner of success and self-respect. Nobody could beat him at fire-building.

Perhaps you can see where this is going? Well, for reasons I no longer remember our scoutmaster decided to organize a competition of merit badge skills. The parents were invited, and brought other relatives and friends to watch their kids perform. Not every kid participated, but the activities were selected so there was a distribution which included many of the boys. Each competition was one on one. Jerry of course was selected for fire-building. But who was going to compete with him? Nobody wanted to do it. The scoutmaster told me to be the other competitor. I expected to lose, but I aimed to do my best, and anticipated my nest of shavings bursting into flame a few seconds after Jerry's. I practiced a little in the days before the competition.

It took place in a school gymnasium, and maybe a hundred or more adults and kids were there. Most of the events were boring to watch, but fire-building was not and it was last on the schedule. Jerry and I each kneeled beside our equipment and at the signal struck our flints. On the first blow several sparks flashed into my nest of shavings. I leapt to my feet, and swirled it as fast as I could. It burst immediately into flame. Jerry was still on the floor. Unexpectedly I had won.

I think I heard a little applause. The scoutmaster came over and shook my hand. I could see my mother and father smiling. Then I walked over to Jerry. His little body seemed even smaller than before, his head hung down, he was crying and would not look at me or speak to me. He shuffled over to his parents and disappeared in the crowd."

I said nothing, and for a long moment my friend too was silent. He neither drank nor smoked. His mind was off somewhere remembering. His voice had a little catch when he resumed.

"I never saw Jerry again. Other kids told me that he refused to go to school, wouldn't play with any of them, hid himself away from everyone. Then his family moved away.

I was to blame for hurting him badly, maybe scarring him forever. He had so little going for him in the game of life, I had so much, and I had taken away the bit that he had. It was only many years later that I read about this in Matthew 13:12. I can still quote the words of Jesus from that wonderful Zondervan Bible - 'Whoever has will be given more, and he will have an abundance. Whoever does not have, even what he has will be taken away.' Some say this is a purely spiritual message, but many of us have seen it happen in real life.

Yes, I have also found it impossible to live without doing harm."

We looked into the fire for a long time and finished our cognac and cigars.

Poems

Poetry
should be
concise,
rhythmic,
intelligible,
and emotive.

And if it may sometimes
cause laughter,
so much the better.

"Say everything as simply as possible,
then cut."

W. Somerset Maugham

Above a Grave

Above a grave I saw it once,
I cannot tell a lie,
HE MARRIED LIVED FOR THIRTY YEARS
AND WAS PREPARED TO DIE.

Beside Me

I lie here and I think of you,
While my true love's beside me.
Why sometimes do I think of you,
While she rests here beside me?

I know I shouldn't think of you,
While she's asleep beside me.
My thought will pass. And joyfully
She'll still be here beside me.

Brokers

"Tonight let's talk of women, not
Stock rumors that we've heard."

"Fine," said the other broker,
"Common or preferred?"

Choices

Sex ends,
Drinking's bad,
Travel's tiring,
Death makes you sad.
Golf's a bore,
Eat and you grow,
Reading's fatiguing,
Investing is slow.
Kids wander off,
Grandkids too,
Aging continues.
What's to do?

Sex is fun,
A small drink's enjoyable,
Travel's amusing,
Most friends are viable.
Par is a thrill,
Good food's like honey,
Reading's a joy,
Investing makes money.
Kids can love you,
Grandkids too,
Aging continues.
What's to do?

Aging continues.
But here's what we'll do.
Remain in love,
Me and you.

Epitaph

Brother, as you're passing by,
As you are now so once was I.
As I am now so shall you be.
Be good before thy soul dost flee.

How?

It must be hard to evolute,
A virus to a man.
If anyone can do it, Lord,
I bet You can.

Some say You aren't needed, and
Just Time alone will do
The job well and unheeded, Lord,
With no regard to You.

They could be right and on the mark,
And Evolution can.
But it seems so hard to evolute
A virus to a man.

Kilimanjaro

You're always as close
As a bottle of pills
To the snows of Kilimanjaro.

Whatever your ills,
A mere bottle of pills,
Will take you to Kilimanjaro.

For to stand and be still
To the Birkenhead Drill
Is a damn tough bullet to chew.

But by night or by day
You are not far away,
From that mountain top where the snow leopards
play.

Just a bottle of pills
Can cure all your ills,
And you'll be on Kilimanjaro.

Lamentation

I shot an arrow in the air,
It fell to Earth,
I knew not where.

I went to see,
Because, you see,
That arrow meant so much to me.

I made it with a head of gold,
From peacock's tail,
Yew strong and old.

T'was made with will,
And love,
And skill.

It took a
Score of years
To do.

Aimed well and high
It left my bow,
then met the sky.

Sent with a song,
And silent prayer,
"Go straight and long."

I watched it go.
It disappeared.
It must, you know.

I searched to see
What fate had done,
Oh arrow, to thee.

I found thee far,
From where I'd aimed,
So very far.
Feathers once bright
Dulled
Beyond twilight.

Mired in dung
Thy golden head,
For which I'd sung

My melody
Of hopes
For thee.

Thy shaft askew,
The winds had not
Been kind to you.

Dear arrow, my little one!
There remains
But lamentation.

Less Than Nine Months

The Nazi general buttoned up.
"In nine months you will have a boy,
And you may call him Adolf, since
I honored you to be my joy."

She smiled and thought, you piece of shit,
You fucking Nazis act like weasels.
Nine weeks from now you'll have my gift -
A rash, and you may call it measles.

Lizzie

Lizzie Borden took an axe,
Gave her mother forty whacks,

When she saw what she had done,
She gave her brother forty-one.

And once she saw what she could do,
She gave her sister forty-two.

Then Lizzie got a lawyer
Who told her what to plead:

A victim of abuse she was,
A lonely child in need.

Her mother wasn't nice to her,
Her daddy was a sot,

Who'd left the family early on,
And told them all to rot.

So Lizzie's angry temper was
Compelled by her abuse.

Poor thing, sometimes she'd lose control
And grab an ax for use.

The lawyer pled, the jury heard,
And Lizzie got 300 years.

She felt a little bad at that,
and even shed some tears.

But then she lost control again,
Brought out a hidden ax,

And 'fore anyone could stop her,
Gave her lawyer forty whacks.

Magnolias Sweet

Daffodils, pink peonies,
Azure iris, robins' eggs,
Magnolias sweet and river birch,
Myrtle trees and plovers' legs.
These have I seen.

Canyons red, valleys deep,
Snow on granite, golden towers,
Bougainvillea, hummingbirds,
Blowing palms and shady bowers,
These too I've seen.

Wind-pregnant sails, salmon wild
In grayish lakes, the resting dove,
Paris lights on winter nights,
Countless stars while with my love,
Are also what I've seen.

The time will come when I shall rest -
Which after all is fair -
And meet the God who blessed me
So fully in my share.
This too I shall see.

Maybe

He ain't that cute, but I sure hope
Now he's asked me to dance
That he won't trample on my feet,
And his wallet's the bulge in his pants.

The Miracle Within the Miracle

Twenty-five years
Of blood, sweat, and tears,
Compass twenty with nights,
Of pure delights.
And I'm still in love with you.

Twenty-five years
Of blood, sweat and tears,
Hold so many mornings
Of satisfied longings.
And I'm still in love with you.

News Item

Men seldom make passes,
At girls with fat asses.
What glasses?

--- Dorothy Porker

Nobody Rides for Free

Ass is a diminishing asset,
Grass only goes so far,
Booze ain't much, and I've
Got adequate gas in my car.

The asset that grows is money.
It's always on my mind,
Mine grows and grows, but I
Must leave it all behind.

So bring your gorgeous body,
And I'll buy two drinks or three.
Since poor or rich, ass, grass, or gas,
Nobody rides for free.

Nonsense

"I wish I were a pair of ragged claws,
Scuttling across the floors of silent seas."
Tell me, Mr. Eliot - tell me anyone -
How that makes sense. Please.

Not Smart

He wasn't smart,
Though he did pull out
When he heard her
Call his name.

But he let it out
After he'd pulled out,
"I guess I shouldn't have came."

Not Snow White

Mary had a little kid,
Its skin was white as snow,
And everywhere that Mary went
That kid is sure to go.
As for Daddy, who can know?
Mary isn't white as snow.

On Baseball

When Adam delved,
And Eve span,
Who was then
A Phillies fan?

On Delmarva's Fair Shore

On Delmarva's fair shore
When you goes out to dine
If you like beer
And don't need wine

For elegance
You takes your picks
From "Big Pecker's", "Hooters"
Or "Dirty Dick's"

Pascal

Pascal was right.
Don't watch TV at night.
Man's troubles arise
From his failure – not wise –
To sit still in a room.
In a quite quiet room
And to think. Or not think.
Or maybe to drink.

Point of View

In sex as in life so much depends
Upon your point of view.
The head of the shaft seems distal to me,
And proximal to you.

Robbers

The robber came into the rich widow's home,
She screamed again and again,
'Til he said he just wanted her money.
"Oh, you're just like all other men."

Savoir-faire

"Please tell me what is savoir-faire?"
The Englishman complained.
"We'll tell you what is savoir-faire,"
Three Frenchmen then exclaimed.

What is zee savoir-faire?

The first began, "You find your wife
In a ménage à trois,
You do not shout, you back away,
You say, "Excusé moi."

Zat is zee savoir-faire.

The second said, "She's in zee bed
with him, imaginez,
You see zem and say calmly, "Ah,
Pardon, continuez!"

Zat is zee savoir-faire.

The third said "No, zee husband comes
With her *you* are zee man,
He says "Pardon, excusé moi,
continue." - AND YOU CAN.

Now zat is savoir-faire!

Shove It

Teasin' ain't pleasin'
Lyin' ain't lovin'
Tryin' ain't doin'
Nothin' ain't somethin'

Fakin' ain't makin'
Stopin' ain't goin'
Takin' ain't givin'
Pretendin' ain't knowin'

Here's the point,
Of what I just writ -
Take it and shove it,
I'm tired of bullshit.

Slippery Slope

The man stood on the slippery slope,
His member full of blisters.
He'd been inside some underpants
And they were not his sister's.

His wife she did forgive him
Though he heard a word or two,
And remember, friend that slippery slope
Is there for me and you,
Yes, it's there for me and you.

Solo Practice

"How are you, Joseph?"
He would say.

Then top his glass
With Tanqueray.

And speak of lives
He'd saved that day.

Next morn renew
His long, hard way.

And later drink
More Tanqueray.

Sonnet on That Time of Year

That time of year I didst in me behold,
When yellowed leaves or none or few do hang
Upon the boughs that shake against the cold.
Bare ruined choirs where late the sweet birds sang.

I went to see my doctor who told me
That I was well, just older by a bit.
He said my solid health was fine to see,
No need to fear or lose sleep over it.

My MRI was perfect and my E
EG benign. The CT scan was good.
My lytes were great, my heart was strong. In me
All organ systems functioned as they should.

So wrong was he I almost had to laugh.
And so, dear friend, you read my epitaph.

Thanksgiving

If only I could have,
By willing it,
A Thanksgiving turkey - without
Killing it.

The Old Man Said

The old man said, and smiled a bit,
"When I was as young as you,
I spent all night a-doing,
What it now takes me all night to do."

The Orator

To fake and lie to everyone,
Is not exactly treason.
An orator's one who persuades
Without resort to reason.

We've seen the work of orators.
Thucydides described
How Athens fell beneath their spell,
Though only few were bribed.

So they invaded Syracuse.
In a Peloponnesian fight
They lost the war from hearing words
The opposite of right.

Herr Hitler worked a German crowd
Like none had ever known.
Eventually, the Germans reaped
What Hitler's words had sown.

Beware the orator, my son!
His words mislead and catch.
Beware the Jubjub bird and shun
The frumious Bandersnatch.

The Teacher Said

Ye who seek for wisdom,
Here's what the Teacher said:
It's vain to seek for wisdom,
And soon ye shall be dead.

So quaff thy drink,
Your work be truth,
And love a lover
In your youth.

For all too soon
The world grows dim.
Let wisdom rest,
And follow Him.

There Must Be

If there's no God, then people are
Just creatures amusing to use.
If there's no God, just kill whom you want,
You've nothing much to lose.

If there's no God, then take what you will,
So what if that causes pain?
If there's no God - if it's fun to do -
Do more of it again.

I pray there's a God, I hope there's a God,
Who judges the good and true.
Oh, there must be a God! And I *know* there's a God
Because He gave me you.

472

Try Harder

They told him to
Try harder.
But he kept mixing up seven times eight and six
times nine.

They told him to
Try harder.
And he ran until his chest hurt and he coughed and
gasped,
But the other boys were faster.

Try harder.
But he could not hear when his trumpet was out of
tune, and
Others winced and turned away.

Try harder.
But college was never a hope.

Try harder as he tried to sell cars, then clothing,
then burgers and fries.

Try harder his wife told him when he lost his job
again.
Then she left with someone else.

Try harder.
But it was already hard enough.

His daughter was depressed and having trouble in
school.
She came to him and cried.

He cried with her. But found himself saying,
Try harder.

And he knew he lied.
You can only try harder when harder is possible.
You can only try harder when harder can make
things better.

He found a high bridge, looked down at the cold
black water,
Decided to jump, then stopped in fear.
Another failure. No! No!

He leaped. And in that weightless moment,
Between the sky and the rushing-up darkness,
He rejoiced.

There was no need any more to
Try harder.

Wave It

We know someone who, don't you,
Found an elephant's wang in her stew.

Said her waiter "Don't shout
Or wave it about,
Or the others will all want one too."

Would they want one? Not true.
Of course it is new, but what can it do?
Now an elephant's snout, I'd wave that about!
It's longer and stronger,
And can feed a whole crew.
The smaller wang I leave to you

Well Known Names

The publisher said, "Well known names
Are only what we deal with."

The author said, "That's fine with me.
Sir, my name is Smith."

What's It All About?

What's it all about?
We laugh and push and shout.

Yet we know it's all a game,
And the end will be the same.

Why Rush?

Someone wrote the Golden Rule
Two thousand years ago,
And yet you've never learned it.
You must be awfully slow.

Why Wait?

Champagne in hand, he poured her glass,
Moved closer with a wink.

"Say when."

"Okay," she then replied,
"Right after the first drink."

Wisdom

Son, money just can't make you happy,
Or make lovely woman adore.
Is a man with thirty-five million
Better off than one with thirty-four?

Writer's Cramp

Balzac, a nympho driven to write,
Hemingway wrote and imbibed day and night,
Faulkner, Fitzgerald, the rest of the crew,
Boozed on and on, sometimes shot themselves too.
Manic, depressive, and driven to drink -
Oh it's hard to create, and it's so hard to think.

Made in the USA
Middletown, DE
28 July 2022

70168762R00275